Thomas B. Akins

History of Halifax City

Thomas B. Akins

History of Halifax City

ISBN/EAN: 9783744790581

Printed in Europe, USA, Canada, Australia, Japan

Cover: Foto ©ninafisch / pixelio.de

More available books at **www.hansebooks.com**

HISTORY OF HALIFAX CITY.

HISTORY OF HALIFAX CITY.

by

Dr. Thomas B. Akins
(1809 - 1891)

Halifax, Nova Scotia
1895

HISTORY OF HALIFAX CITY.

CHAPTER I.

Halifax, the metropolis of Nova Scotia, and the chief City of the Acadian or Lower Provinces, was founded in the year 1749, at the expense of Government, under the direction of the Lords of Trade and Plantations, and was named in compliment to George Montague, Earl of Halifax, then at the head of the Board, under whose immediate auspices the settlement was undertaken.

From the Treaty of Utrecht, in 1713, when Acadia was ceded to the Crown of Great Britain, to the year 1749, no progress had been made by the British in colonizing the country. The inhabitants consisted of a few thousand Acadian peasants, scattered around the shores of the Basin of Minas, Chignecto and the Valley of Annapolis. The Governor resided at Annapolis Royal, a small fortified port, with a garrison of two or three hundred regular troops, and was, in a great measure, dependent on New England for his necessary supplies. This was the only British port within the Province, with the exception of that of Canso, where, during the fishing season, a number of French, with a few Indians and New England fishermen, assembled, and where a captain's guard was usually stationed to preserve order and protect the rights of property. The French population, though professing to be neutral, had refused to take the Oath of Allegiance to the Crown of Great Britain, and were continually in a state of hostility to the British authorities in the country. Their poverty and ignorance placed them completely under the control of a few designing emissaries of the French Governor at Quebec, who incited the people to resent British rule, and frequently put all law at defiance, by assuming to themselves the sole management of municipal affairs in the settlements most remote from the seat of Government. The Governors of Canada had undertaken to claim all the country from the River St. Lawrence to the Bay of Fundy, as comprehended within their jurisdiction, confining the territory of Acadia as ceded under the Treaty of Utrecht, to the Peninsula alone, and had actually commenced to erect forts on the River St. John and the Isthmus while the nations were at peace.

The necessity of a permanent British settlement and Military Station on the Atlantic Coast of the Peninsula, had long been considered the only effectual means of preserving British authority, as well as for the protection of the coast fishing, which, at this time, was deemed of paramount importance to British interests. But lately the continual breaches of neutrality on the part of the French, together with the loss of Louisburg, under the Treaty of Aix-la-Chappelle, in October, 1748, rendered such an establishment indispensibly necessary to the support of the British Crown in Nova Scotia.

The scheme for settlement at Chebucto is said to have originated with the people of Massachusetts,[*] who, in calling the attention of Government to the claims and encroachments of the French, suggested the necessity for, as well as the great commercial advantages to be derived from such an undertaking; and it has also been asserted that a committee of influential citizens had been formed in Boston for the purpose of more effectually advocating the design. No authentic information on the subject, however, has been found beyond the suggestions contained in Governor Shirley's letters to the Secretary of State, in 1747 and 8, in which one extensive plan of British colonization throughout Nova Scotia is proposed and details suggested, many of which, however, did not receive the approval of Government.[†]

A plan for carrying into effect this long-cherished design was, however, matured by the Board of Trade and Plantations, in the year 1748, and submitted to Government in the autumn of that year, and being warmly supported by Lord Halifax, the President of the Board, advertisements soon appeared under the sanction of His Majesty's authority, "holding out proper encouragement to officers and private men lately discharged from the Army and Navy, to

---

[*] One Thomas Corum, whose name appears frequently in the history of the state of Maine, is said to have suggested a scheme for building a town at Chebucto in 1718, and applied to Government for a grant of land, but was prevented by the agents of the Government of Massachusetts Bay, who supposed that such project might interfere with their fishing privileges, and he was compelled to abandon his enterprise. This, however, has not the weight of much authority.

[†] Copies of several of Shirley's letters were furnished Governor Cornwallis on leaving England, as part of his instructions.

settle in Nova Scotia." Among other inducements was the offer to convey the settlers to their destination, maintain them for twelve months at the public expense, and to supply them with arms and ammunition for defence, and with materials and articles for clearing the land, erecting dwellings and prosecuting the fishery. The encouragements appeared so inviting, that in a short time 1176 settlers, with their families, were found to volunteer, and the sum of £40,000 being appropriated by Parliament for the service, the expedition was placed under the command of Col. the Honble. Edward Cornwallis, M. P., as Captain General and Governor of Nova Scotia, and set sail for Chebucto Bay, the place of destination, in May, 1749.*

The fleet consisted of 13 Transports and a Sloop of War. The following is a list of the vessels, with the number of settlers.†

Sphinx Sloop of War, with Gov. Cornwallis and Suite.			
Transports.	Captains.	Tonnage.	Number of Passengers.
Charlton Frigate	Richard Ladd	395	213
Winchelsea	Thomas Cornish	559	303
Wilmington	Thomas Adams	631	340
Merry Jacks	—— Granger	378	230
Alexander	Samuel Harris	320	172
Beaufort	Elias Brennan	541	287
Roehampton	Samuel Williamson	232	77
Canon Frigate	Andrew Dowar	342	190
Everly	S. Dutchman	351	186
London	John Barker	550	315
Brotherhood			27
Baltimore	Edward Cook	411	230
Snow Fair Lady	Isaac Foster		10
			2576

The total number of males, exclusive of children, was 1546; of this number above 500 were man-of-war sailors.‡

The names of the principal settlers, with the rank and calling as they appear in the register, are as follows:

* Cornwallis was gazetted 9th May, 1749.

† Smollet's History mentions 4,000 settlers with their families; this probably was intended to include the Germans and other settlers who arrived between 1749 and 1753.

‡ But one death, a child, occurred during the voyage. This was attributed to the care of the Board of Trade and Plantations in providing ventilators and air pipes for the Transports, a new invention then lately introduced.

Leonard Lockman and Ezekiel Gilman, Majors in the Army; John Lemon, Foot Major and Commissary; Otis Little, Edward Amherst, Thomas Lewis, Benjamin Ives, Frederick Albert Strasburger, and Francis Bartelo, Captains in the Army; David Lewis, George Burners, George Colly, Richard Partridge, Thomas Newton, *John Collier, Robert Ewer, John Creighton,* Thomas Voughan, *John Galland,* Richard Reves, William Joice, Joseph Wakefield, Augustus Graham, *Alexander Callendar,* David Haldame, Robert Campbell, William Bryan, and T. Vaughan, Lieutenants in the Army; James Warren, Thos. Reynolds, and Henry Wendell, Ensigns; John Hamilton, Adam Cockburn, and Wm. Williams, Lieutenants in the Navy; John Steinfort, Dennis Clarke, William Neil, Gustavus Mugden, and John Twinehoe, Lieutenants of Privateers; Chas. Mason, Robert Beatie, Charles Covy, Samuel Budd, John Ferguson, Nicholas Puxley, William Watson, Joseph Tomwell, Henry Chambers, Nicholas Todd, Roger Lowden, Joseph Gunn, John Thompson, Robert Young, Thomas Burnside, Timothy Pearce, Richard Drake, Newbegin Harris, William Vickers, Richard Cooper, Richard Mannering, Thomas Dunster, and Robert Cockburn, Midshipmen in the Royal Navy; John Jenkins, Cadet; Rene Gillet, Artificer; John Grant, John Henderson, Edward Gibson, William Hamilton, and William Smith, Volunteers; Lewis Hayes, Purser; John Bruce, Engineer; William Grant, Robert White, Patrick Hay, Mathew Jones, Thomas Wilson, M. Rush, James Handeside, H. Pitt, George Philip Bruscowitz, Cochran Dickson, Joshua Sacheveral, Thomas Inman, John Wildman, David Carnegie, and John Willis, Surgeons; John Steele, Lieutenant and Surgeon; William Lascells, Augustus Caesar Harbin, Archibald Campbell, John Wallis, John Grant, Daniel Brown, Timothy Griffith, Henry Martin, Robert Grant, and Alexander Hay, Surgeon's Mates and Assistants; Robert Thorckmorton, Surgeon's Pupil; Mr. Anwell, Clergyman, *John Baptiste Moreau, Gentleman and Schoolmaster;* William Jeffery, Commissary; William Steele, Brewer and Merchant; Daniel Wood, Attorney; Thomas Cannon, Esquire; John Duport, and Lewis Piers, Gentlemen; Archibald Hinshelwood, John Kerr, *William Nisbett,* and Thomas Gray, Governor's Clerks; David Floyd, Clerk of the Stores.[*]

---

[*] Governor Cornwallis, in his letter to the Lords of Trade, dated Chebucto, 24th July, 1749, says: "The number of settlers—men, women and children—is 1,400, but I beg leave to observe to your Lordships that amongst them the number of industrious,

On the 21st June, 1749, old style, the Sloop of War, "Sphinx," arrived in the Harbor of Chebucto, having on board, the Honourable Edward Cornwallis, Captain General and Governor-in-Chief of the Province of Nova Scotia, and his suite. They had a long and boisterous passage, and did not make the coast of Acadia until 14th. They had no one on board acquainted with the coast, and did not meet with a pilot until the 20th, when they fell in with a Sloop from Boston, bound to Louisburg, with two pilots for the Government of that place. Governor Cornwallis' intention was first to proceed to Annapolis, but the wind not serving for the Bay of Fundy, and the officers assuring him that in case of foggy weather setting in they might be a long time in getting to Annapolis, he concluded on proceeding at once to Chebucto, rather than risk the possibility of being separated for any length of time from the fleet. He also felt, that by so doing, he would save the Governor of Louisburg the bad and long navigation to Annapolis, and accordingly, he dispatched a letter to Governor Hopson, by the Sloop, apprising him of his intention and desiring him to transport his garrison to Chebucto as soon as possible. The "Sphinx," before making Chebucto, first came to anchor in Malagash Bay, where they found several French families, comfortably settled, who professed themselves British subjects, and had grants of land from Governor Mascarine; they had tolerably good wooden houses covered with bark, and many cattle, and expressed themselves greatly pleased on hearing of the proposed new settlement. It happened that the same day on which Cornwallis arrived in the Harbor of Chebucto, a sloop came in from Louisburg with a letter from Hopson in expectation of meeting him. Hopson was in great perplexity, the French having arrived to take possession under the terms of the treaty, and there were no vessels to embark his troops. It appeared he was fully under the expectation that the ships which were to bring out the settlers would arrive in time to be sent down to him for that purpose, and he had made no other

---

active men proper to undertake and carry on a new settlement, is very small. Of soldiers there are only 100, of tradesmen, sailors and others able and willing to work, not above 200." The rest he reports as idle and worthless, persons who embraced the opportunity to get provisions for a year without labour, or sailors who only wanted a passage to New England, and that many were sick and unfit for settlers, and many without sufficient clothing. He describes the few Swiss who were among the settlers, as "regular, honest and industrious men," and observes that there are "indeed, many come over of the better sort, who, though they do not work themselves, are useful in managing the rest." "I have," he says, "appointed two or three of them as overseers of each ship's company."

arrangements. On receiving this letter, Governor Cornwallis immediately dispatched the Sloop to Boston, with letters to Apthorp & Handerik, whom Hopson recommended for the purpose, to hire vessels with all expedition to transport the garrison of Louisburg to Chebucto; also a letter directed to Governor Mascarine in case they should meet at sea with a vessel bound to Annapolis. At the same time, a Frenchman, acquainted with the country, was dispatched overland by Minas to Annapolis, with orders to Mascarine to come down with a quorum of his Council as soon as possible, that the new commission might be opened and another Council appointed in accordance with the Royal Instructions.*

Governor Cornwallis' first dispatch to England, after arriving at Chebucto, was sent via Boston, and bears date 22nd June, the day after his arrival. In this letter he says: "The coasts are as rich as ever they have been represented; we caught fish every day since we came, within 50 leagues of the coast. The harbour itself is full of fish of all kinds. All the officers agree the harbour is the finest they have ever seen. The country is one continued wood; no clear spot is to be seen or heard of. I have been on shore in several places. The underwood is only young trees, so that with difficulty one is able to make his way anywhere." "De Anvilles' Fleet have only cut wood for present use; they cleared no ground, but encamped their men on the beach. I have seen but few brooks, nor as yet have found the navigable river that has been talked of. There are a few French families on the east side of the bay, about three leagues off. Some have been on board."

Governor Mascarine having received Cornwallis' letter on the 26th, on the following day, ordered Captain Davis to make ready his galley and go round to Chebucto with fresh provisions. Mascarine was waiting the arrival of the new Governor at Annapolis, as appears by his letters to Governor Hopson on the 14th and 26th June, in which he says: "Get ready supplies for the new Captain General who will be here, but the fleet will be at Chebucto." The "Snow Fair Lady" arrived shortly after the Sphinx, and was dispatched to Annapolis to afford Mr. Mascarine the means of transporting his council and part of his garrison to Chebucto. On

---

*This messenger arrived on the fourth day, at Annapolis. "It is," says the Governor in his letter, "25 leagues over to Minas, (now Horton), and the French have made a path for driving their cattle over."

the 26th, the "Fair Lady" was in the harbour of Annapolis ready to receive Governor Mascarine and suite. On the 27th, the transport began to make their appearance off the harbour of Chebucto, and by the 1st July, they had all arrived. As their passage had been extremely good, and none of them had in the least suffered, the Governor found himself in a position to afford vessels to Colonel Hopson the moment the settlers should be put on shore.* Accordingly having countermanded the order to Boston for transports, he dispatched to Louisburg the ship "Brotherhood" on the 1st July, and on the 5th, the "London," "Wilmington," Winchelsea," and "Merry Jacks." On the 8th he received from Louisburg, copies of letters from Governor Shirley of Boston, to Governor Mascarine, giving an account of the French having commenced a fort at the mouth of the River St. John, and on the following day sent Captain Rouse in the "Albany" and a small sloop to attend her, with orders to the commanding officer at Annapolis to furnish him with troops if required, and to proceed immediately to the River St. John, Governor Shirley having previously sent the ship "Boston" to Annapolis for the same service, there to await orders. It appears that the French had fitted out an expedition, under M. Ramey, for this purpose, a short time before the arrival of Cornwallis, and the vessel with ammunition, arms and provisions, bound to St. John River, had passed Malagash Bay a few days before the arrival of the "Sphinx" there; but having put into Port Mouton on her way, the information of their designs was communicated to the authorities of Annapolis.

Governor Mascarine having arrived with several of his Council on the 12th, the following day Governor Cornwallis opened his commission and took the oaths of office in their presence, and on Friday, the 14th July, the Civil Government was organized, and Colonel Paul Mascarine, Captain Edward How, Captain John Gorham, Benjamin Green, John Salsbury and Hugh Davidson were sworn in Councillors† on board the "Beaufort" Transport, and the Commission and Royal Instructions were then read. "The formation of the Board was announced to the people by a general salute from the

---

* The settlers who came out in the transport, afterwards sent to Louisburg, were first landed on George's Island.

† The table around which this Council assembled is now in the small Council Chamber in the Province Building.

ships in the harbour and the day was devoted to festivity and amusement." The four first gentlemen named in the Council were officers from Annapolis; Mr. Green was from Massachusetts, and had been with General Hopson at Louisburg, and the two latter were of His Excellency's suite; Mr. Davidson acted as Secretary.

Early in the month of July, a spot for the settlement was pitched upon near Point Pleasant,* then called Sandwich Point, and people were employed in cutting down the trees; but the want of sufficient depth of water in front, its great exposure to south-east gales and other inconveniences being discovered, it was abandoned for a more eligible situation to the northward, commanding a prospect of the whole harbour and on an easy ascent with bold anchorage close to the shore. Here Mr. Bruce the engineer, and Captain Morris the surveyor, were ordered to lay out the town, which was surveyed, the plan completed and the lots appropriated to their respective owners by the 14th September. The town was laid out in squares or blocks of 320 by 120 feet deep, the streets being 55 feet† in width. Each block contained 16 town lots, forty feet front by sixty deep, and the whole was afterwards divided into five divisions or wards, called Callendar's, Galland's, Ewer's, Collier's and Foreman's divisions, after the names of the persons who were appointed Captains of Militia, each ward being large enough to supply one company.

Buckingham Street was the north and Salter Street the south limit, and the whole was surrounded by a strong palisade of pickets with block houses or log forts at convenient distances. Foreman's new division was afterwards added as far as the present Jacob Street. The north and south suburbs were surveyed about the same time, but the German lots in the north were not laid off till the year following.

Great difficulty was at first experienced in the erection of dwellings; the European settlers being totally unacquainted with the method of constructing wooden buildings. Frames and other materials for building were, however, soon brought from Massachusetts, and before the cold weather set in a number of comfortable dwel-

---

*"From seeing the place only, one would be apt to choose Sandwich Point as the best situation for a town, being very defensible and having the advantage of Sandwich River, (now known as the North West Arm), navigable a great way. This was the general opinion at first, and they began to clear there, the first day they worked, but upon examination we found the strongest objections against it."—*Governor Cornwallis' letter to Board of Trade.*

†The streets are supposed to be 60 feet broad, but none of them are found to exceed 55 feet in width.

lings were erected. Provisions and other necessary supplies were regularly served out in the camp, and every exertion on the part of the Governor made to render the settlers comfortable before the approach of winter. Several transports were detained and housed over to accommodate those settlers whose houses were not complete, and the canvas tent and log hut were soon abandoned for more convenient and comfortable accommodations.

I have, says Governor Cornwallis, in his letter of the 20th August, contracted for frames and materials for barracks and officers' lodgings from Boston. Boards are very high owing to the drought. I have got none under £4 per thousand, and shall be obliged to furnish a vast number to help the people to get under cover, and have sent an officer on purpose to Boston to obtain them at a fair price. Many houses are begun and huts and log houses already up for more than half a mile on each side the town.

Tradition says that on clearing the ground for settlement a number of dead bodies were discovered among the trees, partly covered by the underwood, supposed to have been soldiers of the Duke D'Anville's expedition which put into Chebucto Harbor in 1746,* but the Governor in his letter does not mention the facts.

During the winter months the people were kept actively employed in cutting pickets for fences and wood for fuel, and for erecting new buildings. Mechanics were placed at the head of working parties to direct their labours, and by a judicious division of the people into small parties the more laborious portion of the work was executed with uncommon dispatch. Mills were also erected at the expense of Government for sawing lumber, and a mill master appointed with a salary, and every facility held out to enable those settlers, who had not yet been accommodated, to complete their dwellings on the approach of spring. The Governor in his letter of 27th July, describes the site of the Town as very advantageous. He says : " It

---

* The remnant of this formidable fleet which was destined for the destruction of the British settlements of Acadia and New England, put into Chebucto Harbor in distress in September, 1746. The troops it is said were encamped on the western side of the Basin, near the small Cove about 4 miles from town, which still bears the name of the French Landing. The Duke died of grief at the failure of the expedition, and the Vice Admiral Destourville, ran himself through the body, and was buried on George's Island. His remains, or what was supposed to have been, were afterwards removed to France by his family. Several of the ships of war were sunk on the eastern side of the Basin. The hulls of those vessels were visible in calm weather about 30 years ago, but they have long since disappeared. M. Jonquiere, afterwards Governor of Canada, was also in this expedition.

has all the conveniences I could wish except a fresh water river.* Nothing is easier than to build wharves; one is already finished for ships of 200 tons. I have constantly employed all the carpenters I could get from Annapolis and the ships here to build log houses for stores. I have likewise offered the French at Minas considerable wages to work, and they have promised to send fifty men to remain until October. As there was not one yard of clear ground you will imagine our difficulty and what we have here to do; however, they have already cleared about 12 acres, and I hope to begin my house in two days; I have a small frame and pickets ready."

The following extracts from a letter dated 25th July, 1749, written by a settler,† affords several interesting facts relative to the state of the settlement at this time:—" On our arrival we found the Sphinx, of 20 guns, which had come into harbor a few days before us; as I write the transports are entering the harbor with the two regiments of Hopson and Warberton on board from Louisburg. The assistance, as well as the security we shall receive from them, will greatly forward our settlement; the officers have brought all their furniture, a great number of milch cows, and other stock, besides military stores. We have already cleared about 20 acres, and every one has a hut by his tent. Our work goes on briskly, and the method of employing the people in ships' companies has a good effect, and as the Governor is preparing to lay out the lots of land, we shall soon have a very convenient and pleasant town built, which is to be called Halifax. There are already several wharves built, and one gentleman is erecting a saw mill; public store houses are also building, and grain of various sorts have been sown. We have received constant supplies of plank and timber for building, and fresh stock and rum in great quantities, 20 schooners frequently coming in in one day. We have also a hundred cows and some sheep, brought down to us by land, by the French at Minas, which is about 30 miles distant from the bottom of the bay, and to which we purpose to cut a road. The French Deputies who came to make

---

*At this period when the settlement was confined to such narrow limits the brook known to us as Fresh Water River, in the south suburbs, was considered to be at a distance too far from the pickets to be of much value as a means of supply to the settlers.

†This letter appeared in one of the British periodicals for October, 1749.

submission have promised to send us 50 men for the purpose, and to assist us as far as they are able; we have received the like promise, and friendship and assistance from the Indians, the chief having been with the Governor for that purpose. In short, every thing is in a very prosperous way. But I should be equally unjust and ungrateful, were I to conclude without paying the tribute which is due to our Governor. He seems to have nothing in view but the interest and happiness of all; his zeal and prudent conduct in the difficult task assigned him cannot be too much admired."

The plan of the town having been completed and the building lots marked out, in order to prevent dispute and discontent among the settlers, it was deemed best that they should draw for the lots. Accordingly, at a Council held on the 1st of August, it was resolved that on Tuesday following, the 8th August, all heads of families who were settlers, should assemble at seven o'clock with the overseers, and single men should form themselves into families, four to each family, and each family choose one to draw for them. Mr. Bruce the engineer, being present on the occasion, assisted in distributing the lots according to the arrangement, and the whole were entered in a book of registry which was to be kept for the purpose and to constitute evidence of title and possession.*

The next object of importance was the erection of proper defences for the protection of the settlement. After they had taken possession of the lots, and commenced to build, the Governor endeavoured to induce the people to work for a few days in throwing up a line of defence around their new abode; "but," says he, "there was no persuading them to do it." It was not until the 13th August when the Council voted 1s. 6d. per day to each man employed, that this necessary work was commenced by the settlers. The harbour being broad and easy of access, the difficulty of selecting proper positions for fortifications, which would command the entrance, was at first seriously felt. This had been the great objection on the part of the French to making any settlement at Chebucto, La Have having been chosen by them for the principal post on the Atlantic Coast, being, from its narrow entrance, more easy of defence. In Admiral Durell's plan of Chebucto, the two points that flanked the entrance

---

*This allotment book still remains entire in the office of the Provincial Secretary, in Halifax. It was repaired in 1861 by the Record Commission, and a fac-simile copy made for use, and the original placed out of the reach of injury.

to Bedford Basin were marked as the places proper to fortify. Mr. Cornwallis says, their view must have been to have the settlement within that Bay (the Basin); this would have been subject to great inconvenience. In the first place, it would have been too far up for the fishermen, it being about five leagues from the entrance of the Harbour to those points, and the beach all along as well adapted for curing their fish as can possibly be imagined; no fisherman would ever have thought of going within these forts. Indeed no ship would choose to go so far, as no finer harbour can be than that of Chebucto, which reaches from these points to Sandwich River; so that notwithstanding any forts upon these points, an enemy's fleet might be secure and indeed block up all ships within the bay. He accordingly fixed upon Sandwich Point and the high lands opposite, (now called York Redoubt), and George's Island as the most proper positions for the erection of the necessary defences. On the latter he immediately placed a guard, landed his stores and planned and proposed to build thereon his magazine for powder.

The first act of Government, after the organization of the Council on the 14th, was an audience of the three French Deputies, who had come down to meet the New Governor. They were Jean Melanson, from Canard River; Claude le Blanc, from Grand Pre, and Philip Melanson from Pisiquid. Colonel Mascarine read to the Council the oath which the French inhabitants had before taken. Being asked if they had anything to offer from their several departments, they answered that they were sent only to pay their respects to His Excellency and to know what was to be their condition henceforth, and whether they would be allowed their priests. They were assured that their religion should be protected, but that, as heretofore, no priest should be permitted to officiate within the Province, without having first obtained a license from the Governor. They were furnished with copies of the Royal Declaration, a proclamation issued by Governor Cornwallis, and the oath which had been customary, with directions to return within a fortnight, to report to the Council the views of the inhabitants of the respective districts, and also to notify the other settlements to send deputies as soon as possible. The second meeting of the Council took place on the 17th, when Mr. Wm. Steele was sworn in a member of the Board, and on the following day the Governor's proclamation was read in the camp, prohibiting all persons from leaving the Province without permission, and against the retail of spirituous liquors without license.

On the 18th, Mr. Bruce the Engineer, Lieutenants Ewer, Collier and Mr. John Duport were appointed Justices of the peace, and all the settlers having assembled in separate companies with their respective overseers, each company chose its constables.

The Governor designed opening more perfect means of communication with Minas by constructing a road, which he described as being 30 miles only, in a direct line, and to build a Block House half way, but having only two companies of soldiers with him, one of Hopson's and one of Warberton's regiment, together with about 60 of Goreham's Indian Rangers, and the 50 French, who promised to assist in the work, having disappointed him, he was compelled to postpone the object until after the arrival of the army from Louisburg. Proper access to the interior, by the construction of a good road to Minas, was deemed of paramount importance to the settlement of the country. The inhabitants of the rural districts were so insulated as to be in a great measure independent of all authority. Colonel Mascarine, on returning to Annapolis, received directions to send a Captain, 3 Subalterns and 100 men to Minas, and to erect a Block-house and Battery there, the troops to be first quartered at Grande Pre, where the Block-house was to be built, and the French people were to be hired at fair wages to assist in the work.*

Capt. How, who had been sent to St. John River in the Albany with Capt. Rouse, having returned overland with thirteen Indians, three deputies from the tribes at St. John, the Chief of the Chinecto Indians, and nine others of their tribes. They received an audience on the 14th; they consisted of Francis de Salle, Chief from Octfragli; the Chief Noellobig, from Medochig; the Chief Neptune Albodonallilla from the Chignecto tribe, for himself and tribe. The negotiation was carried on through Martin, the Indian, and André, the interpreter from Minas. They stated to the Council that they had come to confirm the treaty of 1726, and that several of them had been present at that treaty. Terms were drawn up by Mr. Secretary Davidson, and signed by the Chiefs on the 15th August,*

---

*Note.—These Indians are described in a letter from one of the Settlers, to England, dated 19th August, as quite different from the Indians of the peninsula, their faces all rubbed over with vermillion and across their nose and forehead are regularly drawn black lines. Their ears are bored full of holes and adorned with tobacco pipes and ribbons of different colours; their clothes are of the light homespun grey but [...]

1749, and Capt. How was ordered to carry it to St. John to be ratified, and to take with him presents to the Chiefs. It was accordingly ratified on the 4th day of September following, and signed by all the Chiefs and Captains at the River St. John, six in number, in the presence of Mr. How and seven other witnesses; Madame De Bellisle acting as interpreter by request of the Indians. This document is still in existence; also a copy of that of 1726, sent to Governor Cornwallis by the Governor of Massachusetts Bay. This treaty appears to have been little regarded, for in the beginning of October following, news arrived from Annapolis and Canso of further incursions on the part of the Indians, and Government was compelled to raise two new independent companies of Volunteers for that service, which were placed under the command of Major Gilman and Capt. Clapham, on the same footing with the Rangers under Gorham.

After the evacuation of Louisburg the population received a considerable accession; a number of the English inhabitants came with Governor Hobson and became settlers, and many from New England were daily arriving, and upwards of 1000 more from the old provinces had expressed themselves desirous of joining the Settlement before winter. The Governor therefore gave orders to all vessels in the Government service to give them a free passage. The New England people soon formed the basis of the resident population, and are the ancestors of many of the present inhabitants. They were better settlers than the old discharged soldiers and sailors who came on the fleet; most of whom died or left the country during the first three or four years, leaving, however, the most industrious and respectable among them as permanent settlers. Many settlers and traders came out for the purpose of making money; these people infested the Settlement in great numbers, and gave Mr. Cornwallis and his successors much trouble and annoyance, in demoralizing the people by the illicit sale of bad liquors, and in other ways retarding the progress of the country.

---

erably ragged. The French supply them with those articles. Their squaws or women dress equally as gay as the men. They are entire drunkards, and never cease drinking spirituous liquors as long as they can get it. They came on board to the Governor in great form. After the treaty was ratified they received presents and went on board the man-of-war, where they solaced themselves with singing and dancing. As to the songs it is one continued bellowing and noise. Upon their coming off, the man-of-war gave them a salute of 17 guns, as likewise they did on going aboard. They expressed a great deal of satisfaction at the honors done them; so they were discharged and sent in one of Colonel Goreham's sloops to St. John River with presents to the rest of their tribe.

A proposition was made about this time by a French merchant from the West Indies to Governor Cornwallis to bring to Halifax some Protestant families from Martinique with their effects, if he would give them protection and grant them lands, and the Governor was furnished with a list of their names, with what each of them was worth, which approached in all nearly £50,000. This gentleman proceeded to Louisburg to obtain for them a passport, and proposed to have his people on before winter; but it does not appear as far as any information on the subject can be gathered from the public records that any of these French Protestants ever arrived.

The Government found it necessary to check the indiscriminate sale of spirituous liquors by a license duty. On the 28th August an ordinance passed for that purpose, and all such licensed houses were to be closed at 9 p. m. under penalty. On the 31st August the Governor and Council for the first time sat as a Court of Law. This was named the General Court, all authority—legislative, executive and judicial—being vested in the Board. They met on this day for the trial of Abram Goodside, the Boatswain's mate of the Beaufort, who stabbed and wounded two men. A grand jury was summoned who found a bill of indictment; he was tried and found guilty by a petit jury, and hanged under the Governor's warrant on 2nd September, 1749. On 31st August, another Court was held for the trial of one Peter Cartal, for murder. The Acadian Deputies having returned from the country, they were called before the Governor and Council on September 6th, when they presented a letter signed by 1000 inhabitants claiming to take only a qualified Oath of Allegiance.

On the 30th August, a sloop from Liverpool, Great Britain, with 116 settlers, arrived after a passage of nine weeks. They were, however, all quite healthy, not one person being sick on board at the time of their arrival. Two streets were then added to the Town and lots assigned to these people. This was Forman's new division. We have no names of these settlers or the name of the sloop.

Information having reached the Government that the Indians of Acadia and St. John's Island, designed to molest the settlement at Halifax on the approach of winter,* it was deemed advisable to erect

---

* Governor Cornwallis' letter to Secretary of State.

outworks for its defence; accordingly the troops and inhabitants were immediately employed to construct a line of palisades around the town in connection with square log forts which were to be placed at convenient distances. A space of thirty feet was cleared without the lines, and the trees thrown up by way of a barricade, which constituted a complete defence against any attempt on the part of the Indians. Those settlers who had built their houses without the town had arms given them, and their dwellings being built of logs were musket proof; also the Ordnance Artificers, those from New England and such of the settlers as had been in the army, and such others as could be trusted with arms within the town, also received them, and an order was sent to Boston for a supply of lamps to light the streets during the winter nights. Col. Goreham was sent to the head of the Basin with his company of Rangers for the winter, with an armed sloop to assist him, and every preparation possible was made for the protection of the people during the ensuing winter.

The Indians had appeared in the neighbourhood of the town for several weeks, but intelligence had been received that they had commenced hostilities, by the capture of twenty persons at Canso under frivolous pretences, and of two vessels having been attacked by them at Chignecto, when three English and seven Indians were killed. In consequence of this information it was resolved in Council to send a letter to M. Desherbiers, Governor of Louisburg, to recall LeLoutre. On the last day of September they made an attack on the sawmill at Dartmouth, then under the charge of Major Gilman. Six of his men had been sent out to cut wood without arms. The Indians laid in ambush, killed four and carried off one, and the other escaped and gave the alarm, and a detachment of rangers was sent after the savages, who having overtaken them, cut off the heads of two Indians and scalped one.*

These proceedings compelled the government to take more active measures, and orders were given to the commanding officers at the out stations, to destroy the Indians wherever they met them, and a premium of ten guineas was offered for every Indian killed or

* This affair is mentioned in a letter from a gentleman in Halifax to Boston, dated October 2nd, as follows: "About seven o'clock on Saturday morning before, as several of Major Gilman's workmen with one soldier, unarmed, were hewing sticks of timber about 300 yards from his house and mills on the east side of the harbour, they were surprised by about 40 Indians, who first fired two shots and then a volley upon them which killed four, two of whom they scalped, and cut off the heads of the others, the fifth is missing and is supposed to have been carried off."

taken prisoner, this offer was in consequence of the large rewards offered by the French to the Indians for English scalps. Orders were given for raising two independent companies of rangers, one of one hundred men by Major Gilman, who was sent to Piscataqua for that purpose,* the other a company of volunteers by Captain Wm. Clapham, who with Goreham's Indian Rangers, now returned from their stations at the head of the Basin with a company of Philips' Regiment, were to scour the whole country around the Bay. The St. John Indians having kept the treaty, received from Governor Cornwallis a present of 1000 bushels of corn, and an order was also given to purchase at Minas 500 bushels of wheat, to be baked into biscuit for the same purpose. Captain How was intrusted with these and other presents, and was directed to bring back with him, if possible, some of the tribe to go against the Mic-Macs. The preparation necessary to the protection of the town against French-Indian hostilities tended to expedite the progress of the settlement; before the middle of October, about three hundred and fifty houses had been completed, two of the square forts finished and the barricade carried all around. A number of store houses and barrack buildings for the accommodation of the troops had been also erected and the Governor's residence completed. The Council met there on the 14th October. About 30 of the French inhabitants were employed on the Public Works, and in cutting a road from the town to the Basin of Minas. A number of influential and industrious families from New England and other places had already become settlers, and Halifax Harbor was the resort of a large number of fishing vessels.

About this time a destructive epidemic made its appearance in the town, and it is said nearly 1000 persons fell victims during the autumn and the following winter. On the 14th day of October, the Government found it necessary to publish an ordinance, commanding all Justices of the Peace, upon the death of the settlers, to name so many of the neighbourhood or quarter (not exceeding 12) to which the deceased belonged, to attend at the burial and carry the corpse to the grave, and whoever refused to attend without sufficient reason should have his name struck off the Mess Book and Register of Settlers as unworthy of His Majesty's bounty; and again in

---

*Those men were supplied with hatchets and snow shoes for winter warfare.

December, another order was made commanding all householders to report their dead to a clergyman within twenty-four hours.

Owing to the frequent alarms of invasion from the Indians and French stragglers during the winter, it was resolved in Council to organize a militia force for the protection of the settlement, and on the Sunday following the 6th day of December, after divine service, all the male settlers, between the age of sixteen and sixty, were assembled on the parade, and drawn up in the following order:— "Those of Mr. Ewer's and Mr. Collier's divisions to face the harbor, those of the quarters of Mr. Galland and Mr. Foreman to face the Citadel, and those of Mr. Callendar's division at one end of the parade." The proclamation bears date the 7th day of December, 1749. On the 16th, information arrived that a French force had been dispatched overland from Canada, to attack Halifax, and that the Indians were to co-operate with them, also, that two vessels with six hundred men were in the Bay Verte under LeCorne, and with ammunition and stores of all kinds for a winter expedition. The people having been again assembled on the parade after divine service, the proclamation was read and the settlers commanded to fell all the trees around the town without the forts and barricades. No attempt was, however, made upon the town, either by the Indians or French during the winter. These hostilities were being carried on by the Government of Canada, while the two Crowns were nominally at peace, under pretence that the Treaty of Utrecht only ceded to the Crown of Great Britain the peninsula of Nova Scotia proper.

The Governor deeming it expedient that some permanent system of judicial proceedings to answer the immediate exigencies of the Colony should be established, a committee of Council was accordingly appointed to examine the various systems in force in the old Colonies. On 13th December, Mr. Green reported that after a careful investigation, the laws of Virginia were found to be most applicable to the present situation of the province. The report was adopted. It referred principally to the judicial proceedings in the General Courts, the County Courts, and other tribunals.

Before concluding this chapter, which comprehends all that can be collected relative to the affairs of the settlement during the first year of its existence, it will be proper to observe that in founding the City, the spiritual wants of the settlers were not lost sight of by the British Government. Preparatory to the embarkation of the settlers, a letter was addressed by the Lords of Trade and Plantations to the Society for the Propagation of the Gospel in Foreign Parts, dated Whitehall, April 6th, 1749, recommending to the Society to appoint ministers and school-masters for the new settlement at Chebucto, and for such other townships or settlements as should from time to time be formed in Nova Scotia, and requesting the Society to make some provisions for them until arrangements should be made for their sufficient support, by grants of land, etc.* The Society resolved immediately to act on this recommendation, and undertook to send six clergymen and six school-masters, when the settlements should be formed. The first missionaries appointed under this arrangement, were the Rev. William Tutty, of Emmanuel College, Cambridge, and the Rev. Mr. Anwell, who both came out with the settlers in June, 1749. Mr. Tutty officiated in the open air until the necessary church accommodation could be obtained. On laying out the town, a spot was assigned by Government for the church. The site was first selected at the north end of the Grand Parade, where Dalhousie College now stands, but it was changed immediately after for the present site of St. Paul's Church, which was erected at the expense of Government and ready for the reception of the missionary, who preached his first sermon there on the 2nd day of September, 1750. The pews and inside finish were not completed for several years after. The name of Mr. Tutty does not appear among those of the settlers who came with Cornwallis. He probably, however, accompanied him. Mr. Anwell came with the expedition, but his name does not again appear; he died shortly after his arrival. Mr. Tutty spoke German and administered the Lord's Supper to the German settlers in their own language. The other missionary, J. Baptiste Moreau, who came out as school-master, and afterwards went to England for ordination, returned to the settlement and went down to Malignsh with the Germans, 1752. Mr. Halstead was the school-master in charge of the Society's schools at Halifax during the first two or three years.

Governor Cornwallis in 1749, assigned the lot at the south-west corner of Prince and Hollis streets for a Protestant Dissenting

---

*A copy of this letter will be found in the appendix.

Meeting house. The old building known as Mather's, or as it was afterwards called St. Matthew's Church (destroyed by fire in 1859,) was soon after erected on this site. It was appropriated originally to the Congregationalists, many of whom came from New England to settle in Halifax. It was called Mather's Church after the celebrated Cotton Mather, one of the leading divines of that denomination at Boston, in early days. The Presbyterians, and all who did not belong to the Established Church, attended divine service in this building. The Rev. Mr. Cleveland, who came from one of the old colonies, was the first minister who officiated in this building. It afterwards fell into the hands of the Presbyterians and became the property of the Church of Scotland, and the name of Mather's was changed to that of St. Matthew. This old Church was destroyed by fire, which consumed a large portion of the buildings in Hollis Street, in 1859. The lot of ground on which it stood was afterwards sold to Mr. Doull, who erected the fine stone store thereon, now known as Doull and Miller's building.

CHAPTER II.

The winter of 1749-50, as has been before mentioned, was spent in continual apprehension of Indian and French invasion, and in preparations to receive the enemy. On the 7th January, 1750, a number of the inhabitants petitioned that Martial Law should be declared, but the Governor and Council did not consider the danger so great or imminent as to make it necessary. However, stringent regulations with regard to the militia were enacted, and an ordinance was issued compelling all settlers able to bear arms between 16 and 60, to be formed into 10 companies of 70 men each,* and a guard of — officers and 30 men to assemble every evening near the parade to keep guard until sunrise, and all militia men called upon to labour at the fortifications, were to be allowed 1s. per day. Labourers were constantly employed in raising a barricade and continuing it to the water side, and block houses were erected between the forts.

During the winter intelligence frequently arrived from Minas, Pisiquid, and the eastern shore, of attacks being made by the Indians upon stragglers, and several young Acadians were brought from Minas to Halifax for trial, having been found in arms with the Indians. A large reward was offered for the apprehension of LeLoutre, the Indian missionary, and also £10 sterling for every Indian scalp or Indian prisoner. Capt. Sylvanus Cobb, an active and bold sea captain from Massachusetts, was taken into Government employ, and sent to Chignecto with his armed sloop for the purpose of surprising LeLoutre and his gang, and afterwards to search the harbors along the coast for Indians, and bring with him all he captured as prisoners to Halifax. Troops under Capt. Bartilo and others were sent into the interior and other active proceedings taken by the Governor and Council during the months of January and February for the peace of the province. A courier having been stopped at Cobequid, Priest Gourard and the French Deputies, were all brought to Halifax, by Capt. Bartilo, for examination before the Governor and Council; Gourard was detained at Government House until the courier returned, but the deputies were

---

*The Artificers formed one company by themselves, and the whole militia amounted to about 840 men. The Officers behaved well, but, says the Governor in his dispatch, "I cannot say so of the men."

dismissed. He disclosed the fact to the Council that the Mic-Mac Indians of Nova Scotia went every year to Quebec, to receive clothing from the French Government, and that LeCorn had made the French of Acadia take the Oath of Allegiance to the French King. Gourard on this occasion took the Oath of Allegiance to the Crown of Great Britain, and thereupon received a licence to officiate as Priest to the Acadians, and promised not to leave the province without special leave from the Governor.

Among the municipal regulations this winter, was an ordinance that all persons found breaking the liquor license law, should be put one hour in the public stocks, and for the second offence receive twenty lashes. These severe regulations were found to be absolutely necessary, in consequence of the demoralized state of the settlement from settlers and others who infested the town and who were not settlers.

On the 2nd February, 1750, an ordinance was passed in Council, prohibiting the recovery of any debt contracted in England or elsewhere, prior to the establishment of the settlement or to the debtor's arrival in Halifax, in any Court of Law within the province, except for goods imported into the Colonies. There appears to have been some difference of opinion at the Board on the subject; the Council divided, and the ordinance was carried by a small majority.

It was proposed in Council about this time, to build a quay along the shore in front of the town, but several merchants—Mr. Saul, Mr. Joshua Mauger and others, having applied for water lots, and liberty to build wharves on the beach, the subject was referred to Mr. Morris the surveyor, and Mr. Bruce the engineer. They thought the quay was a work of time and required means from England. Licences to build wharves were therefore granted, with a reservation of the right of the Crown in case the quay should be resolved on or the frontage required for government purposes. This scheme was afterwards abandoned by Government, and the licences remained unrepealed. At this period the line of the shore was so irregular, as in some places to afford only a footpath between the base line of the lots, which now form the upper side of Water Street and high water mark;[*] at the Market the tide flowed up nearly to

---

[*]According to the original plan of the Town published in October, 1749, a space appears to have been reserved between the line of the lots and the shore, but no Water

where the [old] City Court House stood, forming a cove, the outlet of a brook which came down north of George Street. Near the Ordnance Yard another cove made in, and this part of the shore was low and swampy many years after the batteries were built.*

The winter passed without any attack on the settlement, and the people were all quite healthy. The number of settlers was daily augmented by almost every vessel which arrived from New England and elsewhere; every thing required was provided for them, that they should be tolerably comfortable before the cold weather set in. The winter was very fine, very few extreme bad days, no heavy snow storms, the navigation never stopped in the slightest degree. More fine days and fewer bad ones (says the Governor) than I ever saw in winter. Spring opened early with fine warm days and thaw, and the fishing schooners began early in March to go upon the Bank.† The snow lay all the winter, from the middle of January; it was, however, only three feet deep in the woods. The healthy condition of the settlers may be inferred from there never being more than 25 in the hospital ship at any one time.

By the 19th March, a place had been erected for a public Hospital, and a school building commenced for the orphan children. The French from the interior engaged freely for money to square timber for the erection of the blockhouses, and preparations were in progress for the completion of the Church.

A meeting of the Governor and Council took place on 19th April, when the French Deputies again appeared with a petition to be permitted to sell their lands and leave the country. The names of

---

Street was laid out—the upper side of the present Bedford Row being the western limit. There were five forts, having each four quadrangular blockhouses, with a barrack in the centre; these were connected by wooden pallisades or pickets.

*A number of licences to erect wharves and buildings along the beach had been granted by Government to individuals engaged in trade and the fishery, before the idea of a general Government breastwork had been abandoned. These titles continued to be held good; a number of wharf proprietors, however, obtained conformation grants from time to time as they required water extension. Mr. Charles Morris, the Surveyor-General, who had the sole management of the land office, in his reports to the Government, advised small spaces to be reserved on both sides in making these conformation grants as well as in subsequent water grants in fee, which have been found of much inconvenience to trade, and a drawback on the progress of the City. No reservation of water was originally made at the foot of the cross streets or hills. At the close of the last and the commencement of the present century, when conformation or extension water grants were asked for, he marked on his plans narrow strips or reservations on the sides of many of these water grants, which for there being in many instances inaccessible, have since proved of no value to the public and a great injury to the proprietors of water property.

† Cornwallis' letter of 19th March.

these deputies were Jaques Teriot from Grand Pre, Francois Granger from River de Canard, Battiste Galerne and Jean André.

Mr. Cornwallis was continually embarassed by letters from the Board of Trade, finding fault with the expenses incurred in planting the settlement. £40,000 had been voted by Parliament, and £36,000 of excess had been demanded as a further vote; this could not be considered so great an expenditure under all the circumstances, as it included the pay and equipment of two regiments of infantry. In his replies, he says, "Not a pound shall be expended "by me unnecessarily, but without money you could have had no "town, no settlement, and indeed no settlers. 'T is very certain that "the public money cleared the ground, built the town, secured it, "kept both soldiers and settlers from starving with cold, and has "brought down above 1000 settlers from the other Colonies. Lots "in Halifax are now worth 50 guineas. If there was no public "money circulating, lots would be given for a gallon of rum. The "money is laid out in building forts, barracks, store houses, "hospitals, churches, wharves, etc., public works all that seem "absolutely necessary. According to your Lordship's directions, I "have discharged the two Government Apothecaries and shall discharge some of the Surgeons' Mates that may be spared. As for "the saw mill, we never had one board from it—it has been a constant "plague from the beginning. Thirty men have been constantly kept "there ever since the affair of the Indians. Gilman has behaved so "ill I shall have to discharge him from all service. I have laid in a "quantity of lumber in the King's yard this spring at a reasonable "price. For want of stock I have been sometimes obliged to pay "£5 per M. The settlers have paid £6. I have got them lately at "£3 10s., £3 and £2 15s. No new boards are given to settlers."

The salaries to the public officers of Cornwallis' Government appear exceedingly small in comparison with the arduous duties which devolved upon them in organizing the settlement. His Aides-de-Camp, Capt. Bulkely and Mr. Gates,* had no allowance except some trifling commission on the issue of molasses and spirits.

In June, 1750, the Governor and Council assigned as a site the spot on which the [old] City Court House stands, for a market for black cattle, sheep, etc., and made market regulations. In

---

* This was the well-known Horatio Gates, afterwards a Revolutionary General.

July, the settlers were ordered to clear the streets in front of their respective lots to the centre. They had begun to clear George's Island and to erect block-houses. Seven 32-pounders had been mounted upon it, and a palisade carried all around the works. The frame of the Church, which had been brought from Boston, was erected and was being covered in, the estimated cost of finishing the edifice being £1000 sterling. The temporary barricades were removed, and the palisades carried completely round the town. 30,000 bricks had been manufactured in the neighbourhood and found very good. The meeting house for Dissenters had not yet been commenced. The town was increasing every day in settlers and the number of its houses, but no improvement of the lands in the neighbourhood had been made beyond a few small gardens. The fishery was prosperous and produced 25,000 quintals the first year.

In the month of August, 1750, three hundred and fifty-three settlers arrived in the ship Alderney; and in September following, three hundred German Protestants, from the Palatinate, in the ship Ann. The Governor and Council were embarrassed in providing for their support, and found it necessary to enter into pecuniary arrangements with the merchants of the town, who at this early period had formed themselves into an association for the benefit of trade. Those who came in the ship Alderney, were sent to the opposite side of the harbour, and commenced the town of Dartmouth, which was laid out in the autumn of that year. In December following, the first ferry was established, and John Connor appointed ferryman by order in Council.

In the spring of the following year the Indians surprised Dartmouth at night, scalped a number of settlers and carried off several prisoners. The inhabitants, fearing an attack, had cut down the spruce trees around their settlement, which, instead of a protection, as was intended, served as a cover for the enemy. Captain Clapham and his company of Rangers were stationed on Block-house hill, and it is said remained within his block-house firing from the loop-holes, during the whole affair. The Indians were said to have destroyed several dwellings, sparing neither women nor children. The light of the torches and the discharge of musketry alarmed the inhabitants of Halifax, some of whom put off to their assistance, but did not arrive in any force till after the Indians' had retired. The night was calm, and the cries of the settlers, and whoop of the Indians were distinctly heard on the western side of the harbour. On the following morning, several bodies were brought over—the Indians having carried off the scalps.* Mr. Pyke, father of the late John George Pyke, Esq., many years police magistrate of Halifax, lost his life on this occasion. Those who fled to the woods were all taken prisoners but one. A court martial was called on the 14th May, to inquire into the conduct of the different commanding officers, both commissioned and non-commissioned, in permitting the village to be plundered when there were about 60 men posted there for its protection.

There was a guard house and small military post at Dartmouth from the first settlement, and a gun mounted on the point near the saw mill (in the cove) in 1749. One or two transports, which had been housed over during winter and store ships were anchored in the cove, under the cover of this gun, and the ice kept broke around them to prevent the approach of the Indians. The attempt to plant a settlement at Dartmouth, does not appear to have been at first very successful. Governor Hobson in his letter to the Board of Trade, dated 1st October, 1753, says, "At Dartmouth there is a small town well picketed in, and a detachment of troops to protect it, but there are not above five families residing in it, as there is no trade or fishing to maintain any inhabitants, and they apprehend danger from the Indians in cultivating any land on the outer side of the pickets."

There is no record of any concerted attack having been made by the Indians or French on the town of Halifax. Many stragglers were cut off during the first years of the settlement, particularly along the western side of the Basin, where the best firewood was to be obtained. It was at length found necessary to send out an armed body when fuel or lumber was required. The enemy usually retired before a regular organized force. The Ranger companies under Goreham and Bartelo, were most efficient for this purpose; they were usually recruited in New England, where men for that service were more readily found.

---

*The Governor in his letter to England mentions 4 men killed, 6 soldiers prisoners who were not upon guard, and our people killed 3 Indians, and had they done their duty well, might have killed many more.

The German settlers who came in the ship Ann, were employed in the public works at 2s. per day, besides a supply of beer and other liquors to each. It was decided that all settlers who came in the previous year, should cease to draw provisions after the 15th September, 1750. This order was afterwards repealed on 29th, and it was determined that all settlers already in the town or who should come before 1st December, should be entitled to one year's provisions from the time of their names being entered on the victualling book.*

It was the intention of Government that the Germans should be sent into the interior of the province; but they having arrived so late in the season, and the want of a sufficient supply of provisions then in store to sustain them through the winter rendered it impossible, and they were retained in the town. They were very sickly, many of them old and unfit for settlers, and their passages not being paid, and there being no person to purchase them, they were employed on the public works to work out their passage money.

About this period a gloom was cast over the settlement by the news of the murder of the Hon. Edward How, one of the Council at Chignecto. "Captain How was employed on the expedition to Chignecto as knowing the country well and being acquainted both with the Indians and the inhabitants, and furthermore he knew personally their leaders, LeCorne and LeLoutre. His whole aim and study was to obtain a peace with the Indians, and get the English prisoners out of their hands, for which purpose he often had conferences with the French officers under a flag of truce. LeCorne one day sent a flag of truce by a French officer to the water side, a small river which parts his people from the British troops. Capt. How and the officers held a parley for some time across the river. How had no sooner taken leave of the officers than a party that lay in ambush fired a volley at him and shot him through the heart, an instance of treacherous brutality not to be paralleled in history, and a violation of a flag of truce, which had ever been held sacred, and without which all faith is at an end, and all transactions with an enemy."—[Cornwallis' letter 27th November.]

---

* See victualling list in the appendix.

The spring of 1751 the five acre lots on the Peninsula were laid out; the people engaged in clearing the land. The uncertainty from surprise by Indians, however, much retarded the work; a large space, however, was cleared around the town before winter set in.

Another vessel having arrived on the 10th June, with German Palatine settlers, they were directed to be employed at Dartmouth in picketing in the back of the town. In July, the arrival of 200 more was reported, and they were ordered to be placed at the head of the N. W. Arm and mouth of the Basin; and those who owed work for their passage, were directed to picket in their stations. Monsieur Dupacquir, who had engaged to bring out 300 Swiss, brought but twenty this year, but more were expected in the following spring.

Ninth July, a proclamation issued to forfeit all lots of the town settlers who only put up slight frames of houses, unless they immediately proceeded to board them in and finish them as dwellings.

On the 18th June, Jas. Stephens and Wm. Harris were hanged for house-breaking; this was the second public execution which took place in the town.

William Piggot had a license granted him to open a coffee house on the 8th April the same year.

In January of this year the Council passed a series of regulations for the General Court and County Courts, and ordered them to be published by the Provost Marshal by reading the same after the beat of drum through the settlement, and on the first day of the next sitting of the General Court and County Courts.

The only matters further recorded worthy of notice during the year 1751, was the dismissal of Mr. Otis Little, the Commissary of Stores, for remissness in his office, and the resolution of the Governor and Council to pay a draft for £882, sent from Quebec, for the ransom of English prisoners taken by the Indians and carried to Canada. It appeared that Lt. Hamilton and upwards of sixty officers, soldiers and settlers had fallen into the hands of the savages, and Priest LeLoutre had agreed to ransom them for the sum above mentioned,

It may here be mentioned that several batteries have already been erected on George's Island,* and expensive earth works had been thrown up.

Towards the close of the year Mr. Joshua Mauger, a gentleman from England, who came out at the commencement of the settlement to trade and distil rum for the soldiers, was charged by government with having attempted to make Halifax the repository for Louisburg merchandize, brought up secretly and to be carrying on an illicit traffic, he being at the time agent victualler to Government. Governor Cornwallis, upon information, caused Mr. Mauger's stores to be searched for contraband articles brought from Louisburg. Much discussion ensued, and the settlement was for some time thrown into commotion, by what Mr. Mauger called in his letter to England, the high-handed proceedings of the Governor.

---

* This Island is called in the old French maps Isle Racket or the Snow Shoe Island, being in the shape of a snow shoe.

CHAPTER III.

In January, 1752, Mr. Collier, who had been acting as Chief Justice, and Captain Frotheringham, were called to the Council in place of Mr. Salisbury and Col. Horseman, who had returned to England. On 3rd February, a public ferry was established between Halifax and Dartmouth and John Connors appointed ferryman for three years, with the exclusive privilege, and ferry regulations were also established. At the same sitting of the Council, an order was passed for the recording of deeds and mortgages, making all papers unrecorded void against those which had been registered. Col. Horseman's stone building was purchased for a prison in place of that before used.

April 29th, Charles Morris, James Monk, John Duport, Robert Ewer, Joseph Scott, John Wm. Hoffeman and Leonard Christopher Rodolf were appointed Justices of the Peace. It was resolved in Council at their sitting on 12th June, that a lottery should be held for building a Light House near Cape Sambro, to raise £450. One thousand tickets at £3 each. Prizes from one of £500 to £7 the lowest. Two hundred prizes, in all amounting to £3000, 15 per cent. to be deducted from the prizes, to be drawn publicly in the Town House at Halifax, under the direction of managers to be appointed by Government.

The winter of 1751-2 had been severe, but the harbour had not been frozen or at all impeded by ice, and the spring opened early, and preparations for prosecuting the fishery were soon in active operation.

The Goverment mills at Dartmouth, under charge of Captain Clapham, were sold at auction in June. They were purchased by Major Gilman for £310.

16th July—An order passed to strike off the victualling lists all the German and Swiss settlers, who had arrived in the Speedwell.

In the spring of 1752, a number of settlers arrived in the Nancy, under the charge of Lt. Young. About the same time the Marquis DeConte, a Sicilian nobleman, and a number of other foreign settlers, came to Halifax from the island of Tercera, one of the Azores, and settled in the town,

Governor Cornwallis having obtained permission to resign the Government, the Hon. Peregrine T. Hopson, was appointed his successor, and was sworn into office before the Council on Monday, 3rd August. Mr. Cornwallis, however, did not leave the province until after the 10th of October, as he appears to have attended the Council held on that day.*

In September, 1752, John Baptist Cope, commonly called Major Cope, a Mic-Mac chief, head of the Shubenacadie Indians, came in with terms of peace, which were agreed to. This bears date the 15th September, in that year. Immediately after this document was signed, Cope left town in a vessel, having requested Capt. W. Piggot should be sent to Indian Harbour, to meet the Indians there, to ratify the Treaty. Mr. Piggot was accordingly dispatched, and brought up with him two or three Indians, who appeared before the Council, after which they were sent back to Beaver Harbour, under the conduct of Mr. Piggot, with blankets, provisions, etc. The terms of the Treaty were agreed to and confirmed in Council, and the whole was engrossed on parchment and ratified on 22nd November, 1752. The names of the Indian delegates on this occasion were, Andrew Hodley Martin, Gabriel Martin and Francis Jeremiah. Mr. Saul received directions to issue provisions, according to the allowance of the troops for six months, for 90 Indians, that being the number of the tribe under Cope, occupying the eastern part of the province.

This treaty does not appear to have been respected by the Indian Chief, who we find, not more than eight months after its ratification, refusing to respect the pass of Governor Hopson to one Anthony Cartel, who had been captured by the Indians, in one of the harbours eastward of Halifax, and carried through the country to Shubenacadie, the head-quarters of Major Cope, from whom he was ransomed by a French inhabitant. It would appear that the terms of amity, entered into by Cope and his men with the Government at Halifax, had been in some manner without the sanction of Abbe LeLoutre, who, when Anthony Cartel was brought before Count

---

*On September 29th, 1752, the first fire regulations were published at Halifax, among which are found the following: Two or three Magistrates may order a house to be pulled down or blown up to stop a fire, the owner to be indemnified by the house owners of the Town. The fire wards to be appointed by the Justices of the Peace, each to carry a red staff 6 feet long, with a bright brass spear 6 inches long on it; and other regulations. This custom is still kept up in the City, or was until very lately.

Raymond at Louisburg, was present, and as Cartel expresses it, inveighed bitterly against Governor Cornwallis, and said if he wanted peace he ought to have written to him, and not to have treated with the tribe of Indians. That he, Cartel, might depart, having been ransomed, but that the first Englishman he caught should be retained until he, LeLoutre, had full satisfaction for himself and his Indians.

In April following, two men named John Connor and James Grace, arrived at Halifax in an Indian canoe, bringing with them six Indian scalps. They informed the Council that they and two others, having put into a place between Tor Bay and Country Harbour, in a schooner, were captured by the Indians, and carried ten miles into the country, where their two companions were murdered; that they had surprised the Indians at night, killed several, whose scalps they secured, and having escaped to the seaside, seized a canoe, and made their way to Halifax. Along the coast, both east and west from Halifax, Indian massacres had been frequent. Those persons engaged in the fishery, who were compelled to land for wood and water, were chiefly the sufferers.

Much had been said and written in Europe at the time, relative to the aggressions of the French, during the suspension of hostilities between the two nations. The Indians, from their religion and trading intercourse, more favourable to the French in Canada and Acadia, were made use of to harass the British settlers, who (though the two nations were then at peace) were looked upon with a jealous eye by the resident French population. A French writer, (I refer to a little work, now a scarce book, published during the second siege of Louisburg), states that the English neglected to cultivate an acquaintance with the manners and customs of the Indians, and it was therefore not surprising at the time, that they should show less affection towards them than towards the French, who had great regard to their humours and inclinations.

"So strong is their aversion to despotic power," says the author, "that force will never do; they will yield to nothing but persuasion. Though they know nothing of precepts or subordination, yet they enjoy almost every advantage derived from well-regulated authority. Their laws and customs appear impressed on their hearts. In order to gain an ascendancy over them, you must gain their esteem, for they never confide in a person whom they do not value, and this esteem is very difficult to obtain."

The savages were exasperated against the English by a speech delivered by Count Raymond, at a meeting of the chiefs, in which, to suit his own purposes, he depicted the most frightful cruelties perpetrated by the English.

During the Indian hostilities, opposition on the part of the Colonists was altogether of a defensive nature. The regular troops, as well as the undisciplined militia, proving unfit for such warfare, it was found necessary to employ the New England Rangers. These were volunteers from the New England provinces, accustomed to Indian warfare, many of them Indians and half-bloods. They ascended the rivers, penetrated into the heart of the province, and attacked the enemy in their strongholds. The Indians finding they were opposed by men equally accustomed to the forest with themselves, soon found it their interest to make peace with the British.*

In 1758, it was found necessary to procure the services of 250 of these Rangers from New England, by promises of high pay and other advantages. Long accustomed to the border war with the Indians and French of Canada, they had become well disciplined, and accustomed to hardships and fatigue, and were perhaps at this time superior to all other provincial troops in America. The Provincials were troops raised in the Colonies at the expense of the Provincial Government, and were distinct from the Rangers, who were independent companies paid by the British Government. They served at Havannah, at Louisburg in the first siege under Pepperell, and with Wolfe at Louisburg and Quebec, and afterwards served to form the groundwork of Washington's army in 1775.

After the fall of Fort William Henry in 1758, it was said that the Marquis de Montcalm sent a number of prisoners taken at that place, in a vessel to Halifax. They were Provincial soldiers, chiefly from the New England provinces. This was said to have been an attempt to introduce the small pox into Halifax, many of the men being ill of the disorder on their embarkation. Providence, however, frustrated this benevolent design. The prisoners being kept on low diet, half starved, and exposed to the cold, soon

---

* Governor Cornwallis reduced the Rangers. He thought Gorcham very incompetent to command them.

recovered, while the French in charge of the vessel, having indulged in the use of wine and strong fare, were thrown down with the disease, and nearly all perished. The vessel was brought into port by the prisoners.*

In the spring of 1751, nine hundred and fifty-eight Protestant German settlers arrived, and in the following year 1000 more.† The latter were from Montbeliard, of the Confession of Augsburgh, and were placed under the spiritual charge of the Rev. J. B. Moreau. They had been induced to emigrate by promises from King George II, which it is said were never realized. Considerable difficulty appears to have been experienced by the Government in providing a suitable situation for settling so large a number of persons. The original design with regard to the foreign Protestants was to place them in the interior of the country, on the lands unoccupied by the French Acadians, it being supposed that their proximity to and intercourse with the French, would be the means of lessening the bad feeling which had been fostered by emissaries from Canada. The project was unfavorably received by the Acadians. There were, however, other difficulties in the way of its accomplishment, of a particular nature, which compelled the Government to abandon the object. The want of sufficient provisions to maintain so many settlers through the winter, the lateness of the season, and the helplessness of a large portion of the Germans, who were unfit for labour, induced the Government to place them in the neighbourhood of Halifax. It was at first proposed in Council to send them to the opposite side of the harbour over against George's Island, and Captain Morris was sent to survey the grounds. The mouth of Musquodoboit River was also suggested, and a survey of that part of the country ordered, but the distance from Halifax and the danger of the Indians, rendered the scheme impracticable. "All I could do," says the Governor, "was to build boarded barracks for them. They must be sustained by Government until they are capable of raising something of their own; most of them are poor and wretched, and have scarce a farthing of money among them."

These people had been collected together by a Mr. Dick, the Government agent for that purpose. He had persuaded these who

---

* This story was related by the late Titus Smith, who received it from his father.
† The names of the settlers who arrived after June and July, 1749, are not to be found among the records of the country.

came out this year to sell everything they possessed even to their bedding, before going on board; and they stated that owing to the want of bedding and other conveniences, many of them died on the passage and since their arrival. Many of these people are represented as very old, and as objects fitter to be kept in almshouses, several of them above 80 years of age. The Governor in his letter to the Board of Trade, says, "On the 26th September last, when the last of these settlers were landed, there were 30 of them who could not stir off the beach, and among the children there were 8 orphans, who in twelve days increased to 14 by the death of their parents. These had to be removed to the public orphan house, and had the best care taken of them." Many of these settlers became discontented with their condition, and went off to the Island of St. John, where they endeavoured to settle themselves. The difficulty of procuring provisions was very great. The Government appears to have been altogether dependent on the contracts of Althorp and Hancock of Boston, and Delaney and Watts of New York, for the necessary supplies for the settlement.

In June, 1753, about 1500 of these German settlers embarked for Malagash Harbour, west of Mahone Bay, where they afterwards built the town of Lunenburg. They were accompanied by a company of Rangers under Major Goreham. The expedition was placed under the command of Col. Charles Lawrence. There were also some regular troops, under Major Patrick Sutherland, who took a very active part in planting the settlement. Lieutenant John Creighton, of Warburton's Regiment, also accompanied the German settlers, and also the Rev. J. B. Moreau, who officiated as their minister.

The Lunenburg settlers were placed under similar regulations with those at Halifax, and received Government allowance for several years after their arrival at Malagash.

After the removal of the Germans from Halifax to Lunenburg, there were but 15 German families left in the north suburbs. Not knowing any English, they formed themselves into a separate congregation for religious worship, and built themselves a small house upon the German burial ground on Brunswick street, in which they had prayers every Sunday. In 1760, a steeple was built on this house, and the next year the Rev. Dr. Breynton, Rector of St.

Paul's, preached there for the first time, and it was on that occasion dedicated by the name of St. George's Church. The congregation followed the English Church rules of doctrine and appointed their Elders and Vestry. This old building still remains in its primitive state, the only monument now remaining of the old German settlement, called Dutchtown.

In October, 1752, Mr. Cotterall was appointed to the Council, and John Duport sworn in Clerk of the Council. An order in Council and proclamation appeared on the 14th of November, forbidding persons from assembling or carrying about effigies on the anniversary of the holiday, called Gunpowder Treason, being the 16th of November, according to the alteration of the style.

At the Council held on the 22nd December, 1752, the Justices were ordered to look out for a proper place for a bridewell or workhouse, and to form a plan for the building of a block-house for that purpose, and to obtain an estimate of the probable expense, and to report rules and regulations for the government of the same. The Constables were to go about the streets on Sundays to prevent disorders, and to make a report to the Justices in the evening after divine service, and to apprehend disorderly persons during the night. Proprietors of land were obliged to fence their quota; on failure, to be liable to an action for the recovery of the charges for fencing the same.

All proprietors of land upon the peninsula of Halifax were directed to clear half their lots by 1st May, 1753, to clear the remainder and fence the whole by 1st May, 1754, otherwise the lots would be forfeited and be disposed of to others who would improve them. And an order was made for permission to John Connors, to assign the Dartmouth Ferry to Henry Wynne and William Manthorne.

Among the local events recorded this year, was a robbery in one of the King's storehouses, which was broken open on the night of the 26th October. There was also a cartel published by Governor Hopson, for the exchange of prisoners with the French Government in Canada.

The most important circumstance of the year, however, was a charge against the Justices of the Inferior Court of Common Pleas, sent in to the Council by a number of the most influential inhabitants, charging them with partiality, and praying for a public hearing. This document was presented to the Council in December, and was signed by Joshua Mauger, Joseph Rundel, Isaac Knott, John Grant, Francis Martin, Edward Crawley, Richard Catherwood, Robert Campbell, William Nesbitt, John Webb, William McGee, Sebastian Zouberbuhler, Samuel Sellon and Isaac Deschamps. These charges came on for hearing before the Council on 3rd January following; they consisted of ten distinct charges against Charles Morris, James Monk, John Duport, Robert Ewer and William Bourn, Esquires, Justices of the Inferior Court of Common Pleas, for the Town and County of Halifax, and were signed by the following inhabitants:

Joshua Mauger,	Louis Triquet,
S. Zouberbuhler,	William Clapham,
Samuel Sellon,	John Webb,
Edward Buckleton,	Robert Catherwood,
James Porter,	John Walker,
Daniel Wood,	Geo. Peter DeBreg,
Jonathan Gifford,	Richard Hollis,
William Schwartz,	Henry Sibley,
Edward Crawley,	Edward O'Brien,
William Jeffray,	Henry O'Brien,
Vere Bous,	Thos. Wynne,
Francis Martin,	John Grant,
John Brooks,	William Vanselsou,
Henry Wilkinson,	Cheyne Brovnjohn,
William Nesbitt,	Richard Tritton,
John Woodin,	Edward Lakey,
James Ford,	Cyrus Janain,
George Featherstone,	John Willis,
Thos. Mattison,	Roger Hill,
Joseph Antony,	Js. Deschamps,
Alex. Kedy,	Robert Grant,
James Fullon,	William McGee,
William Murray,	Joseph Rundel.

This affair arose from a dispute which occurred between the Government and Captain Ephraim Cook, who had been discharged from the Commission of the Peace by Governor Cornwallis for bad behaviour, and appears to have been the result of party feeling.

It resulted in additional numbers being added to the bench of Magistrates, and the Governor and Council availed themselves of this affair to urge upon the Government the necessity of having a Chief Justice.

The necessity of a properly organized Militia force being kept up, had become apparent, in consequence of the continual threats of hostility on the part of the Indians and native French; it was therefore resolved on 22nd March, 1753, that a Militia should be raised and established for the security of the Province, and a proclamation was accordingly issued, compelling all persons (except foreigners, who were to be placed elsewhere) between the ages of 16 and 60, to serve in the Militia.

On the first day of June, another proclamation was issued for a muster of the Militia. Those of the south suburbs to assemble within the pickets opposite the end of Barrington Street, near Horseman's Fort. Those of the north suburbs, between the Grenadier Fort and Lutteral's Fort, and those of the town on the esplanade, near the Citadel Hill.

On the 12th of April, 1753, Claude Gisigash, an Indian who styled himself Governor of LaHave, appeared before the Council, and having declared his intention of making peace, terms of amity were drawn up and signed by the Governor and the Indian Chief, on the part of himself and his people. The terms were the same as those made with Major Cope, and it was arranged that some of his tribe should come up and ratify the treaty.

Governor Hopson went home on leave in the autumn of 1753, and the government was administered by Col. Lawrence. In one of his last letters to the Board of Trade, in reference to the disturbed state of the country, Governor Hopson says, "Your Lordships may imagine how disagreeable it is to me to see His Majesty's rights encroached upon, and those encroachments openly avowed and supported by the Governors of Canada and Louisburg, when it is not in my power to prevent it. I have barely a sufficient force to protect the settlers from the insults of an Indian war, under pretence of which the French take an opportunity to commit hostilities upon His Majesty's subjects. I am informed that the

French have often been mixed among them in the expeditions, and am convinced past doubt that they are fed and protected from our pursuit, and are encouraged to disturb us as openly and in as great a degree as in time of war."

There were three still houses in Halifax in 1753. Mr. Best the master mason, and Mr. Clewley the master carpenter, having been ordered to inspect them. The return was as follows :

> Mr. Richard Bowers, 2 stills in Granville Street.
> Wm. Murray, 1 still in Grafton Street, reported not safe.
> Jonathan Gifford, 1 still in Barrington Street.

October 16th, Mr. John Greenwood presented a petition to the Council, stating that he had paid passage for 12 men, 1 woman and 2 children, foreign settlers, with the Governor's leave. They engaged to serve him for a year, but having been removed to Lunenburg by the Governor's orders, he lost their services ; he was allowed £79 5s., the labour of 12 men for 96 days.

Governor Hopson took leave of the Council on 26th October, and received an address on his departure. He sailed for England on the 2nd November following.

On the 16th November, two Indians appeared before the Council, who had been sent from Lunenburg by Col. Sutherland. They stated they were of the tribe of Cape Sable Indians, which consisted of about 60 people with two chiefs ; that Baptiste Thomas, one of their priests, was one of their chiefs, and the other Francis Jean de Perisse was not a chief, but deputed by the other chief. They stated that they had never joined with the other Indians to molest the English ; that on the contrary they had always exhibited a friendly spirit, in consequence of which they had never received any assistance from the French. The Council gave them 2000 pounds of bread, 3 barrels of pork, 20 blankets, 30 pounds powder, some shot, tobacco and other articles, also two gold-laced hats for their chiefs, and one silver-laced for the deputy.

The close of this year was occupied by the Governor and Council, in investigation of the riots which occurred at Lunenburg, known as the Hoffman Rebellion. It was found necessary to send Col. Monkton with a body of regular troops to suppress the riots. Mr. Hoffman, the supposed ringleader, was brought to Halifax and imprisoned on George's Island. He was afterwards tried and sentenced to a fine of £100 or two years imprisonment.

It may be proper to advert to the religious condition of the settlement at this period. The greater portion of the inhabitants were at this time of the Church of England. The Protestant Germans had nearly all united themselves to that Church, and sought missionaries from the S. P. G. Society.

The Rev. John Breynton succeeded Mr. Tutty in St. Paul's. In 1752, he reported that half of the population had professed themselves members of the Church, and that the actual communicants were between 500 and 600.

Mr. Breynton established an Orphan House, and the Orphan School was under his superintendence. In 1753, fifty poor children were diligently instructed. Ralph Sharrock was the school-master. In 1753, the Rev. Thomas Wood from the Province of New Jersey, was appointed to assist Mr. Breynton, and he remained jointly in charge with Mr. Breynton until 1763, when he was removed to Annapolis.

It may here be observed, that on the establishment of Representative Government at Halifax, in 1758, among the first acts of the Assembly, was that for the support of Religious Worship, which contained a clause for the free toleration of all Protestant dissenters, whether Lutherans, Calvinists, etc., completely exempting them from all charges for the support of the Established Church. By this act, the right of the parishioners of St. Paul's and all future parishes, to present their own minister to the ordinary for induction was declared, and immediately after its publication, the parishioners of the parish of St. Paul's, in the Town of Halifax, presented the Reverend John Breynton and the Reverend Thomas Wood as joint Rectors, or "Rector and Vicar," as they were called, to the Governor, who immediately went through the form of induction, a ceremony thought necessary in order to entitle them to privileges of incumbents. The record of this fact will be found in the correspondence of the Society for the Propagation of the Gospel at that period.

During the winter of 1753-4, there had been no disturbance from the Indians, and the Government availed themselves of the opportunity of sending out proper persons to make a survey of the country around. The winter was mild and the frost not so severe as usual or of so long continuance. The valley of the Shubenacadie had been examined, but it was not found available for settlement, being the principal resort of the Indians under Cope. The Township of Lawrencetown including Chezzetcook, had also been undertaken, and further grants of land in that quarter of the country were sought for in the following spring.

The desertion of many of the lower orders of the German settlers at Lunenburg is mentioned; they appear to have gone over to the French. Governor Lawrence in his letter to the Board of Trade, August 1st. 1754, speaking of the French, says, "They have not for a long time brought anything to our markets, but on the other hand have carried everything to the French and Indians."

At this time the land was being cleared for the Battery at the east side of the harbour, the site probably of the present eastern battery. A fort was also in progress of erection at Lawrencetown when the settlement was progressing, not having been disturbed by the Indians. This settlement had been formed by Governor Lawrence in consequence of the good meadow lands at the head of the harbour, and he granted the township to 20 proprietors and built a blockhouse for their protection. But the undertaking was not prosperous, and finally failed to answer the object intended, owing to its exposed situation and the distance from Halifax.

The arrival of the Vulture, sloop-of-war, Capt. Kenzey, from the Bay of Fundy, produced much excitement in the Town; she brought several prisoners charged with murder, who were lodged in jail to take their trial before the General Court.*

Benjamin Street, Samuel Thornton and John Pastree, were placed on their trial for the murder of one of the midshipmen and a sailor of the Vulcan. It appeared on the trial that a schooner, of which the parties charged were part of the crew, commanded by one Hovey, belonging to Boston or some part of New England, was found trading in the Bay of Fundy and supplying the French with provisions, etc. Capt. Kenzey sent a boat aboard Hovey's shallop, under the idea that he had contraband goods on board. The crew refused to allow the man-of-war boat to come alongside, and fired

---

* Mr. Nisbett was Attorney General at the time. He had been acting in that office since the Spring of 1752.

into her, killing Mr. Jolly and wounding several others. Hovey, the master, appears to have gone below and hid himself during the whole affair. He was discovered in his berth by the officer in command of the man-of-war boat, after the sloop had been captured. This affair occurred in July, 1754, and the trial took place before the Chief Justice in Michaelmas Term of that year. This was the first sitting at which Chief Justice Belcher presided. The three prisoners were acquitted of the murder, but it would appear they were found guilty of the minor offence, as they were sentenced to six months imprisonment, and afterwards placed on board a man-of-war (1755). Joseph Hovey, the master, was discharged, the grand jury refusing to find a bill of indictment against him.

The following appointments were made by the grand jury in Michaelmas Term, 1754: Gaugers of Casks, Paul Pritchard and Lewis Piers; Surveyers of Pickled Fish, Henry Ferguson and Daniel Hills; Cullers of Dry Fish, Charles King and E. Gerrott; Cullers of Hoops and Staves, Dennis Heffernan and Benoni Bartlett; Surveyors of Lumber, etc., Joseph Scott and Joseph Marshall; Surveyors of Cordwood, Samuel McClure, Josiah Milliken and Joseph Wakefield.

On Monday 14th October, 1754, Jonathan Belcher, Esq., was sworn in Chief Justice. The Court then adjourned to the Court House, where His Majesty's Commission was read, appointing Lt. Governor Lawrence, Governor General of the province. Mr. Belcher's appointment bears date in July. At the commencement of Michaelmas Term, the following ceremonies and procession were observed, the first of the kind ever seen in Nova Scotia. On the first day of Michaelmas Term, the Chief Justice walked from the Governor's house honoured by the presence of His Excellency Charles Lawrence, Esq., Lieutenant Governor, and accompanied by the Honourable the Members of H. M. Council, proceeded by the Provost Marshal, the Judge's tipstaff, and other civil officers, the gentlemen of the Bar attending in their gowns, and walking in procession to the long room at Pontach's, where an elegant breakfast was provided, where the Chief Justice in his scarlet robes, was received and complimented in the politest manner, by a great number of gentlemen and ladies, and officers of the Army. Breakfast being over, they proceeded with the commission before them, to church, where an excellent sermon was preached by the Rev. Mr. Breynton, from these words: "I am one of them that are peaceable and faithful in Israel." A suitable anthem was sung, after which they proceeded to the Court House, which upon this occasion was very handsomely fitted up, where the Chief Justice being seated with his Excellency the Lieutenant Governor on his right hand under a canopy, the clerk of the Crown presented His Majesty's commission to the Chief Justice, appointing him to be Chief Justice within the province, which being returned, and proclamation for silence being made, the same was read, and directions were given by the Chief Justice for the conduct of the practitioners, and the grand jury appearing in Court upon the return of the precept, were sworn and charged by the Chief Justice, and the business of the day being finished, the Court adjourned. His Honor the Chief Justice, accompanied and attended as before, returned to the Governor's house. A few days after Mr. Chief Justice Belcher, the Provost Marshal, the gentlemen of the Bar, and other officers of H. M. Supreme Court, and the gentlemen of the grand jury, waited on his Exellency the Lieutenant Governor, when the Chief Justice, in his robes of office, addressed his Excellency in the name of the whole, as follows:

"Sir,—We esteem it our indispensable duty to testify our zeal, as Chief Justice, provost marshal, grand jurors, practitioners and officers of H. M. Supreme Court of judicature, for the interest of this province, and the protection of its laws, our attachment to your person, and our respect and gratitude for your eminent services, by expressing our joy in His Majesty appointing you to the chief command of this his dominion of Nova Scotia. We shall ever consider it as essential to our fidelity in the execution of the laws, to exert our most vigilant endeavors for the ease and success of your administrations, and not only to suppress any measures subversive of your consultations for the public good, but at all times affectuate the means prescribed by you for the prosperity of the province. Our solicitude for the advancement of justice under the laws, cannot be more fervently expressed, than by the tender of our ardent wishes for your being and happy continuance in the chief chair of this Government."

To which his Excellency the Lieutenant Governor was pleased to make the following answer:

"Mr. Chief Justice and gentlemen of the Supreme Court and grand jury:

"I have the highest sense of this testimony of your zeal for the public welfare and your esteem for me. I should be much wanting in my duty if I did not embrace this opportunity of returning my thanks for the late pious, learned and eloquent charge from the Bench, and I doubt not, gentlemen, but your vigilance and fidelity in the service of your country will have its desired effect.

"While I have the power to sit in the chair, be assured the authority of Government shall be ready to support the law, for the law, gentlemen, is the firm and solid basis of civil society, the guardian of liberty, the protection of the innocent, the terror of the guilty, and the scourge of the wicked.

"CHARLES LAWRENCE."

Governor Lawrence in his letter of 12th January, 1755, says, " I am now preparing to build three batteries of 10 guns each in front of the town, and contemplate finishing them in good time. These batteries were erected along the line of the shore. The middle or King's battery stood where the Queen's wharf now is, there was another at the present Ordnance Yard, another near the site of Fairbanks wharf, and a fourth at the present Lumber Yard, which latter still remains."

The batteries along the front of the town were completed during the summer of 1755, and a plan of them sent to England in June of that year, They were twelve feet in height above high water mark, two hundred and forty feet in length, and sixty-five in breadth. The parapet raised on these was seven feet high, and the materials consisted of logs and timber framed and filled up with gravel, stones, earth and sand. The materials consisted of 9500 logs of 25 feet, 1280 tons of square timber and 25,000 tons weight of gravel and earth, the whole expense about £5,300. The work was commenced in January, 1755, and completed late in the summer. 20 guns were mounted on these three batteries in July of that year — the other batteries were afterwards added.

An attempt was made this year to involve the Government in a dispute with the Indian tribes. Paul Laurant, an Indian Chief of the

Mic-Mac tribe, appeared before the Council on 12th February, 1755, and informed them that he and another Indian Chief named Algamud, had set out from Beausejour for Halifax in order to treat of peace, but that the Chief had fallen sick at Cobequid and had intrusted him with the proposals. They demanded the whole eastern section of the Province, from Cobequid to Canso, to be set apart for them as feeding and hunting grounds. Being asked what security he could give that the Indians would keep the peace, he said he could say nothing to that, being only desired to bring in the terms. The Council dismissed him with a promise of an answer in writing. An answer in writing was drawn up and signed by the Governor on 13th February, 1755, which expressed a willingness on the part of the Governor and Council to allow them such lands as would be sufficient for their purposes. It mentioned the perfidious breaches of all former treaties on the part of the Indians, and where their conduct was complained of that the Tribes themselves had disallowed all authority on the part of their Chiefs to make such treaties, and that the Governor and Council demanded a full attendance of Chiefs before them, with full power to treat, before any further proceedings could be taken.

On the 3rd and 4th July, the Council was engaged with the French Deputies, again on 14th, 15th and 28th same month.

The defence of the settlement was the next subject of deliberation and the protection from the incursions of the French along the Bay of Fundy and from Louisburg, both nations being at the time arrayed against each other in open warfare.

On the 18th February, 1755, Mrs. Green, wife of Hon. Benj. Green, and her family, Captain Horatio Gates and Mrs. Gates, with Captain Hale and their servants and baggage, were received on board Captain Rogers' sloop for Boston. Captain Gates had been one of the Aides-de-Camp of Governor Cornwallis, he was afterwards a General in the American Revolutionary Army.*

The loss of the Mars, a 70 gun ship, occurred off the harbour in May, 1755. It was in an easterly gale and supposed to be the fault of the pilot. Guns and crew were all saved. The Mars rock at the western entrance of the bay marks the spot. The guns and stores were brought to Halifax. Admiral Holborn's letter announc-

---

* See Biographical note in the last Chapter.

ing the loss of the ship bears date the 28th May, off Halifax Harbour.

30th December, 1755, Montague Wilmot and Charles Morris, having been appointed to the Council, were sworn in. The other members were John Collier, Mr. Cotterell, Robert Monkton and Captain Rous.

A number of French prizes, taken by the fleet under Admiral Boscawen, were this summer brought into Halifax. There were in these 19,998 gallons of rum and brandy.

A Mr. Ellis had for several years held the office of Governor of Nova Scotia, and received the emoluments, but never came out. Lt. Governor Lawrence received the appointment of Governor-in-Chief on the resignation of Mr. Ellis, and Colonel Monkton became Lt. Governor; their commissions were read and they sworn into office on 23rd July, this year.

The following census of the town appears to have been taken about 1755 or 1756 :—

Masters of families paying poor tax	256
Male children between 12 and 21 years of age	182
Male children under 12	291
Transient persons who pay no taxes	108
	837
Married women	241
Girls unmarried above 12 years old	261
Girls under 12 years of age	345
Women servants	71
	918
	1755

The only other event of this year worthy of notice was the following melancholy affair detailed in Col. Sutherland's letter from Lunenburg, dated 12th September. "Yesterday," he says, "I received the melancholy account of Mr. Payzant's house being burned in Mahone Bay, and that he himself and other people who were with him, were killed by the Indians. I immediately sent out an officer and party, which returned this morning, by whom I am informed that on Payzant's Island the house is burned, he with another young man killed and scalped, a woman servant and child also killed and scalped near the water side. His wife and four children missing. The young man was son to a family which lived on Captain Rous's Island. As his hands were tied the gentlemen immediately conjectured some further mischief was done there, and on their arrival they found the man thereto belonging, likewise scalped. It appears that Captain Rous's is the most advanced settlement, that they first came there and took the boy to conduct them to Payzant's.'' Mr. Payzant came to this country with a strong recommendation from Mr. Pownall, secretary to the Board of Trade. The death of James Payzant, Esquire, a clerk in the office of the Secretary of State, of the age of 100 years is announced in the London Gazette for 1757. This was probably the father of the gentleman who came out to Halifax, to whom Mr. Secretary Pownall's recommendation referred.''

1756. January 26th, the term of Henry Wynne and William Manthorn's licences of the Dartmouth and Halifax ferry having expired, John Rock petitioned and obtained the same on the terms of his predecessors.

On the 30th June, 1757, Lord Loudon arrived at Halifax with the troops from New York, destined for the invasion of Cape Breton.

Saturday, 16th July, 1757, His Excellency acquainted the Council that the Earl of Loudon had this day represented to him that a fever had broken out among the troops, under His Lordship's command, occasioned by the great quantities of rum that were sold to the soldiers by unlicensed retailers, and if continued must prove of fatal consequences to the service; and unless steps were immediately taken to effectually stop the same, he would feel himself justified in ordering all liquors found in the possession of such unlicensed retailers to be destroyed. The Council empowered the Provost Marshal and his deputies to enter such houses, seize the liquors and place them in the King's store until the army and navy departed.

On the 1st November, 1757, the grand jury of the County of Halifax petitioned the Governor and Council on behalf of the inhabitants of the town, that the town should be put into some state of defence "for the preservation of the place, the inhabitants, their families and effects." They stated that the property, etc., was insecure from the want of proper defences; that the people were willing to assist in the work, and intimated that if their prayer could not be heard, humbly beg that they " may immediately know it in order to take the first opportunity of conveying themselves, their families and effects, to a place of safety in some of the neighbouring Colonies." A previous petition had been presented to the Governor, to which no answer had been returned. The names attached to the petition were, Robert Saunderson, Joseph Rundell, John Anderson, Paul Pritchard, Hugh McCoy, Joseph Fairbanks, William Schwartz, Robert Campbell, William Pantree, John Killick, John Brooks, Henry Wilkinson, Walter Manning, John Slayter, Richard Catherwood, Joseph Pierce, Alexander Cunningham, Richard Tritson, Jonathan Gifford and Benjamin Leigh.

The boundaries of the Township of Halifax were settled by order in Council 20th May, 1758, as follows: That until said township can be more particularly described, the limit thereof shall be deemed to be as follows:

To comprehend all the lands lying southerly of a line extending from the westernmost head of Bedford Basin, across the northerly head of St. Margaret's Bay, with all the Islands near to said land, together with the Islands called Cornwallis Island,* Webb's and Rous' Island.†

Minutes of Council 21st June, 1758: Mr. Josiah Marshall proposed to build a workhouse, 50 feet long, 20 feet wide and 8 feet high, in the town. The timber to be laid close, with a roof double boarded and shingled; to have 4 windows on each side, each window to have nine panes of glass and three iron grates; to have a staircase in the entry and a whipping post. The building to be placed on a good dry wall. Mr. Marshall's tender for £200 sterling, finding materials and labour, was accepted.

To Charles Morris, Joshua Mauger and Charles Proctor, Esquires. " Whereas, it has been thought proper to convert to the " use of the public, a piece of land called Goreham's Point and the " lands next ajacent, lying in the north suburbs of Halifax, " formerly allotted to sundry persons, who have cleared and " improved the same and erected some buildings upon them; they

---

* Now McNab's.
† Now known as Lawlor's and Devil's Islands.

"were directed to value the lands and proportion each owner's extent therein, and report to His Excellency. Dec. 9th, 1758."

This is the site of the Commissioners' House in the present Dockyard.

December 9th, 1758. Peter Marquis de Conte and Gravina, convicted for intent to commit rape on a child under the age of ten years, was sentenced by the Court to walk between the hours of 11 and 12 this day from the north to the south side of the Parade, and from thence to the jail with a paper placed on his breast with his crime inscribed thereon, and to be confined for three months and fined thirty pounds; to remain in jail till the same be paid. Governor Lawrence remitted the first part of this sentence. The Marquis de Conte was a Sicilian nobleman; he had been an officer in Gorsham's Rangers.

December 29th. 1758. It appears by an advertisement of this date, that Governor Lawrence had wells sunk and pumps erected as reservoirs against fires, and that they had been damaged by some unknown person. His Excellency caused them to be put in repair.

Governor Lawrence, in his letter to the Board of Trade, 3rd November, 1759, mentions that the masoury of Sambro Light House had been some time finished, and that the lantern was then in progress of erection. That a chart of the harbour was also in progress, as also proper directions for piloting in ships with safety. Copies of these directions were enclosed in his letter.

It appears that in the year 1758, the Governor appropriated out of the old crown duty money for the Light House £1,000, for the Work House £500, for the Church £400, and for the Meeting House £100.

Again in 1760, for the Light House £987 5s. 5d.
" 452 10 10
" 685 6 8

£2075 2s. 11d.

For the Work House £5,456, for the Church £350 18s. 6., Meeting House £174 0s. 4d., Jail £208 11s. 9d.

Captain Rous was placed in charge of the Light House, a post which he occupied for many years. This was not Captain John Rous, the member of Council, but a relative of his from New

21st December, 1758. The Governor and Council appropriated the sum of £400, raised by duties on liquors, towards the church in Halifax, under the direction of Benjamin Green, John Collier, Charles Morris, Robert Saunderson and Henry Newton, commissioners for that purpose.

[Extract of letter from Louisburg, June 9th.]

"Admiral Saunders, with the squadron under his command, arrived in good condition on the 21st April off Louisburg, but on account of ice blockading the harbour, was obliged to bear away on the 26th for Halifax, whence he arrived on the first of May."

June 16th, 1759. Peter Marquis de Conte and Gravini, was released from his imprisonment, he having paid his fine. This gentleman died at Halifax. His will is recorded in the probate office.

Thursday 16th August, 1759, William Cotteral, Robert Grant and Montague Wilmot, Esquires, Councillors, being absent from the Province, the Governor appointed Richard Bulkeley, Thomas Saul and Joseph Gerrish, who were this day sworn in and took their seats.

February, 1760, two Indian Chiefs attended the Council, and were presented with laced blankets, laced hats, etc. They were informed that the same would be sent to the Chief of the St. John's Indians, and that the treaty of peace would be ready to be signed to-morrow, and if the wind was favourable they should embark on Sunday.

In Council 11th March, 1760, the Governor appointed the Hon. Jonathan Belcher, Benjamin Green, John Collier, Charles Morris, Richard Bulkeley, Thomas Saul and Joseph Gerrish, Esquires, and William Nesbitt, John Duport, Joseph Scott, John Creighton, Sebastian Zouberbuhler, Edward Crawley, Charles Proctor and Benjamin Gerrish, Esquires, to be justices of the peace for the town and county of Halifax. Charles Morris, John Duport, Joseph Scott, Joseph Gerrish and Edward Crawley, Esquires, to be justices of the Inferior Court of Common Pleas for the county of Halifax, to the several of whom His Excellency then administered the oath requisite.

CHAPTER IV.

Notwithstanding the advantages held out by Government to the settlers at Halifax, and the repeated large grants of money by Parliament, the people were rapidly removing to the old Colonies. Little progress had been made in clearing the country. The fishery, one of the main inducements of the settlement, was almost altogether neglected, and the population was reduced to much less than half its original number. They subsisted chiefly on the money expended by the Army and Navy, and were dependent on Boston for their provisions and many other necessary supplies.

In 1755, Dr. Breynton, the minister at St. Paul's, estimated the inhabitants of Halifax at 1,300, eight hundred of whom professed themselves members of the Church of England; and again in 1763, eight years later, according to the Doctor's returns to the Propagation Society, the number was still found not to exceed one thousand and three hundred souls; nine hundred and fifty of them being of the Church of England, and three hundred and fifty Protestant Dissenters and Roman Catholics.

Up to the year 1757, the enormous sum of £560,000 sterling had been expended on the settlements, and though in some respects the Colony had been considered a failure, yet in a military point of view it was of incalculable importance to Great Britain, and to its position as a naval and military depot may be ascribed in a great measure the downfall of the French power in America.

On 30th June, 1757, Lord Loudon with his transports and 12,000 regulars and provincials arrived at Halifax, and on July following, Admiral Holborn arrived with his fleet. This armament, which was destined for an attack on Louisburg, left Halifax early in August, but having proved a failure the fleet returned to England in September, but Loudon returned with his army to New York; they both left Halifax on the same day, 16th August. Holborn arrived at Louisburg on 20th, where finding the French fleet superior to his own, he continued to cruise off Louisburg harbour until 24th September, when he encountered a severe gale of wind which scattered his fleet, several ships were lost, eight sail got safe to

Portsmouth, and the rest got to New York. This powerful armament consisted of 13 sail of the line—the Newark 80 guns, Invincible 74, Grafton 68, Terrible 74, Northumberland 68, Captain 68, Bedford 64, Orford 68, Nassau 64, Sunderland 64, Defiance 64, Tilbury 64, Kingston 60, Windsor 54, and the Sutherland 50, with several others which afterwards joined them, and 16 smaller vessels of war. The naval forces amounted 10,000 men, and the land forces to 12,000, six thousand of whom were provincial troops. Loudon left three regiments at Halifax, and several of the vessels remained to winter here.

In May of this year the Governor and Council offered a bounty for sowing land with grass on the peninsula of Halifax, also for the erection of stone fences around the lots, and for raising grain and potatoes.

Loudon was succeeded in the supreme command by Abercrombie, another incompetent — a debilitated old man who remained in command for a short time. He was succeeded by Sir Jeffrey Amherst.

In the following spring about 12,000 troops arrived at Halifax, under the command of General Amherst. They were soon followed by Admiral Boscawen from England with a large fleet consisting of 23 ships of the line and 18 frigates. This great fleet arrived in Halifax harbour in May, 1758, accompanied by 120 transports. The land forces amounted to 12,260 men. On Sunday, 28th May, they set sail from Halifax, 157 vessels in all. They were met by General Amherst, with part of the force, as they went out of the harbour. Governor Lawrence accompanied the army and took command of one of the Brigades, Colonel Monkton being left in command during his absence.

After the siege, which was protracted for two months, part of the fleet and army returned to Halifax, and some of the vessels remained to refit. The colony was sacked for provisions and the town turned into a camp for the troops. A number of the provincial soldiers and others, having enriched themselves with the spoils at Louisburg, became settlers in the town. All the ammunition and stores, with a quantity of private property, were removed to Halifax, and the town once again began to assume a prosperous appearance.

This year was also memorable as the one in which Representative Government was established in Nova Scotia. The subject of calling a Legislative Assembly had undergone much discussion. It had been represented by the Governor and Council, to the authorities in England, that such a step at that particular time would be fraught with much danger to the peace of the colony. Chief Justice Belcher, however, having given his opinion that the Governor and Council possessed no authority to levy taxes, and their opinion being confirmed in England, it was resolved in Council on 3rd January, 1757, that a representative system should be established and that twelve members should be elected by the province at large, until it could be conveniently divided into counties, and that the township of Halifax should send four members, Lunenburg two, Dartmouth one, Lawrencetown one, Annapolis Royal one, and Cumberland one, making in all twenty two members, and the necessary regulations were also made for carrying into effect the object intended.

Much discontent prevailed in the town, and also in other parts of the province, in consequence of the opposition of Governor Lawrence to the calling of a Representative Assembly. Hitherto the Government had been carried on solely by the Governor and Council, who possessed both Legislative and Executive authority. Under the Royal instructions the Governor was directed to call a Representative Assembly as soon as the circumstances of the country would permit, but the Governor was of opinion that it would be injudicious to proceed to a popular election until the country was better prepared for it. After repeated remonstrances from the people of Halifax and some pressure from his Council, it was on the 7th January resolved in Council that an assembly should be called, and a plan was drawn up and submitted to the Board of Trade for the sanction of the home government. We find, however, that in February following it was resolved by the inhabitants of Halifax to petition the Crown against the conduct of Governor Lawrence, not only as regards his unwillingness to establish a representative government, but his oppressive and overbearing conduct in other respects to many of the leading inhabitants. This petition was entrusted to one Ferdinando Paris, a gentleman in London, accompanied by affidavits and a power of attorney, conferring on him authority to represent the subscribers before the Privy Council and the Board of Trade and Plantations. A subscripton was set on foot, and about £120 sterling subscribed, to meet the expenses of the application to Government. These documents were certified by Chief Justice Belcher as authentic, on 14th March. As these proceedings bear date in February, 1757, it is probable that the resolution of the Council of the 7th January had not been made known. The petition and power were signed by the following residents of the town who reputed themselves as a committee appointed by the people for the purpose of forwarding their views: Robert Saunderson, William Pantree, Malachi Salter, Jonathan Binney, Otto Wm. Schwartz, Robert Campbell, Henry Ferguson and John Grant. These papers were also accompanied by a copy of an address from the people of Halifax to Lt. Governor Robert Monkton, praying that certain sums of money, collected as rum duties, etc., might be expended on the fortifications of the town as a protection to the inhabitants, and offering to contribute both labour and money for the purpose. It also complains of the "miserable management of those who have had the direction of the defences." This petition bears date 19th October, in the same year. The language of one of the letters addressed to Mr. Paris, the request on the subject of the Halifax grievances and the overbearing military rule of Governor Lawrence, bespeak much excitement to have existed in the town on the subject. The feeling appears to have prevailed principally among the leading inhabitants. We find that the list above referred to was signed by Mr. Binney, Mr. Salter, Mr. Pantree, Mr. Schwartz, Dr. Grant, Mr. Saunderson, Mr. Fairbanks, Mr. Robt. Campbell, Mr. Butler, Mr. Suckling, Mr. Vanput, Mr. G. Gerrish, Mr. Gibbon, Mr. Wiswell, Mr. Mason, and many others.

On the first of November following, the Grand Jury of Halifax petitioned Governor Lawrence that some immediate steps may be taken to fortify the town so that the inhabitants might be placed in a more secure position in case of invasion. They refer to a petition presented to Lt. Governor Monkton on the same subject, to which no reply had been made, and concluded by asking that they might know without further delay what they were to expect; that if no further security is to be provided for the settlement they may have an opportunity of conveying themselves, their families and effects to a place of greater safety in some of the neighbouring Colonies. The names of the Grand Jury were Robert Saunderson, Joseph Rundell, John Anderson, Paul Pritchard, Hugh McKay, Joseph Fairbanks, William Schwartz, Robert Campbell, William Pantree, John Killick, John Brooks, Henry Wilkinson, Walter Manning, John Slayter, Richard Catherwood, Joseph Pierce, Alexander Cunningham, Richard Tritton, Jonathan Gifford and Benjamin Leigh.

On Monday, the 2nd of October, 1758, the newly elected members met in the Court House in Halifax, pursuant to summons from the Provost Marshall; their names were as follows:

Joseph Gerrish, Robert Saunderson, Henry Newton, William Foy, William Nesbitt, Joseph Rundell. } Esquires.	William Best, Alexr. Kedie, Jonathan Binney, Henry Ferguson, George Suckling, Robert Campbell, Willm. Pantree, Joseph Fairbanks, Philip Hammond, John Fillis, Lambert Folkers, Philip Knout. } Gentlemen.

They sent Messrs. Nesbitt, Newton and Rundell, to wait on the Governor, who sent Messrs. Morris and Green from the Council to swear them in. They then chose Robert Saunderson their speaker, which was confirmed by the Governor, who addressed them as follows: " Gentlemen of the Council and House of Representatives: His Majesty having been most graciously pleased by his royal instructions to his Governors of this Province to direct the calling an assembly of the freeholders to act in conjunction with his Governor and Council as the Legislative Authority, when such a measure should be found essential to his service; I am to assure you that it is with particular pleasure I now meet you convened in that capacity, in consequence of a plan some time since formed here for that purpose, with the advice and assistance of His Majesty's

Council, and by me transmitted to the Lord Commissioner for Trade and Plantations to be laid before His Majesty for his approbation.

"Gentlemen of the House of Representatives:

"I entertain the most sanguine hopes that you are come together unanimously disposed to promote the service of the Crown, or in other words, the real welfare and prosperity of the people whom you have the honour to represent, in every point to the utmost of your authority and capacity.

"This, I presume, you will conceive is justly to be expected, not only from the immediate regard due to the Civil Rights and Interests of your constituents, but likewise from the unspeakable obligations you are under to demonstrate in their behalf your dutiful sense of His Majesty's paternal concern for the prosperity and security of those his subjects in those distinguishing marks of his royal favour and protection which we have from time to time so happily experienced in the fleets and armies sent out for our immediate preservation when we were under the most imminent danger of being swallowed up by a merciless enemy; also in the ample supplies of money for so many years annually granted for the support and encouragement of this infant colony; and moreover still, in the continuance of His Majesty's royal bounty for that purpose, when from the seeming inclination of the inhabitants to have an assembly convened some time since, it might have been presumed, and indeed by an article of His Majesty's Instructions, which I shall order to be laid before you, it has been judged that the Colony has become capable of providing for the necessary support of government here, as has been usual in all His Majesty's other American Dominions.

"Gentlemen of both Houses:

"As my Military occupation requires my attendance as early as possible upon the Commander-in-Chief of the Forces to the Westward, and as the Lieutenant Governor is now necessarily employed, and will be for some time to come, upon an enterprise of importance in a distant part of the province, there is not at present an opportunity of entering upon such particulars as might otherwise call for your attention; I am therefore earnestly to recommend to your serious consideration the expediency, or rather

"the necessity of unanimity and dispatch in the confirmation of
"such Acts or resolutions of a legislative nature, as the Governor
"and Council under His Majesty's Royal Instructions have found
"expedient, before the forming of an assembly and indispensably
"necessary for promoting the welfare and peaceable Government of
"this people.

"You may depend upon it, Gentlemen, on my return to the
"Government you will find me perfectly disposed to concur with
"you in enacting such further laws, making such amendments to
"the present ones, and establishing such other regulations as shall
"appear upon more mature deliberations to be consistent with the
"honour and dignity of the Crown and conducive to the lasting
"happiness of His Majesty's subjects where I have the honour to
"preside.
"CHARLES LAWRENCE."

The House then resolved that the members should all serve without pay for the session. The calling of the Legislature had been delayed till the autumn in consequence of both the Governor and Lt. Governor being absent with the Army at Louisburg. Governor Lawrence came up to Halifax from Louisburg specially to meet the Legislature.

The Governor in his letter to the Board of Trade about this time noticed particularly the serious effects on the settlement of the enormous importation and retail of spirituous liquors, and expressed a hope that the Legislature would check it.

On 2nd July, 1761 (second session) the House voted £50 for a public clock in the Town.

The following year (1759) Halifax was again the rendezvous for part of the fleet and army both before and after the siege of Quebec; not a few of the more enterprising settlers followed the camp and enriched themselves during the war. Admiral Darell with 4 ships of the line arrived in Halifax Harbor in April and left for the St. Lawrence on 5th May.

At the news of the victory, the town was illuminated, and fire works, bonfires and other public entertainments lasted several days.

Between the years 1759 and 1763 the harbor had been the constant resort of the squadrons under Lord Colville and others;

the place was enlivened by the presence of a large army and navy, and at the close of the war several gentlemen of condition were induced to become settlers.

Peace having been proclaimed in 1763, the 28th day of December of that year was solemnized at Halifax as a day of thanksgiving on account of the termination of the war. Though the town possessed all the advantages to be derived from the presence of the naval and military forces, the resident population did not increase. From the notitia parochials of the Rev. Dr. Breynton, the Rector of St. Paul's, the number of inhabitants in the town did not exceed 1300 souls. However, in 1769, six years after, the Doctor makes the following return : Inhabitants in and about Halifax including Garrison, Acadian French and fishermen, by the late public survey 5000 souls, of which 200 are Acadians and 55 protestant dissenters. The number of births that year was 200 and the deaths 190.

Among the local occurrences of the year 1759, was the trial of Thomas Lathum, baker, for the murder of Lieutenant Collins of the Royal Navy. It appeared that Mr. Collins, Captain Sweeney, Doctor Johns, Mr. Fulton and others of the Navy, had been sipping at the house of one John Field, and late in the evening proposed to go out in search of some women with whom one of them had made an engagement. They knocked at the door of one Hewitt, and inquired for Polly. On being refused admission, it appeared that Thomas Lathum, the brother-in-law of Hewitt, who lived in the neighbourhood, hearing the noise, came to his own door and demanded of the gentlemen in the street whether they intended to rob Mr. Hewitt. They replied that they were gentlemen and not robbers. Some further words provoked a scuffle, in which Fulton was dragged by Lathum into his house. The affair terminated in Lathum discharging a gun after the party, and mortally wounding Collins. Captain Sweeny had previously called the guard, who shortly after the affair arrived and took Lathum into custody. Lathum was tried on the 24th April, 1759.

The names of the grand jury, who found the bill of indictment, were Michael Francklin, foreman, Charles Proctor, Abraham Bowyer, Walter Manning, James Quinn, Nathan Nathans, J. Pernette, John Craig, Terrence Fitzpatrick, John Kerby, Jonathan

Pierce, James Porter, Henry Sibley, J. Flanagan, Michael Moloney, Robert Cowie, Charles Terlaven, Jonathan Gifford and James Browne.

On the 11th March, 1760, the following gentlemen were appointed Justices of the Peace for the county of Halifax, viz.: The Hon. Jonathan Belcher, Hon, Benjamin Green, Hon. John Collier, Hon. Charles Morris, Hon. Richard Bulkeley, Hon. Thomas Saul, Hon. Joseph Gerrish, William Nesbitt, John Duport, Joseph Scott, John Creighton, Sebastine Zouberbuhler, Edward Crawley, Charles Proctor and Benjamin Gerrish, and on 30th December following, Malachi Salter, Alexander Grant, Jonathan Binney and John Burbidge were added to the number. Messrs. Morris, Duport, Scott, Gerrish and Crawley were appointed Justices of the Inferior Court of Common Pleas.

Governor Lawrence, who had been for 7 days ill, died of inflammation of the lungs on the morning of the 19th October, 1760. The Council were immediately summoned, and Chief Justice Belcher sworn in to administer the Government. A question had arisen on a previous occasion, between Mr. Belcher and Mr. Green, as to the eligibility of the Chief Justice to the office of administrator of the Government, which was decided in favour of the Chief Justice, but some years after, the question was determined by the British Government declaring that the two offices of administrator of the Government and Chief Justice, should never be held by the same person.

It was resolved in Council, that the funeral of the late Governor should be at the public expense, and a monument to his memory was afterwards voted by the Assembly to be placed in St. Paul's Church.*

The funeral of Governor Lawrence took place on the Thursday following, 24th October, at 4 p. m. The procession began from Government House as follows:—

The Troops in Garrison, the Military Officers, two field pieces 6 pounders, the Physicians, the ministers, the corpse in a coffin covered with black velvet, and the pall, to which were affixed

---

* The inscription to be placed on this monument is given at full length in the Gazette of that day, but it was not to be found among those which cover the walls of old St. Paul's. There is, however, an escutcheon with the arms of Lawrence on the east gallery.

escutcheons of His Excellency's arms, supported by the President and the rest of His Majesty's Council.

The Mourners, the Provost Marshall, the House of Assembly, the Magistrates, the Civil Officers, the Freemasons and a number of the inhabitants. The Bearers, Clergy, Physicians and all Officers, Civil and Military had linen and cambric hat-bands.

The corpse was preceded near the church by the orphans singing an anthem. The pulpit, reading desk and the Governor's pew, were covered with black and escutcheons, and a most pathetic Funeral Sermon was preached by the Reverend Mr. Breynton, Rector of the Parish, after which the corpse was interred on the right side of the Communion Table.

Minute guns were fired from one of the batteries, from the time the procession began, until the interment, when the whole was concluded with three volleys from the troops under arms.

The Supreme Court, which began on Tuesday following, was hung in mourning and escutcheons.

The following fulsome eulogium, to the late lamented Governor, appeared in the newspapers of the day : " The Lieutenant Governor " was possessed of every natural endowment and acquired, accom- " plishment necessary to adorn the most exalted station, and every " amiable quality that could promote the sweets of friendship and " social intercourse of human life.

" As Governor, he exerted his uncommon abilities with unwearied " application, and the most disinterested zeal in projecting and " executing every useful design that might render this Province and " its rising settlements flourishing and happy. He encouraged the " industrious, rewarded the deserving, excited the indolent, protected " the oppressed and relieved the needy. His affability and masterly " address endeared him to all ranks of people, and a peculiar great- " ness of soul made him superior to vanity, envy, avarice or " revenge.

" In him we have lost the guide and guardian of our interests, " the reflection on the good he has done, the anticipation of great " things still expected from such merits, and circumstances which, " while they redound to his honour, aggravate the sense of our " irreparable misfortune."

About the end of October, Commodore Lord Colville arrived in the harbor with the Northumberland and three other ships of the line and several frigates from Quebec. The Sloop-of-War England also arrived from England with dispatches and next day sailed for Louisburg and Quebec. Several transports also came in about the same time with Col. Montgomery's Highlanders to relieve the two battalions of the 60th Royal Americans.

Among the advertisements in the Halifax Gazette of 1st November, 1760, is the following:

" To be sold at public auction, on Monday the 3rd of November, at the house of Mr. John Rider, two Slaves, viz.: a boy and girl, about eleven years old; likewise, a puncheon of choice old cherry brandy, with sundry other articles."

1759. Among the town officers nominated by the Grand Jury this year were, John Fillis, Richd. Wenman, Richd. Gibbon and Wm. Schwartz as Commissioners of the poor for the town.

Surveyors of Highways, Chas. Morris, Esq., Chas Proctor, Esq., Mr. Wm. Prescott and Mr. John Rider.

This year an Act of the Legislature was passed to regulate the Sambro Light House at the entrance of Halifax Harbor, which had been erected the previous year at the expense of £1000. The Work House was also erected this year. Firing guns within the town and peninsula was forbidden in 1758 under a penalty.

The accession of King George the Third was proclaimed at Halifax on the 11th February, 1761, with great ceremony. The proclamation was first read at the Court House door,* then at the north gate of the town,† at Government House, at the south gate,‡ and lastly on the Parade, where the troops were drawn up and a salute fired by the artillery. Lord Colville's fleet being in the harbour at the time, " each ship fired a Royal Salute, beginning with his Lordship's flagship the Northumberland."

The order of the procession on this occasion was as follows:—
1st, A Company of Grenadiers ; 2nd, Constables of the Town ; 3rd,

---

* Now Northup's corner, Buckingham and Argyle Streets.
† At this period there was a fence on the north side of what is now called Jacob St. and a gate near the opening of Brunswick St., in front of the North Barrack old parade, some say further north.
‡ The situation of the south gate is uncertain ; there were several south gates. It was along Salter Street, probably in a line with the old forts known as Luttrell's and Horseman's Forts.

Magistrates; 4th, Civil Officers of Government; 5th, Constables; 6th, The Provost Marshall with two deputies on horseback; 7th, a Band of Music; 8th, Constables; 9th, The Commander-in-Chief of the Province, the Honorable Jonathan Belcher, with Admiral Lord Colville and Colonel Foster, commandant of the Garrison, and the members of His Majesty's Council; 10th, the Speaker and the members of the House of Assembly, followed by the principal inhabitants. At three o'clock the company waited on the Commander-in-Chief at Governor Lawrence's head tavern, where a very elegant entertainment was provided for them, and after dinner His Majesty's health was drunk under Royal Salute from the Batteries, also other toasts, and the evening concluded with great rejoicings and illuminations, bon-fires and artificial fire works, played off by the Royal Artillery. A sermon was afterwards ordered to be preached (13th February, 1761) in St. Paul's Church, on account of the decease of the late King, and all public amusements were ordered to cease for one month from that day. The 17th was accordingly set apart and the sermon preached by the Rev. T. Wood, the Curate. Part of St. Paul's church was hung in black, and minute guns were fired for an hour and a half, and the flags on the Citadel and George's Island were half-mast during the day.

On the 11th day of February, 1760, two Indian Chiefs of the Passamaquoddy and St. John River tribes, came to Halifax with Colonel Arbuthnot and appeared before the Council, and by their interpreter, settled with the Governor terms of peace, renewing the Treaty of 1725 and giving hostages for their good behaviour. At their request truck houses were established at Fort Frederick. Benjamin Gerrish, John Collier and Thomas Saul were appointed a Committee to prepare the Treaty in French and English, which was to be taken back with them to be ratified by their tribes. It was arranged that Colonel Arbuthnot should accompany them, and that they should be sent back at the public expense, after which His Majesty's health was drunk and the Chiefs returned to the quarters assigned them by the Governor. On the 13th the Treaty was ratified in Council and the Indians and the Governor and Council settled the table of the prices to be established at the truck houses. The Indians stated that the number of their tribes, men, women and children, was about 500. During the sitting of the Council on the

13th, Roger Morris, one of the Mic-Mac Indians, appeared and brought with him three Frenchmen who were lately arrived from Pictou, and another Indian called Claude Renie, who said he was Chief of the Tribe of Cheboudie Indians. He stated that he had left 70 of his people at Jeddore; the men were out killing moose and their families were in want of provisions. It was arranged that provisions should be sent to them and that the men should forthwith come up and conclude a peace.

Treaties of peace were afterwards concluded on 10th March following with three Mic-Mac Chiefs, viz., Paul Laurent, chief of the Tribe of LaHave, Michael Augustine, chief of the Tribe of Richibucto, and the before-mentioned Claude Renie, chief of the Cheboudie and Musquodoboit Indians; the treaty was signed in Council on that day and they received their annual presents. Another treaty of peace was signed in Council on 15th October, 1761, with Jannesvil Peitougawash, Chief of the Indians of the Tribe of Pictock and Malogomish, and the merchants and traders were notified that the Indian trade to the eastward would be thrown open under regulations in the following spring. The following summer Joseph Argunsault, Chief of the Mongwash Indians, with a number of followers, appeared before the Council and executed a final Treaty of peace. The members of Council and Legislature, with the Magistrates and public officers, attended on the occasion.

The Abbe Mallaird being introduced, interpreted the treaty to the Chief, who was then addressed by the Hon. Mr. Belcher, the Commander-in-Chief. The treaty was respectively signed by the Commander-in-Chief and the Indian Chief, and witnessed by the members of the Council present, the Speaker of the Assembly and Mr. Mallaird.* The Chief then addressed Mr. Belcher in the following manner: That he had formerly paid obedience to another King, but that he now acknowledged King George 3rd for his only lawful Sovereign, and vowed eternal fidelity and submission to him; that his submission was not by compulsion, but that it was free and voluntary with his whole heart, and that he should always esteem King George 3rd as his good father and protector. That he now buried the hatchet in behalf of himself and his whole tribe, in token

---

*Note.—This document is not to be found among the papers preserved in the Secretary's office at Halifax.

of their submission, and of their having made a peace which should never be broken upon any consideration whatever. The Chief then laid the hatchet on the earth, and the same being buried the Indians went through the ceremony of washing the paint from their bodies, in token of hostilities being ended, and then partook of a repast set out for them on the ground, and the whole ceremony was concluded by all present drinking the King's health and their Haggas. This ceremony is said to have been performed in the Governor's garden, westward of the old English burial ground, where the Court House now stands. Benjamin Gerrish, Esquire, was appointed Commissioner of Indian Affairs, and additional truck houses were built and other arrangements made throughout the Province for more effectually carrying on the Indian trade.

On the 30th December, 1760, Malachi Salter, Alexander Grant, Jonathan Binney and John Burbidge were appointed Justices of the Peace for the Town of Halifax. Mr. Burbidge was a member of Assembly; he afterwards removed to the country and settled in Cornwallis township, where his descendants now remain.

The French having invaded the British settlements in Newfoundland, and captured the fort of St. John, a council-of-war was called at Halifax, for the purpose of consulting on means of the defence of the town in case of an attack. This Council was composed of Lt. Governor Belcher, Col. Richard Bulkely, Halifax Militia, Major General Bastead of the Engineers, Col. William Foster, Lt. Col. Hamilton, Lt. Col. Job Winslow, and the Right Honorable Lord Colville, commander-in-chief of the squadron. They met on the 10th July, 1762, and continued their sittings until 17th August. They recommended to Government the embodying a portion of the militia force, and that the Batteries on George's Island, Fort George, Point Pleasant and East Battery should be put in repair and guns mounted, and the erection of such works around the town and at the Dockyard as might be considered necessary for the protection of the place. The whole to be placed under the superintendence of General Bastead of the Engineers. Some of the old works were put in repair and others added on this occasion, but the cause of alarm having subsided, further expense was deemed unnecessary.

At the first settlement it had been found necessary to occupy not only every elevated position in the vicinity, but also large spaces around the town as at first laid out, for the purposes of defence and other military objects. After the necessity for those defences had ceased, it frequently occurred that the military commanders would lay claim to the grounds as military property, and in this way obstacles had continually arisen to the extension of the town, a grievance which has continued to be felt until the present time. Those whose duty it was to plan and lay out the town appear to have been guided more with a view to the construction of a military encampment than that of a town for the accommodation of an increasing population. The narrow blocks and small dimensions of the building lots have been found to be a continual drawback on the comfort, the health and the convenience of the inhabitants, and of late years these inconveniences have been severely felt in the business parts of the city. This, however, was not the case in laying out the north and south suburbs; here the lots were of ample dimensions, and though the streets were not of the width frequently met with in modern cities, yet of sufficient dimensions to ensure comfort. It is to be regretted that the town and city authorities, during the last 35 years, have not, as in other places, exerted their authority in the arrangement and laying off of building lots, and by wholesome regulations, prevented the crowding of buildings on pieces of land not sufficiently deep to admit of proper ventilation. It is also a matter of the utmost importance to the future welfare of the city that those lands now in the hands of the military and naval boards in various directions around the city which are not immediately required for military works should be handed over to the Civil Government for public promenades and other useful purposes.

July 18th, 1768. The Chiefs of the tribes of Indians of St. John's River, named Pierre Thomas and Ambroise St. Aubon, appeared before the Council with the following requests: They said the use of rum and spirituous liquors was too common among them, and requested that a remedy might be thought of to prevent it. They also required lands for cultivation, and that they should not be required to bear arms in case of war with any of the European powers. That some further regulations of prices in their traffic should be made, and several other matters, all of which appear to have been granted them. They desired to return home as soon as possible, that their people might not be debauched with liquor in the town.

This year (1768) Mr. Joshua Mauger retired from the office of Agent of the Province in London. Mr. Mauger came up from Louisburg with the army and resided in the town as a distiller of rum, and followed the camp for several years. He received grants of land from the government in various parts of the province. The beach at the south-west extremity of Cornwallis Island, now known as McNab's Island, was named after him. Mr. Mauger was afterwards elected a member of the British Parliament.

In the month of May of this year was presented to the Legislature the celebrated revolutionary document known as the Massachusetts or Boston Letter. This was a letter addressed by Speaker Cushin of the House of Representatives at Boston, to the Speaker of the Assembly in Nova Scotia. It bears date February 11, 1768, and was on the subject of the differences existing between the British Government and the American Colonies, then on the eve of revolt. This letter is couched in very moderate but firm language; it appears to have been received, however, with great indignation by the House, who declined to have it read. A memorial was presented to the Governor and Council in March, 1767, by Colonel Dalrymple, then commander of His Majesty's troops at Halifax, complaining of the undue occupation of grounds about the town, on which there had been palisaded forts and lines of defence. It appeared that Governor Lawrence had granted certain small tracts of land on which a palisaded line of defence had formerly been, and that such tracts of land could not be supposed to come into use on any future occasion for fortifications. That Colonel McKellan of the Engineers had advised the situation of the Work House with an enclosure, in the front of said line, and that a whole bastion of two curtains of Lutterell's fort were covered by it, and that Governor Lawrence had further laid out more of such grounds on which part of the palisading of Horseman's Fort formerly stood, all of which it appeared he did by an undoubted right of the power given him by the King's Commission, to erect and demolish fortifications, and therefore to convert the ground to other uses, it being no more serviceable for the former purposes. But it also appeared that none of the Barracks were ever granted or admitted into private occupation. That Governor Lawrence had admitted the occupation of some of the ground reserved for fortification, on condition it should be surrendered when the King's service should again require it, by which it was evident that the King's rights in their lands had been sufficiently secured. Horseman's fort occupied the ground in the vicinity of the present Roman Catholic Cathedral. Lutterell's fort stood where the old Poor House and County Jail formerly stood. In June, 1763, the Council recommended the Governor to make a grant of the Common for the Town of Halifax to trustees for the benefit of the inhabitants. The Trustees were John Collier, Charles Morris, Richard Bulkeley, William Nesbitt, Charles Proctor and Richard Best. Some question having arisen as to the limits of the common, the Council were unanimously of the opinion that the lands which had been granted without the town were not within the limits of the Common as appeared by the plan thereof laid before the Lords of Trade, and which had not been disapproved of by their Lordships. No copy of this plan is now to be found.

The number of families residing in and around the town in 1763 was estimated at 500, which would make the population about 2500 souls. There was also supposed to be, at this time, about one thousand Acadian French in and about the town.

In June, 1763, the Hon. Montague Wilmot was sworn in Lieut. Governor in place of Mr. Belcher. In the following year he received the appointment of Governor-in-Chief.

On the 29th day of September, 1766, the Germans, who had been located to the west of the peninsula, the settlement now known as the Dutch Village, petitioned the Government that a convenient road should be laid out for them to their settlement. The Surveyor was ordered to report on the petition. He reported that he found the road from the north German lots to the southward of George Bayers' stone wall, now laid out, in the most convenient place, and that the road should be at least four rods wide. That from George Bayers' stone wall the road should be on the south side of said wall and thence to run until it meets the public road leading to the town.

About this time, at the request of the Magistrates, the Hospital was granted for an alms house. This hospital was established very early for the use of the settlers, and stood on part of the land now occupied by the Government House, to the north of that building.

The church of St. Paul's had now been for some years finished, and the Town and vicinity had been, by an Act of Legislature, constituted into a parish with corporate powers in the church wardens and vestry. After the death of Mr. Tutty, the Reverend Thomas Wood, from the Province of New Jersey, was appointed to assist Dr. Breynton, and he and the doctor were jointly inducted into the parish in 1758; Dr. Breynton as rector, and Mr. Wood as vicar or curate, to assist. Mr. W. continued at St. Paul's until 1763, when he was removed to Annapolis Royal with the consent of the Governor and the church wardens and vestry, when the whole duties of the Mission at Halifax devolved upon Mr. Breynton. Mr. B. was in the habit of officiating to the Germans in their own language. In 1761, he preached in German and English to the small congregation in the old Dutch church in Brunswick Street, on occasion of its being dedicated as the church of St. George. In 1770, at the solicitation of the Governor and Council, the Chief Justice and the congregation of St. Paul's, he received from the University of Cambridge the degree of D. D., to which he was entitled from his standing in the University. Early in his ministry the Doctor established in the Town an orphan school, and provided for the tuition of 50 poor children, through the assistance afforded him by the Society for the Propagation of the Gospel. Mr. Ralph Sharrock, a discharged soldier, was his first schoolmaster. In 1776, Dr. Breynton mentions in his report to the Society, having administered the Lord's Supper to 500 men of the Baron de Sciltz's German regiment in their own language "whose exemplary and regular behaviour" he says, "did them great honour." The following extract from a document, in reference to Dr. Breynton, said to have been written by a Dissenter, is given by Mr. Hawkins, from the records of the Propagation Society: "As a person who, during a residence of upwards of twenty years in this Province, has deservedly gained the good will and esteem of men of all ranks and persuasions. He preaches the Gospel of peace and purity, with an eloquence of language and delivery, far beyond anything I ever heard in America." He lived to a good old age, preserving the esteem of his fellow townsmen to the last. He appears to have lived on terms of Christian fellowship with the clergy of other denominations, as we find that at the annual meeting of the Church Society, which took place in St. Paul's in 1770, the dissenting ministers all attended at the Church to hear the doctor preach his

Visitation Sermon. One of the last acts of his ministry was the establishment of a Sunday School in the city. This was about 1783, perhaps a little later, and was the first Sunday School instituted in Nova Scotia.

In the month of July, 1769, a large number of Indians, many of whom at this time appear to have been Protestants, attended divine service in St. Paul's Church, when prayers were read by the Reverend Thomas Wood, in the Mic-Mac language, the Governor and many of the principal inhabitants being present. The Indians sang an anthem both before and after the service. Before the service began a Chief came forward, and kneeling down, prayed for the prosperity of the Province and the blessing of Almighty God on King George, the Royal family and the Governor of the Province. He then rose up, and Mr. Wood, who understood the language, at his desire explained the prayer in English to the whole congregation. When service was ended the Indians returned thanksgivings for the opportunity they had of hearing prayers in their own language. In the following year Mr. Wood again performed divine service at Halifax in the Mic-Mac language at the residence of Colonel Joseph Gorham, where a number of Indians were assembled. He had obtained great influence with the Indians through his friendship with the Abbe Maillard, and particularly from his behaviour to him a little before his death. He was in consequence frequently called on both by the Indians and French to baptize their children and visit the sick in the absence of a priest of their own church. In one of his letters to the Society for the Propagation of the Gospel, in 1762, he mentions having attended the Abbe Maillard during his illness of several weeks, and at his request, the day before his death read to him the office of visitation of the sick in presence of many of the French, and having performed the funeral service of the Church of England, in French, on his remains in the presence of the principal inhabitants of Halifax and a number of French and Indians. The Governor and all the public functionaries attended the funeral of M. Maillard, who was highly esteemed and beloved in the community, and the members of His Majesty's Council were the pall bearers.*

---

* It must be understood that M. Maillard did not leave the Roman Catholic Church, but there being no priest of his own persuasion in Halifax at the time, he availed himself of the pious offices of his friend, Mr. Wood, whom he no doubt esteemed as a good Christian.

Mr. Wood was shortly after removed to Annapolis Royal, where he died in the year 1778. While there he applied himself to a closer study of the Mic-Mac language, and by assistance of papers left him by M. Maillard was enabled to prepare a Mic-Mac grammar and dictionary. He sent the first volume of his grammar, and a Mic-Mac translation of the Creed and Lord's Prayer to England in 1776. He continued occasionally to minister to the Indians in their own language until his death.

February 26th, 1769. Halifax harbour was so full of ice that vessels could not come in, which had not been the case for (says the Gazette for that day) ten years. The cold was intense, snow between four and five feet deep in the woods and on the peninsula, an instance of which had not been known for several years.

May 9th, 1769. Major Leonard Lockman died after a lingering illness in the 73rd year of his age; he was interred under the old German church in Brunswick Street, and a monument to his memory, with coat of arms, is yet to be seen in that church. Major Lockman was one of the leading settlers among the Germans. The street running between the German lots and Water Street in the north suburbs bears his name.

In the fall of this year the town was visited by a severe gale of wind from the S. W., which caused the destruction of much property and some loss of life.

Among the principal merchants in Halifax in 1769, the Hon. John Butler, uncle to the late Hon. J. Butler Dight, Robert Campbell on the Beach, John Grant, Alexander Brymer, Gerrish and Gray appear most prominent. Among the shopkeepers and tradesmen who advertized during the year were, Robert Fletcher on the Parade, Bookseller and Stationer, Andrew Cunod, Grocer, Hammond and Brown, Auctioneers, Robert Millwood, Blockmaker, who advertized best Spanish River Coal at 30s. per chaldron.

The period between 1770 and 1776 was one of great public excitement, emissaries from the revolted colonies were numerous, and the Governor and Council deemed it expedient as early as 1770, to prohibit all public meetings of a political nature.* The

---

* Among the various exhibitions of public feeling at this period was the erection of a gallows, on the Common, with a boot suspended from it as a token of disapprobation of Lord Bute's Government.

same spring the general election took place, after which the House sat for fourteen years without being dissolved.

In 1771, Governor Lord William Campbell issued a proclamation forbidding horse races as tending to gambling and idleness.

October 8th, 1773. Governor Legge was sworn into office.

The subject of fortifying the town came under the consideration of the Council in the following year. It was considered that the ground being rocky in many places around the town, it would not admit of entrenchments being made, and that the only practical fortifications would be temporary blockhouses and palisades, and it was resolved that the Engineers under Col. Spry do immediately proceed to fortify the Navy Yard in that manner, which may be defended by the people of the town, and afford a retreat for them. Any attempt at fortifying the Citadel Hill this season was thought to be out of the question, the season being too late, the scarcity of workmen very great, and there being no troops for its defence.

The Governor proposed and it was agreed in Council to collect a force of 1000 men with pay and provisions, and that four companies of light infantry now forming at Lunenburg be ordered up, and that 100 Acadians from Clare and Yarmouth, and two light companies from Kings County do march immediately to Halifax. The public authorities appear to have been kept in a constant state of apprehension of invasion, while a continued suspicion of many of the leading inhabitants being favourable to the revolt, seemed to have taken possession of the mind of Governor Legge, who, having differences of opinion with some of his officials, attributed their disagreement with him on subjects of finance, etc., as marks of disloyalty. He at length became so obnoxious to those in authority, that it was deemed advisable to remove him from the Government. His quarrels with Jonathan Binney, Governor Francklin and other leading men of the town, are disclosed in the official letters and minutes of Council of that day.

It was found necessary to remove the Military Stores to George's Island for safety, and additional batteries were erected there. The officers of the Town Regiment of Militia were called on to subscribe the Oath of Allegiance before going on duty. Those who subscribed were Col. Butler, Major Smith, Captains Vanput, Brown, Finney and Millet, Lieutenants Pyke, Piers, Solomon, Clarke and

Fletcher, Second Lieutenants Tritton, Jacobs, Schwartz and Kerby, and Adjutant Peters. Among them we recognize several family names, the grandsires of some of our present citizens.

Among the magistrates appointed in 1771 were Joseph Gray, John Amiel and Captain Thompson of His Majesty's Ship Mermaid.

The bureau of Governor Legge, at the Government House, was broken open in 1744, and a reward of £100 was offered for the detection of the thief.

The condition of the Orphan House, and the children therein, was considered bad, and an order was issued for immediate steps to be taken for its being put on a better footing.

During the winter of 1774, Sambro Light House was without light for five successive nights in consequence of Mr. Woodmass, the contractor, not having sent down a supply of oil, for which he was dismissed by Order of Council.

The following year William Nesbitt, speaker of the House of Assembly, was appointed Custos of Halifax County, and the names of Thomas Bridge and Thomas Proctor added to the Commission of the Peace.

Col. Butler, commanding the militia force, reported that the sickness in the town, together with the daily labour of the inhabitants, rendered it difficult to make up the number of men ordered for the town guard, which duty the people considered a hardship. The guard was accordingly ordered by the Council to be discontinued.

The scarcity of provisions in the town was at this time so great that the government found it necessary to dispatch the Snow Elizabeth to Quebec for flour for the inhabitants.

The impressment of men for the Navy had been a great grievance; the trade of the country was not only injured, but the town was becoming deprived of fish and fuel in consequence of the scarcity of fishermen and labourers. The merchants petitioned the Governor and Council on the subject. The memorial was sent to the naval commander of the station; it does not appear, however, that any further attention was paid to the remonstrance.

In September, 1775, it was proposed to throw up some temporary works in addition to the old works on Citadel Hill, and to entrench about the naval yard. On consideration, it was thought too late in this season to do any earth work on Citadel Hill. Col. Spry, however, proposed the erection of Blockhouses in the neighbourhood of the town. It is probable the old Blockhouses at Fort Needham and Three Mile House, the remains of which are within the recollection of many of our citizens, may have been originally constructed about this time. They were in full repair during the war of 1812.

A continual influx of strangers from the old colonies caused Martial Law to be proclaimed on the 30th of November of this year, and it was deemed necessary by the Council that a proclamation should be issued requiring all persons not being settled inhabitants of the town, who had arrived since September, to give notice of their arrival and names to two Magistrates, and all inn and tavern keepers were required to report arrivals at their houses, and vessels were forbidden entering the North West Arm without license. One thousand militiamen were ordered for the defence of the town. The constant arrival of loyalist refugees from the revolted colonies, during this and the subsequent years, rendered provisions scarce, and in addition to these troubles, the small-pox broke out in the town about the middle of July. The King's troops had all been removed from Nova Scotia to the revolted provinces, and the Governor was informed by the home authorities that no troops could be spared, and that the inhabitants themselves must defend the town. The town guard was accordingly again composed of militia.

1775. The fifth General Assembly held this year its seventh session from 12th June to 20th July. Mr. Nesbitt was Speaker. Chief Justice Belcher presided at the quarter sessions this summer, and gave a very loyal address to the Magistrates and public functionaries present; all Magistrates and town officers took the Oath of Allegiance. The general feeling throughout the town appeared to have been eminently loyal; some of the leading citizens, however, though firm in their allegiance to the British Crown, yet thought that self government in the Colonies in fiscal matters was the correct policy. This threw several under suspicion; Mr. John Fillis, Mr. Malachi Salter and Mr. Smith, who were natives of Boston, were among the number.

Mr. Legge, the Governor, proposed to raise a regiment in Halifax, to be commanded by himself, but was unsuccessful owing to his unpopularity.

In the autumn of the previous year, a difficulty had arisen regarding the importation of some tea, in which Mr. Smith and Mr. Fillis were concerned; and it having been understood that Fillis had said the measures of Government were oppressive, these two gentlemen were ordered to be removed from all offices under Government. The year previous a quantity of hay belonging to Joseph Fairbanks, intended for the King's service, had been burned. Some one in Halifax sent to Boston a statement charging Fillis and Smith as being privy to the act. They complained to the House of Assembly, then in session, when the following resolution was passed: That this House do esteem Mr. Fillis and Mr. Smith to be dutiful and lawful subjects to the King, etc., and that the "House is unanimously of opinion that the said reports are base, infamous and false, and that the authors thereof merit punishment." The garrison having been reinforced by King's troops, the Governor concluded on bringing no further drafts of militia to the town.

1776. This was a memorable year for Halifax. The British forces under General Howe having evacuated Boston, a fleet of three men-of-war and 47 transports arrived in the harbour on 30th March, with troops and a number of inhabitants of Boston. These were followed on 1st April by many more transports, nearly 100 in number, with the remainder of Howe's army and a number of Loyalist refugees. Howe demanded accommodation for 200 officers and 3000 men, and about 1500 loyalists with their families, with supplies of fresh provisions, etc. Rents of houses in the town were consequently doubled and the town soon presented the appearance of a military camp.* Many complaints appear against the soldiers for pulling down the fences and demolishing the stone walls on the peninsula. One Christopher Schlegall had been killed in one of the numerous affrays with the soldiers. Three soldiers were arrested and tried for murder, but no convictions occurred. Several persons were called on to give security for their good behaviour in the town.

Among the events of this year was the appearance in one of the Halifax newspapers of copies of treasonable articles from the Rhode Island and Boston papers. The printer was brought before the

---

* The engravings of the town published in 1777 show the Common, west of the Citadel, and Camp Hill covered with tents, where a large part of the troops appear to have been encamped.

Council and reprimanded and cautioned against permitting any such publications again to appear in his paper.

The names of the Members of Assembly for Halifax County and Town in 1776 were Wm. Nesbitt and Henry Smith, and Thomas Bridge and Joseph Fairbanks. Mr. Fenton was still Provost Marshall with jurisdiction throughout the province, there being then no County Sheriffs at this time. Henry Newton was Collector of Customs at Halifax, James Burrows, Comptroller, Lewis Piers, Gauger of Liquors, etc.

The Magistrates of the town were John Creighton, John Burbidge, Malachi Salter, Benjamin Green, John Cunningham, George Cotnam, John Newton, Winkworth Tonge, Jos. Desbarres, Charles Morris, Junior, George Smith, J. Gray, Giles Tidmarsh, George Deschamps, Dan. Cunningham, Thomas Proctor and Thomas Bridge.

The death of Chief Justice Belcher occurred this year. Mr. Morris, one of the assistant judges, was appointed to fill the office of Chief Justice until another should be appointed.

1777. The jail at Halifax was at this time in a very insecure condition. Criminals were continually escaping from it, several of whom had been found guilty of being in arms against the King. The jailor was infirm and his wife took charge. There were no regulations enforced for visiting the prisoners at night, and the shackles on the prisoners were found not to be sufficient. The Provost Marshall was suspended and Mr. Bridge appointed to act in his place.

Malcolm McIntyre, Thomas Crow, John Chalk, John Sewlock, Samuel Miller, Robert McMullen, Tulley McKilley, Cornelius O'Brien, Thomas Whitteny, John Cribben and John McIntyre, all fishermen of Herring Cove, were this year rewarded for attacking and taking a shallop and apprehending seven persons, being part of the crew of an American privateer which had been driven on shore and destroyed by the armed brig Hope, off Canso, from which they had made their escape in the shallop.

1778. The names of John Hosterman, Thomas Stevens and Edmund Phelan appear as Commissioners of the Poor, John Woodin, Keeper of the Poor House, and Thomas Brown, Schoolmaster at Halifax.

On the 13th July, 1779, the Revenge, privateer, Capt. Sheppard of Halifax, was taken and destroyed by two American armed vessels. In December following, H. M. Sloop-of-War North and the armed sloop St. Helena, in coming into the harbour from Spanish River, Cape Breton, the night being very dark and a south-east storm, were driven on shore about a league from the light house; both were lost and 170 persons perished.

1780. This year the following gentlemen were in the Commission of the Peace at Halifax: William Nesbitt, Winkworth Tonge, John Burbidge, Benjamin Green, John Cunningham, John Newton, Isaac Deschamps, William Russell, W. Phipps, J. F. W. Desbarres, Charles Morris, junior, George Smith, Enoch Rust, Joseph Gray, Giles Tidmarsh, John Fillis, George Deschamps, Daniel Cunningham, Thomas Proctor, Thomas Bridge, George W. Sherlock and John George Pyke.

A public slaughter house was erected this year in the town and John Woodin, senior, made keeper.

March 12th, 1780. John O'Brien advertizes as keeper of the tavern known as the Golden Ball, formerly kept by Edward Phelan. The Golden Ball was situate at the corner of Hollis and Sackville Streets, opposite the building now called Variety Hall, occupied by W. Harrington. The hotel called the Pontac, at the corner of Duke and Water Streets (now Roger Cunningham's corner) was at this time kept by one Willis. It was here the Town Assemblies, Public Balls and Entertainments were held.

The Court House stood at the north-east corner of Buckingham and Argyle Streets, where the store of Messrs. Northup & Sons now is. Chief Justice Belcher presided here when first appointed. This building was, some years after, burned down and the lot on which it stood, sold.

On the 15th January, this year, the town was illuminated and there were great rejoicings throughout the day for the success of the British troops in Georgia.

The Governor being informed from England that a large armament was fitting out at Brest, it was resolved in Council that the town militia should be called out for duty and a portion of the country militia got ready to march to Halifax if required. General McLean, then in command of the Garrison, was directed to put the fortifications in working order. The Halifax militia was employed in the erection of bomb batteries. Drafts of militia from the country came down and were employed for three weeks on the works.

At this period the means of communication between this country and England had been very uncertain. The intercourse of Halifax with the old colonies having been cut off, Governor Sir Richard Hughes urged on the British Government the necessity of a line of packets being established between Halifax and England. Several privateers, during this and the following years, were fitted out at Halifax to cruise in American waters. The Revenge, Capt. James Gandy, and the Liverpool, Capt. Young, the former mounting 30 and the latter 8 guns, sailed for Halifax early this spring. They were accompanied by the Halifax, Robert E. Foster, master, owned and fitted out by Alexander Brymer, one of the principal merchants of the town.

The 18th January being the Queen's birthday the citizens and militia had a Ball at Willis' rooms in the Pontac.

In May, the Revenge brought in a richly laden Snow, bound from Cadiz to Chesapeake Bay. The Blond Frigate and an armed sloop both brought in American prizes.

For several years two large ships, the Adamant and St. Lawrence, were regular traders between Halifax and Great Britain. They were regular in their trips, spring and fall, and the merchants of Halifax depended chiefly on them for their supplies of British merchandize.

A government armed vessel called the Loyal Nova Scotian, and several other small vessels, were kept to cruise off the mouth of the harbour to prevent surprise from the pirates and privateer cruisers which infested the coast. Several were captured and brought into Halifax during this and the two following years.

In May, 1779, an election for the County took place in Halifax. John George Pyke and Francis Boyd were the candidates. Pyke was returned.

General McLean left Halifax in June with a force for the reduction of Penobscot. In August, a squadron, consisting of several men-of-war and some merchant vessels, among which were the Adamant and St. Lawrence, sailed from Halifax for his relief.

The town continued to be infested with Press Gangs for the ships of war. The inhabitants complained to the Governor and Council. Several riots on the wharves having occurred in consequence of the press, proclamation was issued demolishing all impressments except under the sanction of the Governor and Council.

October 26th, 1780. The committee of the House of Assembly, at this date, reported the sum of £1500 to be granted for the erection of a "proper and convenient building in the town for a public school, and a sum not exceeding £100 per annum for a master, and £50 for an usher when the number of scholars shall exceed forty." The trustees were to be five in number, to be appointed annually by the government, and the £1500 was to be raised by lottery. This lottery was carried into effect, but the building does not appear to have been erected. How the proceeds of the lottery were disposed of is not mentioned. The Halifax Grammar School had its origin from this proceeding. It was established in the old building at the corner of Barrington and Sackville Streets, from which it has only lately been removed to the private residence of the Rev. Doctor Gilpin, the Head Master. This building was originally occupied as a place for the meeting of the Legislature, and was previously at one time used as a Guard House. It appears to have undergone very little alteration since 1780, until sold a year or two ago. It is one of, if not the oldest building in the city, except St. Paul's Church, and the old Dutch Church on Brunswick Street. The Rev. William Cochran, afterwards Vice-President of King's College, was the first head master. He was succeeded by the Rev. George Wright, who was Garrison Chaplain and minister of St. George's. On his death, in 1819, the Rev. John Thomas Twining received the appointment. He retired from the school in 1848, when the Rev. Edwin Gilpin, succeeded him.

CHAPTER V.

At the commencement of the year 1781 many of the Loyalist refugees who came to Halifax after the evacuation of Boston by the British Army, had left the town, and the price of provisions was beginning to come down. The constant influx of strangers, however, from the revolted colonies, with the prisoners taken in the prizes brought into the port by the privateers and ships of war, tended again to augment the population. Captains of men-of-war, when vessels were in port, in order to fill up their complements of men, undertook to impress in the streets of the town without authority from the civil magistrate. On the 6th January an armed party of sailors and marines assisted by soldiers and commanded by naval officers, seized in the streets of the town, some of the inhabitants and several coasters belonging to Lunenburg, who had come up in their vessels to sell their produce; bound their hands behind their backs, carried them through the streets and lodged them in the guard houses, from which they were conveyed on board the ships of war in the harbour. The Grand Jury were in session at the time and presented the outrage to the Sessions, who requested the Governor, Sir Richard Hughes, to interfere. The Governor issued his proclamation declaring all such impressments, without the sanction of the civil authority, to be illegal and an outrageous breach of the civil law, and calling upon all magistrates, etc., to resist such proceedings and to bring the offenders to justice. It does not appear, however, that the proclamation was sufficient to procure the release of the unfortunate coasters. The names of the Grand Jury on this occasion were William Meaney, William Graham, Robert Kitts, Peter McNab, John Boyd, William Mott, William Millett, junior, John Moore, William Carter, James Creighton, John Cleary, Richard Jacobs and Charles Hill.

On the 13th January, this year, died Malachi Salter, Esq., aged 65 years. He was one of the first members of Assembly for the town. His colleague in the representation was Joseph Fairbanks. Mr. Salter came from Boston to Halifax, very soon after the town was commenced, and carried on business as merchant. He is said to have visited Chebucto Harbour while engaged in the fishery, several years before the arrival of Cornwallis in 1749. The old building at the corner of Salter and Barrington Streets, formerly the residence of the late Hon. William Lawson, afterwards owned by John Esson, was originally built by Mr. Salter, and was his residence for many years. This is one of the oldest houses now remaining in Halifax. It received improvements, and was enlarged by Mr. Lawson, about 60 years ago.

The School Lottery, before mentioned, was carried on this year. It was divided into two classes. The first to consist of 5000 tickets, at 20s. each, was advertised on the 25th September. The highest prize was $2000. The prizes in all came to £4,250, leaving a balance of £750 for the purposes of the school.

The most exciting occurence of the year was the arrival of the Charleston Frigate, the sloop Vulture, and the armed ship Vulcan, in July, after a sharp conflict with a French Squadron. The Charleston had left the harbour a short time before in convoy of some transports, and while out had taken several prizes, which had been sent in a few days previously. On the 10th July, the Charleston discovered near Spanish River, Cape Breton, two French Frigates, of 40 guns each. Captain Francis Evans, of the Charleston, having thrown out signals for the transports to make for a port, bore down upon the enemy. The Little Jack, convoy to the Quebec fleet, being in company, supported the Charleston and the Vulture. Some time after the action began, Capt. Evans being killed by a cannon shot, Lt. McKay, the succeeding officer of the Charleston, under the direction of Capt Dennis George,* of the Vulture, continued the action with the greatest coolness and bravery. Nor was the Vulcan, armed ship, in the least deficient in giving signal proof of the resolute determination of the troops on board, under command of Capt. Ewatt, of the 70th Regiment. But notwithstanding the superiority of the French, after an obstinate resistance they were enabled to sheer off and bear away, and Capt. George conducted his much-shattered little squadron into Halifax Harbour.

---

* Afterwards Sir Dennis George, Baronet. He was father of the late Sir Rupert D. George, Secretary of the Province for many years, and of Sir Samuel Hood George, who was for a short time member of Assembly for the County of Halifax. Capt. George married Miss Cochran, of Halifax.

The Little Jack stuck to one of the French Frigates of 42 guns, but was afterwards recaptured. On the 31st, the remains of Captain Evans, were interred with military honors, under St. Paul's Church, where his monument is still to be seen on the east side of the chancel. He was a young man of great promise, and his premature death was a loss to the service, and shed a gloom over the town, in which he had made many friends.

This year (1781), Lord Charles Montague, who had been Governor of one of the West India Islands, arrived at Halifax, with 200 of his disbanded corps from Jamaica. This nobleman died at Halifax, from the effects of fatigue, in travelling over land from Quebec to Halifax, in winter. He was buried under St. Paul's Church, where a monument to his memory is to be seen near that of Capt. Evans. He was a younger son of Robert, Duke of Manchester.

1782. The continual intercourse at this time carried on with the revolted colonies, rendered it necessary that a more strict system of inspection should be adopted with respect to vessels and passengers entering and leaving the port; accordingly Capt. Thomas Beamish was appointed Port Warden. His duty was to grant passes to all vessels and boats leaving, and to visit all those entering the harbour. No vessel or boat was allowed to pass George's Island, in the night time, or leave the harbour without sending a boat to the island, and also producing a pass from the Port Warden; and all vessels coming in were to be hailed from the island, and ordered to send their boat on shore to the Market Slip, or public landing, to be examined by the Port Warden before landing in any other part of the town. The Port Warden's office was in the old building which formerly stood at the corner now known as Laidlaw's Corner on Water Street, just above the Steamboat Wharf. At this time the water came up as far as the spot on the wharf, where Bauld and Gibson's store or shop now stands.

The Governor, Sir Andrew Snape Hammond, went to England this year, and was succeeded by Governor Parr. He received a very flattering address from the inhabitants of the town. Hammond was esteemed a good Governor, and had gained the good will of the people by his courteous manners and desire to meet, as far as possible, the wishes of the inhabitants in all municipal matters.

This summer 57 transports with troops, and the Renown, a fifty gun ship, put into Halifax on their way to New York and Canada. In October the Renown sent in a prize, laden with a rich cargo of silks, etc. The annual ships Adamant and St. Lawrence made their trips this season in 35 days.

Among the occurences this year was the conviction and sentence of a man named William McLean, for street robbery, and the murder of a Mrs. Ann Dunbrack in July, by persons unknown. The grand Jury recommended McLean to mercy, but the Governor and Council saw no reason to grant a reprieve, and he was executed. Street robberies were at the time of frequent occurence in the town.

Articles of peace between Great Britain and the United States of America were signed in November of this year, and with France in January following.

The principal public amusements in the town during the year were subscription assemblies, held at the Pontac, and at Mrs. Sutherland's Coffee House, every fortnight. The latter establishment was in Bedford Row, opposite the Commissary offices. The national societies dined together, and levees were held and parties given at Government House on all public holidays. The Garrison consisted of the 70th, 82nd and 84th Regiments, with Baron de Seitz's* Germans. Night riots were frequent, and continual complaints appear to have been made before the Sessions, of signs being removed from shops, and windows broken.

The views of the town and suburbs at this time show the fortifications at Citadel Hill, Fort Needham and Point Pleasant. They were supposed to have been taken by one Colonel Hicks, and were engraved and published in London. These views were mere outlines. Copies of them are to be seen at the Provincial Museum, where there are also a series of views, very neatly executed in copper plate, of the Government House, St. Paul's Church and other parts of the town. These latter were published about 1776, some six or seven years before those of Colonel Hicks.

---

* Baron de Soltz died at Halifax in the following year. He was buried under St. Paul's Church with military honors, with his full uniform, sword and spurs, according to the ancient custom in Germany when the last Baron of the race dies. His monument, a quaint old German performance, may be seen in the east gallery of St. Paul's, with his armorial bearings, etc. Among his effects advertized for sale was his diamond ring and coach with 3 horses.

Governor Parr and family came out in the ship St. Lawrence, and assumed the government in October.

Benjamin Green, Esq., son of the Hon. B. Green, one of the first members of Council, was elected member of Assembly for the town in February, without opposition. Mr. William Shaw was at the time Sheriff of the County.

In December, 1782, a large quantity of heavy ordnance was brought to Halifax from Charleston, South Carolina; also 500 refugees, men, women and children, arrived about the same date.

In August, 1783, a number of Negro refugees arrived from New York. It was resolved that they should be settled in different parts of the Province; however, not a few remained in Halifax, and became servants and labourers.

The Loyalists continued to come from the old Colonies, many of them in a destitute and helpless condition, until the population of the town was increased to three times its former number, and much temporary suffering in consequence prevailed. Yet many intelligent and enterprising settlers were at this period added to our population, giving new life and spirit to the town. Many spacious and commodious buildings began to be erected, taking the place of the low gamble-roofed and picketed buildings of an early day. It is very remarkable, however, that in the year 1791, only seven years after this great influx, the population had again so decreased as scarcely to exceed 5,000. In 1783, Governor Parr estimated the population at only 1,200. This was before the Loyalist emigration from New York. In 1784, one hundred and ninety-four Negro men, women and children arrived in Halifax from St. Augustin's, in a destitute condition; they did not remain in the town, but were distributed by the Government throughout the interior parts of the Province.

Governor Parr in his letter to England of November 20th, 1783, says, "upwards of 25,000 Loyalists have already arrived in the Province, most of whom, with the exception of those who went to Shelburne, came to Halifax before they became distributed throughout the Province."

Again in his letter of 15th January, 1784, he says, "In consequence of the final evacuation of New York,[*] a considerable

---

[*] New York was finally evacuated by the British Troops on the 25th November, 1783.

number of refugee families have come to Halifax, who must be provided for at the public expense. They are in a most wretched condition, destitute of almost everything—chiefly women and children, all still on board the vessels, and I have not been able to find as yet any place for them, and the cold is setting in very severe.*

On the 20th October, 1784, an advertizement appeared in a Halifax paper, for sale, "All that land near the entrance of the harbour and opposite to Cornwallis' Island, called Mauger's Beach, containing by particular grant 5 acres according to the plan attached to the grant." This beach had been formerly occupied for curing fish, and had buildings erected thereon for that purpose.†

The Penal Statutes had been repealed in 1783. The Roman Catholics in the town, chiefly emigrants from Ireland, having become numerous, purchased a piece of ground in Barrington Street, where they built a Chapel, which was dedicated to St. Peter. The frame was erected on 19th July, 1784, and many of the inhabitants, both Protestants and Roman Catholics, attended the ceremony. This building stood in from the street, directly opposite the head of Salter Street. It was painted red, with a steeple at the western end. It was removed in or shortly after Bishop Burke's time, on the completion of the new stone church, now St. Mary's. The Rev. Mr. Jones was the first officiating priest. The Rev. Edmund Burke, who came from Canada, officiated at St. Peter's for many years before he was appointed Bishop.

A number of emigrants arrived in Halifax this year from England. Three hundred passengers came in the Sally transport, in a great measure destitute of clothing and provisions. Fresh provisions became very dear, and the merchants of Halifax had flour up to £3 10s. per cwt. The Governor and Council, in consequence, ordered the admission of provisions from the United States to afford relief to the inhabitants.

---

* NOTE.—Tradition says that the town was then so crowded by refugees and soldiers, that the cabooses from the transports were removed from the vessels, and ranged along Granville Street in rear of Government House, for the accommodation of the people.

† The tower now on Mauger's Beach was not built until about the commencement of the present century.

The House of Assembly was dissolved this year; it had sat fourteen years without being dissolved, in consequence of the American troubles. The only alteration in the Halifax representation was the return of Capt. William Abbott for the County. Mr. Francis Green, second son of old Councillor Green, was again chosen Sheriff of Halifax in 1784.

1785. January 3rd, Mr. Sampson Salter Blowers, a barrister from Boston who came among the Loyalists, was appointed Attorney General in the place of Mr. Gibbons, who had received the appointment of Chief Justice for the Island of Cape Breton, then a separate province.

The Orphan house being no longer in use, was ordered to be let on a lease for one year.*

In September, 1785, a number of whalers from Nantucket came to Halifax; three brigantines and one schooner, with crews and everything necessary for prosecuting the whale fishery, which they proposed to do under the British flag. Their families were to follow. A short time after they were joined by three brigantines and a sloop from the same place.

On the twentieth of October following, the Chief Land Surveyor was directed to make return of such lands as were vacant at Dartmouth to be granted to Samuel Starbuck, Timothy Folger, and others, from Nantucket, to make settlement for the whalers. The Town of Dartmouth had been many years previously laid out in lots which had been granted or appropriated to individuals, some of whom had built houses, and others though then vacant, had been held and sold from time to time by their respective owners. Most of these lots were reported vacant by Mr. Morris, the surveyor, and seized upon by the Government, as it is said, without any proceeding of escheat, and re-granted to the Quakers from Nantucket, which caused much discontent, and questions of title arose and remained open for many years after.

At a Court of Admiralty held on Friday, the 27th August, 1785, for the trial of piracies committed upon the high seas, M. Buckley and Relitham Taylor were tried, committed and sentenced to death for running away with the schooner John Miller of Chedabucto and

---

* The locality of this orphan house is uncertain.

her cargo. Two men were also hanged this year for robbery committed to the eastward of Halifax.

The death of the Chief Justice, Bryan Finucane, having occurred this year, Judge Isaac Deschamps filled the office until the appointment of Chief Justice Pemberton. Judge Finucane was buried under St. Paul's Church. His escutcheon is in the gallery.

A general election occurred in 1785, when Mr. S. S. Blowers, John George Pyke, Richard John Uniacke and Michael Wallace were returned for the County, and John Fillis and William Cochran for the town.

The whale fishery was the chief subject which engaged the attention of the public during the year. Much advantage was expected to accrue to the commerce of the place from the Quakers from Nantucket having undertaken to settle in Dartmouth. They went on prosperously for a short time, until they found the commercial regulations established in England for the Colonies were hostile to their interests, and they eventually removed, some of them, it is said, to Wales and other parts of Great Britain, where they carried on their fishery to more advantage.

A petition was presented this autumn to the Governor and Council from a number of merchants, tradesmen and other inhabitants, praying for a Charter of Incorporation for the Town. This was the first occasion on which the subject was brought prominently before the public. It was, however, not deemed by the government "expedient or necessary" to comply with the prayer of the petition. The reasons are not given in the Minute of Council, which bears date 17th November, 1785. The names of the Councillors present were Richard Bulkeley, Henry Newton, Jonathan Binney, Arthur Goold, Alexander Brymer, Thomas Cochran and Charles Morris. The functions of His Majesty's Council at this period of our history embraced all departments of executive authority in the Colony. They were equally supreme in the control of town affairs as those of the province at large. The magistrates, though nominally the executive of the town, never acted in any matter of moment without consulting the Governor and Council. The existence of a corporate body having the sole control of town affairs would in a great measure deprive them of that supervision which they no doubt deemed, for the interest of the community, should remain in the Governor and Council.

1786. It was customary at this period to celebrate the Royal birthdays and almost all public holidays by a levee at Government House, a review of the troops in garrison on the Common, and occasionally a public ball, either by the Governor at Government House or by the inhabitants of the town at the public assembly room. This custom continued in Halifax until about the year 1844 or 1845, when it was broken through by Governor Falkland. On the 18th June, 1786, Queen Charlotte's birthday was celebrated in the town by a levee and review, and in the evening by a ball in the old Pontac building. The confectionery on this occasion was very superb. It was prepared by one Signor Lenzi. The ball commenced at half-past eight, supper was announced by the elevation of a curtain that separated the two rooms. In the middle of the table there arose an artificial fountain, with the temples of Health and Venus at the top and bottom, all constructed of sugar. The Gazette of the time says, they "did not go home till morning."

A regular post communication was opened this summer with Annapolis; a courier was engaged, who went through once a fortnight with the mail between Halifax and Annapolis. John Howe, who had lately come to Halifax from Boston and had established a newspaper, was at this time postmaster; he succeeded Mr. Stevens. The following spring (1786) the town was so enveloped in smoke for many days as almost to impede business, caused by a great fire which raged in the woods in the neighbourhood.

On 10th October, 1786, arrived His Majesty's Ship Pegasus, commanded by His Royal Highness Prince William Henry. He was received at the King's Slip by Governor Parr and Major General Campbell, then in command of the Garrison, and conducted to the Government House, which stood in the square now occupied by the Province Building, where he was waited upon by the military and the principal inhabitants. The Prince expressed a desire that all display should be laid aside, but the people illuminated their dwellings, and by 8 o'clock the whole town was lighted and the streets crowded with people.

In the Gazette of the 9th February, 1786, appears a resolution and engagement entered into by the merchants and others at a public meeting lately held in Halifax, wherein they pledged themselves neither to buy nor sell articles imported from the United States, prohibited by the Governor's proclamation. The document is signed by 75 persons.

On 28th February, a German Society was formed in Halifax, when John W. Schwartz was chosen President, Doctor F. Gschwint, (pronounced Swint) Vice-President, Godfrey Schwartz Treasurer, Henry Uthoff Secretary. In 1790 Adolphus Veith was secretary of this Society.

On 4th March, the jail was broken open and the prisoners, six in in number, all escaped, of whom five were re-taken. Mr. Green was then Sheriff. Inquiries were instituted, but no information obtained. The delapidated and insecure state of the jail at the time was the subject of public comment.

The money collected for Liquor Licences in the town, between 31st May, 1784, and 31st May, 1785, amounted to £531. Mr. Francis Shipton was Clerk of Licences.

Three vessels were fitted out during the summer of 1786 for the whale fishery,—the schooners Parr and Lively, and the ship Romulus.

This year the merchants and shipowners formed themselves into a society called the Halifax Marine Association, for the benefit of trade. The following year Nova Scotia was erected into a Bishop's See. The Right Reverend Charles Inglis was appointed Bishop. He arrived from England on 16th October, and made Halifax his residence.

On the 3rd July, 1787, the Pegasus, frigate, commanded by Prince William Henry, arrived again at Halifax, 15 days from Jamaica. On Friday, at half-past two o'clock, the troops were drawn up in double line from the wharf to Government House. The Prince landed at the slip under a salute from the artillery on the King's Wharf. He was accompanied to Government House by the Governor and Council, where he received an address from the inhabitants. There was a dinner and ball at Government House in the evening, and a brilliant illumination of the town.

This month two whalers returned bringing 1,060 barrels oil and 72 cwt. whalebone. It is not mentioned whether these vessels belonged to the Quakers or to some of the merchants of the town.

On the 24th June, the Freemasons had a grand procession. They walked to St. Paul's Church, where they heard a sermon from the Rev. Mr. Weeks. The Prince reviewed the troops in garrison on 30th July, consisting of the 57th and 37th Regiments, and the first Battalion of the 60th Regiment.

On the 7th July the fleet, consisting of the Leander, Commodore Sawyer—Pegasus, Prince William Henry—Ariadne, Capt. Osborne, the Resource, and the Brig Weazel, Commander Hood, fell down to the beach, intending to proceed to Quebec the first fair wind. They sailed on the 14th. The Pegasus, with the Prince, returned to Halifax early in November. He received an address on the 6th, from the House of Assembly then in Session. At two o'clock on that day, the barge of the Pegasus with the Royal Standard flying, preceded by the Commodore in his barge, with his pendant, and the Captains of the other ships of war in their barges, proceeded slowly in procession from their ships to the King's Wharf, where the party landed under a salute of 21 guns. They were received at the stairs by the Governor, Council and Assembly, and the troops, under General Ogilvie, being ordered up, they proceeded to Government House, where a number of members of the Legislature were presented to him. They then proceeded through the lines of troops to the Golden Ball,[*] where a handsome dinner was prepared, and where the Prince dined with the members of [†]Assembly and the principal officers of Government. He retired at 6 o'clock, after which a ball was given in the evening at Marchington's new building in Water Street, adjoining the Ordnance Yard, called the British Coffee House. The Prince entered the ball room a little after 8 o'clock, and at 12 the company were conducted into the supper room. The table was handsomely decorated and contained places for 200 people. The Prince is said to have displayed great affability in conversation on the occasion.

An Act was passed this Session authorizing the sale of the Orphan House, the Court House, the Public Slaughter House, and the Old Jail, and to erect a Jail, and also to erect on the Lower Parade a Public Hall, a Province House of Brick or Stone for the setting of the Legislature and Public Offices. The Commissioners

---

[*] S. W. corner of Sackville and Hollis Streets.
[†] The House afterwards voted £700 for the cost of the day's entertainments.

appointed for this purpose were John Newton, Richard John Uniacke, John George Pyke and Mr. Taylor. Such parts of this Act as have been executed were afterwards repealed by Act of 1797.

1788. An Election for Members for the Town took place this winter, which was attended with extraordinary excitement. On the 20th February the poll opened, at the Court House, in Halifax; the candidates were Mr. Charles Morris and Jonathan Sterns. It closed on the Friday following, when it stood: Morris, 415; Sterns, 274. Majority for Morris, 141. Mr. Morris was carried through the Town and then taken home to his father's house. Hand-bills had been posted up reflecting on the government. Serious riots at the election occurred and many persons were hurt, some of whom received fractures of the skull and other severe injuries. Armed persons paraded the Town assaulting individuals. As this was a very remarkable election, and resulted in more turbulence and riot than had ever before occurred in the town on such occasions, we here copy the following extract from Anthony Henry's *Gazette* of 25th February:—" The unwearied and spirited exertions of a num-
" ber of respectable gentlemen in a great measure calmed the minds
" of the people, and prevented their violence being carried to any
" very great length; nevertheless it was utterly impossible, in such
" confusion, to prevent many persons from being wounded and
" hurt, two of whom, we are sorry to inform the public, remain
" in a dangerous state; one having his skull fractured by some
" persons who rushed out of Laycock's house on the beach, and
" the other having been dangerously wounded by a shot from a
" window in the same house. We are likewise sorry to inform
" the public, that Mr. Benjamin Mulberry Holmes and his son,
" have been much beaten and abused by the populace on Friday
" night, and were it not for the very fortunate and timely inter-
" position of Mr. Tobin's man and some others, it is probable
" they would have fallen a sacrifice to an enraged multitude."

The excitement had been caused partly by certain proceedings on the part of the judges of the Supreme Court against Mr. Sterns and Mr. Taylor, two practising lawyers in the town, whose names had been struck off the roll by Chief Justice Deschamps. One of the gentlemen, Mr. Sterns, was the defeated candidate at the election.

On the 3rd June, Bishop Inglis held his primary visitation of his

Clergy, when he delivered a charge, received an address, and held a confirmation in the afternoon at St. Paul's, when one hundred and twenty young persons went through the ceremony of confirmation.

A heavy rain-storm occurred on Saturday, 5th July, when the streets of the town were very much injured by the torrents of water which poured down the hills. It was estimated that the rainfall was upwards of 186 tons of water to an acre, which, allowing the rain to have fallen equally on the whole peninsula, would make the fall of water on that small space equal to 345,000 tons, in four hours.

July 30. Arrived five sail of whalers, having on board the following valuable cargoes:

 Sloop "Watson," Danl. Ray, Master, 150 bbls. sperm,
  50 do. headmatter.
 Brigt. "Lucretia," J. Coffin, Master, 250 bbls sperm,
  300 bbls. black oil, and 3000 cut bone.
 Brigt. "Somerset," S. Gardner, Master, 230 bbls. sperm.
 Brigt. "Sally," P. Worth, Master, 200 bbls. do.
 Brigt. "Industry," W. Chadwick, Master, 84 bbls do.
  26 bbls. headmatter, and 300 do. black oil, also
  3000 cut bone.

The "Andromeda," frigate, commanded by Prince William Henry, from England, arrived on 17th August, 1788; he was again received with the usual honours and the town was illuminated. The Prince attended a sham-fight on the Common, on 10th September, in which, the 4th, 37th, and 57th Regiments took part. Three soldiers were wounded by bursting of their muskets during the performance.

On 21st October, the new Chief Justice Jeremiah Pemberton, took, the oaths and his seat on the bench, and his patent was then read in open Court.

Wednesday, Oct. 22nd, was launched at the south end of the town, a handsome brig, the property of Messrs. Gouge & Pryor; she was the first vessel of the size ever built in the town.

The following gentlemen composed the Magistracy of the town this year, viz:—Benj. Green, John Cunningham, John Newton, Charles Morris, George Smith, William Sherlock, John George Pyke, Thos. Cochran, Anthony Stewart,[*] W. Taylor, Stephen N. Binney, J. M.

---

[*] Anthony Stewart was a gentleman from the province of Maryland; he was the father of the late Judge James Stewart, who married a sister of the late Chief Justice Sir B. Haliburton and who died in 1830, and was succeeded on the Supreme Court Bench by R. J. Uniacke, junior.

F. Bulkeley, Revd. Michael Houseal, James Gautier, William Morris, Charles Morris, junior, Daniel Wood, junior; Matthew Cahill was High Sheriff.

It appears that the rank of Esquire was not applied to any person, at this or any previous period, except Magistrates and high public functionaries, and persons to whom it was accorded in consequence of their personal wealth and rank in society. Being a member of the House of Assembly did not confer the title.

There was then no regular police establishment in the town, the Magistrates, by turns, attended to police duties with the aid of the town constables, who were annually appointed. All special matters were discussed and settled at the special sessions, which was generally a private meeting of Magistrates in the back office in conjunction with the Clerk of the Peace. Criminal charges of a delicate nature, or when private character was likely to be affected, were usually investigated with closed doors, and no information made public until found to be necessary for the ends of justice. This system continued until Mr. John George Pyke received the appointment of Police Magistrate, about 60 years since. His duties were merely to relieve the Magistrates from the more onerous duties of attending daily at the Police office. Colonel Pyke became incapacitated by age about the year 1825 or 6, when Mr. John Liddell was appointed, who had to his aid three or four Police Constables, two of whom had attended his predecessor, and the valuable assistance of David Shaw Clarke, the clerk of the peace. Such was the arrangement until the Act of Incorporation in 1848.

The "Royal Gazette" was published by Anthony Henry, until about 1801, when it fell into the hands of Mr. John Howe, from Boston.

The "Weekly Chronicle," another paper, was at this time established by Mr. William Minns, stationer, in Barrington Street, opposite the north-end of the Grand Parade. It was commenced in 1787, and continued to exist until about 1828 or 9.

Among the merchants who advertized in these papers we find the names of James Vetch, opposite the woodyard; David Hall & Co., in Hollis Street, opposite Government House, (Crown Prince Building); and George Bell, Granville St. The shops appear to have contained both groceries and dry-goods, like the country stores of the present day. A. & R. Leslie were at the corner of Duke and Water Streets, near the Pontac. Lawrence Hartshorne, Hardware, corner of Granville and George streets, between the market house and the parade. This old corner, so many years known as Hartshorne & Boggs' corner, had a gun at the corner of the platform which extended down the hill to the lower corner, occupied by one Hart, a Jew, afterwards known as Martin Gay Black's, and now occupied by the new building of the Merchant's Bank; this walk was the resort of the merchants in the morning, and the fashionable and idle in the afternoons.

1789. On the night of Friday, the 23rd January, Cochran's buildings, a range of three-storey buildings in the market square, were totally consumed by fire. Firewards were John Fillis, J. G. Pyke, R. J. Uniacke, Michael Wallace, Geo. Bell, Lawrence Hartshorne, William Lawlor, Charles Hill.

On 9th February, an advertisement appeared in the "Gazette," as follows: " I am directed by His Excellency the Governor, to " acquaint the several gentlemen called upon on Friday last to form " a Fire Company, that he desires their attendance at the ' Golden " Ball " on Thursday next, at twelve o'clock, to agree to rules and " regulations. (Signed) Jas. Gautier."

On 15th August, the jail was broken open, and a prisoner for debt, one Livesay, who had been imprisoned at the suit of William Stairs, escaped, for which Sheriff Green was prosecuted; Green stated that he had repeatedly represented to the Council the insecure state of the jail. Mr. James Clarke succeeded Mr. Green as Sheriff of Halifax, this year.

The Dockyard at this period was in full operation. The Commissioner in charge was the Honorable Henry Duncan, who was also a member of His Majesty's Council. Doctor John Haliburton, father of the late Chief Justice Sir Brenton Haliburton, was Surgeon of the Naval Hospital, Mr. Provo Wallis was Master Superintendent, Elias Marshall, foreman of shipwrights, William Lee foreman of carpenters, Alexander Anderson and Provo F. Wallis, Chief Clerks.

A great scarcity of bread was felt in the town this summer. Vessels sent to Canada for wheat, returned empty. On the 9th July, the Governor received a letter from the Governor of Canada, stating the great scarcity of provisions in the Province of Lower Canada or Quebec, that a famine was dreaded, and requesting him not to obstruct the exportation of corn and flour from Halifax to Quebec. But the Justices of the Quarter Sessions presented a memorial which had been laid before them by the bakers of Halifax, setting forth that there is not more of flour in the town than sufficient to provide bread for three or four days, whereupon it was ordered by the Council that no vessel be permitted to clear out with bread or flour to Quebec, except the brigantine " Ceres," until further consideration.

There were amateur theatrical performances this winter at the Pontac. It would appear that the old theatre in Argyle Street, in the recollection possibly of some of the oldest inhabitants, was in operation this year. We find plays advertized to take place there in February and March. This building stood on the spot on which the present Acadian School was afterwards erected. It was the only theatre in the town during the time of the Duke of Kent. It was afterwards occupied by Walter Bromley as a public school upon the Lancaster plan, until removed to make way for the present building, in the year 1816.

The first Agricultural Society was formed in Halifax in the year 1789; the Hon. Richard Bulkeley was the first president, and Mr. James Clarke,* (afterwards Sheriff Clarke,) was the first secretary.

The old Block House on the Citadel Hill being in a ruinous condition, was taken down this year, but the flag and signal staffs which were on it, were preserved.

June 1, 1789. The old gaol and garden were offered for sale at auction. This old building was in Hollis Street, nearly opposite the present Halifax Hotel, and was formerly the property of the late Mr. Robert M. Brown.

On the 16th June, in comformity with the Act of the Legislature formerly passed, the Governor was pleased to nominate Hon. Henry Newton, Hon. Thos. Cochran, James Brenton, John Newton and R. J. Uniacke, Trustees of a Grammar School forthwith to be erected in the town. " These gentlemen chose Mr. William Cochran, of " Trinity College, Dublin, and lately Professor of the Greek and

---

*Sheriff Clarke was father of the late David Shaw Clarke, for many years Clerk of the Peace, and one of the Police Magistrates of the town.

"Latin languages in Columbia College, New York, to be master.
"Mr. George Glennie, who was regularly educated in the University
"of Aberdeen, to be usher, and Mr. Thomas Brown, already well
"known in this town, to be teacher of writing, arithmetic and
"mathematics. It is thought proper to give this early notification
"to the public, but until a suitable building can be provided, the
"school will be opened without delay in the room where the
"Assembly of the Province meets."

The Legislature after this met in the building known as Cochran's building, which was erected at the Market Square after the fire before mentioned, and the old building appropriated permanently for the Grammar school, which remained so until lately, when the school was removed to the private residence of Mr. Gilpin, the head master, and the old building sold.

The following advertizement appeared in the "Royal Gazette:" "Information for Masters of Vessels. The Block House on Citadel "Hill, which was a conspicuous object, is removed, having been in "a ruinous condition. The flag and signal staffs remain." "The "hulk of the large ship, sometime since stranded at the back of "Thrum Cap, was beaten to pieces in the last gale."

On the 15th October, Charles Hill advertized for sale at auction, the ground where the Court House stood, now known as Northup's Corner; measuring on Buckingham Street, 94 feet, and on Argyle Street 43 feet. On the 17th July previous, the old Court House, and the building adjoining, known as Kirby's soap-house, and other buildings, were destroyed by fire.

1790. In the month of July, this year, the whaling fleet arrived, after a successful voyage. The brig Prince William Henry, Capt. Pinkham, with 110 barrels of sperm oil; brig "Hibernian," Capt. Worth, 100 barrels sperm and 32 black oil; ship "Parr," Capt. Chase, 480 sperm and 100 black oil, and brig "Harvest," Capt. Kelly, with 200 sperm. In August following arrived the "Romulus," with 170 bbls. sperm oil.

Among the chief merchants of the town at this time were William Forsyth, Philip Marchington,* Brymer & Belcher, Hardware

---

*Mr. Marchington was a Loyalist from New York. He commenced business in Halifax soon after his arrival, and accumulated a large landed property in the town. He owned all the land on the north side of the lane, known by his name, leading from the ordinance into Argyle Street, since called Bell's Lane, also the wharf adjoining the

merchants, successors to Thomas Robic; Michael Wallace, retail store-keeper; James Moody, Hollis Street; Sabatier, Stewart & Co., Chas. Geddes, dry goods, lower side of the Parade; Richard Kidston, general merchandize; George Deblois, William Millet, Charles Hill, Hugh Kelley, all auctioneers. John W. Schwartz kept store at the corner of Granville and Buckingham Streets; Lawrence Hartshorne, at his corner, had a general assortment of cutlery, etc., D. Hall & Co., in Hollis Street, opposite Government House; Ann Bremner kept a dry goods shop at the north-west corner of the parade; Peter Lynch kept a hat store at the sign of the "King's Arms;" C. C. Hall & Co. was the chief dry goods store in the town; Benjamin Salter, Ship Chandlery, Water St.; John Fillis & Son and G. & J. Thirlock were among the wholesale dealers; Linnard & Young were the fashionable tailors; Richard Courtney had a shop at the lower side of the parade, William Sellon in Granville Street, King & Story in Marchington's buildings, John Butler Dight, wholesale store in Marchington's buildings; C. C. Hall & Co. had this year removed to Marchington building; Winkworth Allen, general dealer, in Cochran's new building. Mr. Wm. Millet the auctioneer, on the 9th Sept. advertized for sale, " a negro man and sundry " other articles." In the following year, James Forman & Co. occupied a store on Copeland's wharf, also Benjamin Salter. The British Coffee house was kept by John Gallagher at the head of Marchington's wharf. Mrs. Sutherland's coffee house, was at this time, one of the chief places of resort for Public Committees and Societies, as well as for Public entertainments; concerts were held here throughout the winter, commencing in September. The Halifax Marine Society, which had been established in Halifax for several years, held their quarterly meetings at this house. There was a house of entertainment then kept on McNab's Island by one Mary Roubalet, for tea parties in the summer. It was called the Mansion House.

On the 12th day of January, 1790, James Clarke and George Geddes, Church Wardens of St. Paul's, advertized that in consequence of the inclemency of the weather on Sunday there was so small an attendance in church, that the contributions towards the

Ordnance yard, long known as Marchington's wharf, afterwards the property of Tim. Connors. He died at Halifax; he was the grandfather of Major Welsford, killed in the Crimean War, whose monument is to be seen in the old English burial ground.

clothing of the children in the Sunday Schools in the town, were so small, that they desired to invite contributions from the inhabitants for the relief of the orphans and others attending the schools. In February following, the church wardens again advertized the distribution of clothing to the poor children of the Sunday Schools: 15 great coats, 64 shirts and shifts, 70 pairs stockings and 35 pairs strong shoes, which cost £30. 7s. 2d. The St. Paul's school had nineteen boys and sixteen girls in attendance.

On the same day, there was a visitation of the Halifax Grammar School by the Governor, the Bishop, the Trustees and others. The attendance during the winter was usually about 60. The school was addressed on this occasion, by one of the elder boys, and after the examinations in the Latin classes, writing and arithmetic, several scholars repeated pieces and dialogues. Mr. Cochran was the headmaster; he shortly afterwards accepted the charge of the Academy at Windsor; and the Rev. George Wright was appointed in his place. His salary was £150 per annum from the Legislature, with what he could get from the pupils. The number of scholars was 68. He states his loss in the shape of discount on his Treasury warrants amounted to from 15 to 20 per cent, in consequence of the delay in payment.

The winter was very severe; The harbour was frozen over, and the destitute condition of the poor very great. The gentlemen amateurs of the theatre, sent £25 to the Rev. Mr. Weeks, of St. Paul's, Dr. Andrew Brown, of the Presbyterian meeting house, and Mr. Houseal of St. George's in Dutchtown, for the poor of their respective parishes. The overseers of the poor, Jonathan Tremain, James Gautier, James Kerby and Andrew Belcher, met at the "Golden Ball," to assess the inhabitants of the town for the poor rates.

The Court House having been destroyed by fire, the Quarter Sessions held their sittings on the 19th February, in the long room of the "Golden Ball," for the trial of offenders. The "Golden Ball" was kept by Edward Phelan this winter, who occupied the north end of the building as a store for general merchandise.

An Act of the Legislature had been passed this year, and was published early in May, reciting that the destruction of the Court House by fire, and the inconvenient situation of the present Assembly House, made it necessary that a more suitable place should be provided, and the state of the Province finances not being such as to admit of the expense of erecting a proper and suitable building, it was therefore enacted, that Commissioners be appointed to treat with Thomas James and William Cochran, for their building opposite Government House, for £200 per annum, and to expend £100 in furniture for the purposes of the meeting of this Legislature and the Courts of Law. This building lately erected after the fire, stood on the spot now occupied by the new Dominion Public building, and continued to be the place of holding the General Assembly, the Courts of Law, etc., until the Province Building was completed for their reception in 1820. The building in which the Legislature formerly held its sittings, and which was now appropriated for the Grammar School, was this year repaired at the public expense.

In June, the Grand Jury addressed Chief Justice Strange on his arrival from England. The names of the Jury were:—Richard Kidston, foreman, William Millet, Lawrence Hartshorne, Godfrey Schwartz, Winkworth Allen, John Davis, J. Forbes, James Lewis, Benjamin Salter, James Strachan, William Lawlor, Martin Shier, John Boyd and Alexander Copeland.

In the autumn, the Secretary of the Province announced to the people of the town, that in the event of a war with Spain, and the withdrawal of the troops from the Province, it would be necessary to call out the Militia for the defence of the town, and the Colonels of regiments were called upon to hold themselves in readiness, and to make returns of the state and condition of their respective regiments.

About this time, Captain Stack was a regular trader between this port and Ireland, and sold his cargoes of beef, salt pork, lard, etc., at auction, at Charles Hill & Co.'s rooms.

The Halifax Bar addressed Chief Justice Strange, on his leaving for England on a visit, this autumn. The address was signed by S. S. Blowers, R. J. Uniacke, James Sterns, E. B. Brenton, James Stewart, Daniel Wood, Foster Hutchinson, J. Prout and W. H. O. Haliburton.

At a Court of Quarter Sessions, held at Halifax, in June term of this year, the Sheriff, pursuant to law and by virtue of a warrant directed to him by the Justices of the Sessions, to lay out a road in the north suburbs of the town, reported that he had laid out the road by a jury, in the manner following, viz :—Beginning at the north-east corner or angle of Lot No. 2. on the road leading from the Dockyard to the Naval Hospital; thence to run north 28 west, 40 feet; thence north, 59 east, 238 feet, which leaves a road of 40 feet wide, between Allbright's ground and the Hospital fence; thence north, 28 west, 660 feet; thence north 20 west, 664 feet to the road leading to Fort Needham, leaving the road 50 feet wide between the shore at the Narrows at high-water mark, and the Lots Nos. 3 and 4. This notice was published, that all persons who might think themselves aggrieved by the laying out of the road might have an opportunity of being heard before the sessions, on Tuesday, the 5th September, 1790. It was signed by Thomas Wood, Clerk of the Peace.

This road was intended as a continuation of Water Street northward, to meet the road which leads up from the water to Fort Needham, but it does not appear to have been on the line of the present road, but to have gone through the northern end of the Hospital grounds, along the water side, below the site of the old magazines.

At the session of the House of Assembly in 1790, several articles of impeachment against the Judges of the Supreme Court, as before mentioned, passed the House, which were laid before the Executive Council by the Governor, on 7th April. It was proposed to suspend Chief Justice Deschamps and Judge James Brenton, in conformity with the request of the Assembly.

1791. Governor Parr died on 25th November this year, in the 66th year of his age, and the ninth of his government. He was buried with military honours, under St. Paul's Church, on the 29th of the month. The procession moved from Government House to St. Paul's Church, in the following order :—All the Lodges of the Freemasons, (His Excellency having been the Grand Master,) the 20th regiment as the firing party, the Church Wardens, the Physicians of deceased, the Clergy, the Bishop, the body covered by a pall adorned by eight escutcheons, Pall-bearers, Hon. A. Brymer, Major Boyd, the Commissioner of the Dockyard, the Admiral, the Hon. S. S. Blowers, Hon. Thomas Cochran, Major Rawlinson, the General, the relatives and servants of deceased, particular friends, the Sheriff of the county, members of Council, viz., Morris, Bulkeley and Newton, Judges Brenton and Hutchinson, the treasurer of the province, the Speaker of the House of Assembly, Custos of the county and Justice Binney, Magistrates of the town, the bar, staff of the army, officers of the navy and army, officers of militia, gentlemen of the town, and the whole garrison all under arms, lining the streets. Minute guns were fired by the men-of-war in the harbor and by the Royal Artillery, during the procession. The service was performed by the bishop, Dr. Charles Inglis, and the body was buried under the middle aisle.

During the autumn and winter, a number of black people from different parts of the province were brought to Halifax, to be removed to Sierra Leone. Michael Wallace was agent, who on 5th December, advertised for 1000 tons of shipping, for the purpose. Ships "Venus," "Parr," "Eleanor;" Brigs "Betsy," "Beaver," "Mary," "Morning Star," "Catherine," "P. W. Henry;" Schrs. "Liberty," and "Two Brothers," the whole commanded by Lieutenant Clarkson, having on board the colored people, all sailed for Sierra Leone on 15th January, 1792. The hire and damages amounted to £3965 8s. 0d. sterling. This expense was borne by the Sierra Leone Company. These colored people were chiefly those who came from the old provinces with the Loyalists. They formed a colony in Africa, called the "Nova Scotia colony,"* which still exists, and about 15 years since several old negroes were living who recollected the removal from Halifax, when children. The fleet arrived at their destination after a passage of 40 days. The number embarked was 1139. The day of arrival was 28th March, and the 28th March in every year is still kept up by the adherents of the Lady Huntingdon Congregation at Sierra Leone, as the anniversary of the arrival of their fathers in the colony.

Until these Nova Scotian adherents of Lady Huntingdon's connection could erect a chapel for themselves in their new home, they united with the other coloured congregations of Methodists and Baptists. Mr. Zachary Macaulay, who was at one time Governor of this colony, says: "There were five or six black preachers among the Nova Scotians

---

*Among those negroes was a coloured preacher, the Rev. John Marrant, who had been ordained in London in 1785, as a minister of Lady Huntingdon's connection. He laboured among the people of his own colour while in Nova Scotia, and having accompanied them to Sierra Leone, officiated among them there for several years. He returned to England, and died in 1791.

"raised up from their own body, who are not without a considerable "influence." Among these, was John Ellis, who was Superintendent of the churches; he was succeeded by Anthony Elliot, a young Nova Scotian negro; he acquired several of the native dialects and became an active Christian missionary in Africa. He died in 1854 at the advanced age of 80. Elliot followed the avocations of a fisherman and pilot as the means of livelihood, and on the Sundays he preached to the people the Word of Life.

The population of the city and suburbs, in 1791, had fallen to 4,897.

The returns on the census this year, are as follows:—

    1301 males over 16 years of age.
     935 " under " "
    2209 females.
     422 black people.

The Agricultural Society of Halifax, offered premiums this year, and published a volume on husbandry.

A gold medal and 10 guineas was offered for the best essay on the natural history of the Hessian fly, and the method of stopping its progress in the wheat crop. A volume of the Society's proceedings, was this year published at Halifax by John Howe.

1792. On the 17th April news arrived of the appointment of Mr. John Wentworth as Governor. He had resided in Halifax for seven or eight years, having held the office of Ranger of woods and forests, and had been Governor of New Hampshire. On 12th May, the "Hussar," frigate, Capt. Rupert Denis George, arrived, having on board Governor Wentworth, etc. He landed at the King's wharf under a salute fired from the parade and a guard of honour from 21st regiment. On the 14th he was sworn into office. In the evening the town was brilliantly illuminated.

On 17th August a fire broke out in the property of John Welner, soap-maker in Granville Street. Six tenements and the Ordnance laboratory were consumed; Welner and his wife, two aged persons, were burnt to death. The sum of £140 was raised by subscription for the sufferers at the fire. The principal sufferers, however, declined to receive any aid, and a committee was appointed to examine the claims and distribute the fund.

Folger and Starbuck, the Quaker whalers, who settled at Dartmouth a year or two since, left Halifax this year, for Milford Haven, in Great Britain, where they expected to carry on their whale fishery with greater facilities than at Dartmouth.

Died at Halifax, on 27th September, 1792, Mrs. Hester Godfrey, aged 101 years.

The Grand Jury at Halifax, for 1792, were as follows, viz:— George Smith, foreman, Andrew Liddell, John Masters, Philip Marchington, Benjamin Mulberry Holmes, Rufus Fairbanks, Peter Smith, Michael Wallace, John Steeling, Richard Jacobs, John Kirby, Thomas Filles, Charles Hill, J. W. Schwartz, William Cochran, John Butler Dight,[*] Thomas Russell, Alexander Brymer, George Grant, William Williams and George Deblois.

Several petitions were presented this year to the Governor and Council, from the merchants and others of Halifax, on the subject of trade regulations and the collection of debts. Among the signatures to these petitions, we find the names of James Forman & Co., James Moody, William Veitch, George Grant, Winkworth Allen, William Kidston, Samuel Rudolph, Benjamin M. Holmes, James and Alexander Kidston, Chas. Geddes, Wm. Forsyth & Co., Thomas Russell, Hall, Bremner & Bottomry, William Taylor, Burnes, Liddell & Co., P. Smith, Jonathan Masters, Williams & Lyons, Geo. Deblois, John Moody, and S. Hall & Co.

Again 1793: Brymer & Belcher, Forman & Grassie, John Steeling, Jonathan Tremain, P. Marchington, Andrew Liddell, George Sherlocke, Francis Stevens, Geo. Bell, Geo. Moren, Edward Butler, Nathan Hatfield, Thomas Watson, Peter McNab, Benjamin Salter, Frederick Major and John Brown.

The town Assemblies were held this winter in Mrs. Sutherland's rooms in Bedford Row, opposite the Commissary offices.

On Thursday evening, Dec. 20th, 1792, Governor and Mrs. Wentworth gave a grand ball. The decorations in the supper room were very elegant. The ladies sat down and the gentlemen waited on them. Among the decorations were the exact representations of

---

[*] John Butler Dight was the nephew and heir of the Hon. John Butler, one of the early councillors. Under the will of his uncle, he assumed the name of Butler only and was afterwards known as John Butler Butler. He first was engaged in keeping a shop in the town; having acquired a fortune by the death of his uncle, he became a member of council and obtained a situation in the Commissariat department, after which he was removed to the seat of war with the army under Lord Wellington and others. Being owner of a large property near Windsor, he came back to Halifax in about 1833, and died at Windsor. He was the father of Colonel Edward S. K. Butler of 35th regiment, who afterwards settled and died at Windsor.

Mr. Jonathan Tremain's new flour mill at Dartmouth, of the windmill on Halifax Common. A model of the red light house at Shelburne, and the tract of new road from Pictou, was delineated in the most ingenious and surprising manner, as was also the representation of our fisheries.

To all these inimitable ornaments, corresponding mottoes were attached, so that not only taste and elegance were conspicuous, but encouragement and genius were displayed. Such was the description of this affair as it appeared in the newspapers of the day.

Cochran's buildings were again on fire, 30th January, 1793, but the fire was extinguished without much damage.

War with France was announced by letters from the Secretary of State to the Governor, dated 9th February, 1793. Orders were also received to raise a provincial regiment. This regiment was to be called the Nova Scotia Fensibles; they were to be raised in Halifax, but were not to have half pay, and the Commissions were to be given to half pay officers. Young Haligonians were thus excluded. It was about the same time decided on embodying a part of the Militia force for the defence of the town. 1050 effective men were accordingly marched into the town from the country, who were to receive pay from the British Government while on duty. The Governor published his thanks to the militia on 2nd November, for the alacrity with which they obeyed his orders in marching to Halifax. By the month of May the number of men enlisted for the Nova Scotia regiment, amounted to 100, the enlistments were afterwards increased to 600 men.

Apprehensions appear to have been entertained of an attack on the town by the French fleet. Every precaution appears to have been taken by Governor Wentworth for the protection of the Capital. In his letter to the Secretary of State of 23rd July, the Governor says, "In twenty minutes I could put under the command " of General Ogilvie, 900 militia men, and in a few hours a second " battalion of 600, who reside in the neighbourhood of the town."

The Halifax Militia Artillery, commanded by Capt. J. Tremain was a most effective body of men. It had been this year formed and consisted of sixty freeholders of the town. The Town Regiment of Infantry was commanded by Col. John George Pyke. 550 men of the Town Militia assisted the Garrison in repairing and mounting the batteries on Citadel Hill and elsewhere. On the 2nd April, two French Prizes were brought into the harbour by H. M. Ship Alligator, with cargoes valued at £40,000.

Among the events of the War was an expedition fitted out at Halifax to attack the Island of St. Pierre, in Newfoundland. It consisted of the Alligator and Hussar, men-of-war, with a body of troops under General Ogilvie. Before leaving, the two ships of war received permissions from the Governor and Council to press through the town and complete their crews. The place surrendered without fighting, and the Governor, M. Danseville, with several hundred prisoners and stores were brought to Halifax. They landed on the 20th of June. Governor Danseville was placed on parole, and resided at Dartmouth for many years in the house known as Brook House, now or lately the residence of the Hon. Michael Tobin, junr., about a couple of miles or more from Dartmouth town. The old gentleman displayed some taste in beautifying the grounds at Brook House. He built a fish pond and laid out walks among the beech and white birch groves near the house. The pond still remains, but the walks and most of the trees have long since disappeared. He remained a prisoner with an allowance from Government until the peace of 1814, when he returned to his own country a zealous royalist. Mr. Mizanseau was his aide-de-camp; he married a farmer's daughter in the South East Passage, and left a family who bear his name in that neighbourhood.

Governor Wentworth proposed to place the French prisoners who had been brought to Halifax from time to time, on an Island in the North West Arm, afterwards known as Melville Island, but the General preferred the Cornwallis *Barracks. The Island was not the property of the Government at this time, but hired by Governor Wentworth for this purpose of a prison. It afterwards became Admiralty property.

A poll tax existed at this time. It had been imposed by Act of the Legislature in 1791. One shilling per head was imposed on all males above 21 years of age. The law also contained a tax on cattle, with an extra tax on certain trades and occupations. It was ostensibly for the purpose of reducing the provincial debt. It does not appear, however, to have been regularly collected in the town.

NOTE.—* Uncertain as to where the Cornwallis Barracks were situated.

1794. On the 10th May, His Royal Highness Prince Edward arrived at Halifax in the Blanche Frigate, twelve days from St. Kitts. He landed immediately under a salute of 21 guns.

A levee took place on the 14th and an address was presented to him couched in the most fulsome and ridiculous language. On the 24th there was a garrison review under the command of General Ogilvie.

On the 22nd January, the following year, he set out by land for Quebec. He was at Boston on 5th February, where he remained 10 days and then embarked for the West Indies. It appears, however, that he was in Halifax on 25th February.

1794. This year a number of merchants of the town agreed to underwrite policies of insurance on vessels and goods, and appointed Benjamin Salter the broker, who, on the 10th May, advertised attendance every day during "change" hours at the "Coffee Rooms."

The town was again harassed by press gangs from Admiral Murray's ship. The Admiral had persuaded the Governor and Council to allow him twenty-four hours power over the inhabitants to man his fleet—though Capt. Home had been previously refused the privilege in January.

In December the Marine Society, which had been established by the merchants of Halifax several years previously, was re-modeled and extended in its operations. About this time a project had been formed by Governor Wentworth for uniting the waters of Halifax Harbor with the Bay of Fundy by a canal from the River Shubenacadie, and rendering the river navigable. Suggestions on the subject had been made to Governor Wentworth by persons whom he supposed competent to judge of the feasibility of the project, and was very sanguine of success in the work if not interrupted by hostilities. It does not appear, however, that any attempt was made this year towards effecting the object, but three years after (1797) the sum of £250 was voted for a survey of the projected canal.

All public lands in the town were this year granted to trustees. A grant of part of the King's Stores for a fishmarket was made, also the Province Building ground and the Grand Parade. The old English burial ground opposite the present Government House on Pleasant Street had been originally set apart, in 1749, as a genera burial place for the inhabitants of the town. It consisted of two acres and a quarter, but the title had not passed out of the Crown. It was this year granted to the Church Wardens and Vestry of St. Paul's Parish. They have been considered to hold it in trust for the original purpose for which it was dedicated. The old poor house burial ground was also included in this grant.

The French prisoners brought from St. Pierre and Miquelon, who had been lodged in the town with others who had been taken in prizes, were sent, in the month of July, to the Island of Guernsey.

We find Captain George of the Hussar receiving permission from the Council to fill up the complement of his men by impressment. In July following a similar application from Capt. Knowles of the ship Daedalus was refused. Admiral Murray, it appears, obtained another license in September to press through the town for seven days.

Commodore George informed the Governor that intelligence of the state of the defences of the town had been, or was likely to be, communicated by the French prisoners, through persons from the United States, to the French ambassador at Washington, and suggested an embargo on all vessels going to the United States for the present until he should receive intelligence from Admiral Murray. The Collector of the Customs at Halifax was accordingly ordered not to clear any vessels to the United States until further orders.

The following gentlemen were added to the Magistracy of the town: Michael Head, M. D., George Sherlock, Francis Green, J. M. F. Bulkeley, J. B. Dight, John Phillips, M. D., Jonathan Tremaine. James Clarke was Sheriff. Among the advertisements which appeared in the newspaper this and the previous year was a notice that sedan chairs would stand for hire in Barrington Street, also at the Court House, for the convenience of the public. The principal merchants and ship owners in the town between 1787 and 1795 were Geo. Bell, Hardware and Glass Store in Granville Street, near the town guard, then kept in the old house behind Masons' Hall; Peter Smith, Wines & Groceries; James Veitch, Groceries and General Store, shop opposite the wood yard; David Hall & Co. Dry Goods Store in Hollis Street, opposite old Government House; Charles Handesayde, Boot & Shoe Maker in Granville Street; Alex.

and Robert Leslie, Dry Goods Store at the corner of Duke & Hollis Streets, near the Pontac; Lawrence Hartshorne, Hardware Store at corner of Granville Street, between the Market House and the Parade; Wm. Forsyth & Co., Importing Merchants; Linnard & Young, Tailors, in Marchington's Buildings, Upper Water Street; George DeBloise, General Dealer; John Butler Dight, Importing Merchant, and Winkworth Allen and the Messrs. Cochran. William Minns, Stationer, Benj. Salter, Importing Merchant, Chas. Geddis, Watch Maker & Jeweller, lower side the Parade; John Hill, Cutter, Hollis Street; Edmond Phelan, "Golden Ball" tavern, Hollis Street; Wm. Brindley, Wines, etc., Forman, Grassie & Co., Importing Merchants, store on the Long Wharf (late Copeland's); Hall, Bremner & Bottomley, Dry Goods, etc.

Between '95 and '99. James Romans, Boot & Shoe Maker, corner of Duke & Granville Streets; Wm Dickie, Dry Goods, Phebe Moody, Dry Goods, Matthew Richardson, General Store, Robert Chrisley, Dry Goods, John McMasters, Dry Goods, Edward King, Livery Stable, John Kidston, General Dealer.

In 1798 the firm of L. Hartshorne & Co. was changed to Hartshorne & Boggs.

Moody & Tidmarsh, Dry Goods, Thos. Wallace, Dry Goods, etc. opposite wood yard; J. Hemmiongton, Grocer, near the Navy Yard; Lyon & Butler, General Dealers, Saml. Leddiet, Soap Boiler from Liverpool, kept the London Porter House above the Grand Parade; Philip Garrell, Tailor, Fraser, Thom & Co., Importing Merchants, Marchington's Wharf; Robert Scaiff, successor to Wm. & Thos. Williams, Hardware, Jewellery, etc., Forsyth, Smith & Co., Importing Merchants, James Leaver, Lower Water Street, Dry Goods, David Seabury, Auctioneer, Joseph Davis, Dry Goods, Michael Head, Apothecary, Saml. Hart, Dry Goods, D. Marshall and D. Fraser, both Importing Merchants, Wm. Annand, Groceries, etc., Saml. Greenwood, Mast Maker, Ed. Bartlett, Dry Goods, Marchington's Wharf; Jacob Miller & Son and Philis, Boyd & Philis, Importing Merchants, Tremain & Boggs, opposite the fuel yard, Hardware, etc., Thomas Roby, Merchant, Granville Street, Brymer & Belcher, John Grant, Wm. Forsyth & Co., Jonathan Tremain, Merchants, James Moody, Grocery & General Store keeper, Hollis Street, Michael Wallace, Wines, Groceries, etc. C. C. Hall & Co.

appear to have been the leading dry goods shop keepers; their store was in Marchington's buildings near the Ordnance. Charles Hill, Auctioneer, James Forbes, Wine, Groceries, etc., Water Street, near Fairbanks' Wharf. Andrew Gallagher kept the British Tavern opposite Marchington's Wharf. Sabatier, Stewart & Co., General Merchants; their firm was dissolved in 1790. William Millett, Auctioneer, King & Stoc, Shop-keeper, No. 6 Marchington's buildings, near the British Tavern; Thomas Russel, shop-keeper, store near the Coffee House; Alex. Morrison, Bookseller, Thos. Donaldson, Confectioner, Etter & Tidmarsh, corner of the Parade, British Merchandise, D. Curry & Co., Dry Goods, James Frame, Cabinet Maker, Jonathan & John Tremain, Hardware, etc., David Rudolph, near the Golden Ball, Dry Goods & Groceries, Richd. Woodroffe, Furrier, near the South Barracks.

1795. At the request of Prince Edward, the men of the Militia were employed on the fortifications in the neighborhood of the town during the summer. At this time the French prisoners in the town became very riotous; they were ordered to be removed to a place of confinement and none to be permitted at large. Several French prizes were brought in during the summer by Capts. Cochran and Beresford, of the Hussar and the Thetis, Sloops-of-War. An armed Snow named the Earl of Moira was kept by the Provincial Government for the protection of the coast. The most stirring event of the year was the arrival of the Hussar and Thetis after a long cruise bringing with them two French ships-of-war which they had captured; part of the enemy's squadron bound from the West Indies to Virginia.

Several Halifax ship masters lost their vessels and were made prisoners by French privateers in 1795. The names of Capts. Jacobs, Lloyd, Ewing and John Pryor appear among them. They suffered much hard usage at Guadaloupe where they were detained. A project for building a bridge across the Narrows was contemplated about this time. A petition was presented to the House of Assembly dated 11th March, 1796, from a number of persons praying for an Act to authorize the building of a bridge across the Narrows.

Between January, 1795, and January, 1796, the Halifax markets appear to have been well supplied. The newspapers of the day mention that 786 head of fat cattle, 80 cows and calves, besides sheep and swine had been brought into the town,

1796. St. George's day was celebrated with much festivity by the English Society. They had a dinner in the evening at which Governor Wentworth and Prince Edward were present. Among the decorations were sixty variegated lamps. Genl. Ogilvie and Chief Justice Strange were among the guests. The Prince arrived and departed under a royal salute and, during the dinner, sat under a canopy of white satin and gold lace.

During the spring of 1796 Halifax suffered from a scarcity of provisions. The inhabitants were indebted to Messrs. Hartshorne and Tremain, whose mills at Dartmouth enabled them, through the summer, to obtain flour at a reduced price and to afford a sufficient supply for the fishery.

The 4th June, old King George's birthday, was celebrated this year with the usual ceremonies. There was a levee and a review of the troops, and Sir John Wentworth entertained the Prince and a number of the principal inhabitants at a Ball, when the old Government House was brilliantly illuminated. There was a dinner the same afternoon among the merchants at the British Tavern, Marchington's buildings.

St. Patrick's day, this year, was also celebrated by a levee at the Government House and a dinner at Gallagher's hotel. The society sat down to dinner at five o'clock. His Royal Highness Prince Edward, Governor Sir John Wentworth, several members of Council, the Speaker and a number of members of the House of Assembly attended. The Prince and the Governor retired early, but the society kept up their festivities to a late hour.

On July 21st, vessels arrived in the harbor with five hundred Maroon negroes from Jamaica. The Maroons were the descendants of a number of African slaves, who, when Jamaica was conquered from the Spaniards, took refuge in the Island. They continued in a state of insubordination, but occasionally made treaties with the English. At this time they were in open hostility, but had been conquered, and it was arranged that a number of them should be sent as settlers to Canada. They put into Halifax on their way. They were under the superintendence of Colonel Quarrell of Jamaica, who had letters from the Governor of Jamaica to Sir John Wentworth. Prince Edward was commander of the garrison at the time, and on inspecting the people was so much pleased with the athletic proportions of the young mulatto men that he proposed to detain them to work on the fortifications of the town, which were then in progress under his direction. The French squadron under Admiral Richery was then off the coast, and it was expected that he would visit Halifax. The fortifications at the mouth of the harbor having fallen into decay were under repair, but not sufficiently forward to afford protection in case of an attack. The proposal was accepted by the Maroons; some were accordingly accommodated with sheds, and others placed in barns and such places of shelter as could be found in the town for their temporary accommodation. A number were sent to work on Citadel Hill, and one of the bastions there was called the Maroon Battery. The assent of the Secretary of State having been obtained for their settlement in Nova Scotia, land was assigned them in the Township of Preston. Col. Quarrell did not like the treatment they received. Many of the Maroons were permitted to come to town and seek work among the inhabitants. It was about this time that Sir John Wentworth proposed, as has been before mentioned, to open communication between Halifax and the River Shubenacadie which was to be performed by Maroon labor. This was the first proposal to be met with in reference to the Shubenacadie Canal which, in after years, caused so much loss and suffering by its failure. Differences arose between Col. Quarrell and the Governor, the Maroons refused to work, and discontent increased. Sir John and Prince Edward had a project of forming them into a corps of militia, and bestowed militia commissions on several of the young men among the Maroons, and two of their leading men, Montagu and Johnson, were appointed Colonels. Jarret, Bailey, Mayers and others were made Majors and Captains, which gratified their vanity.

The winter of 1796-7 was very severe, the want of provisions was felt, and the scarcity of flour threatened a famine in the town. The expenses of supplying these people had hitherto been borne by the Jamaica Government. Land had been purchased at Preston and the large building known as Maroon Hall, afterwards the property of Lieut. Katzmann, was erected as a residence for the superintendent. Some difficulties arose with the Jamaica Legislature. Quarrell left Halifax in the spring of 1797, leaving the Maroons discontented and refractory. It was finally arranged that they should be sent to Sierra Leone. Eight years previously a number of negroes had been sent there from Halifax. The Maroons were to be united with them in the hope that the union would be a check on the turbulent conduct of the Nova Scotia colony, which at that time had been the source of some trouble to the Sierra Leone Company. They were accordingly embarked in the autumn of 1800, and arrived on the coast of Africa in October.

Sir John Wentworth had received intelligence in September which led him to apprehend some attempt on Halifax by the French forces now in Newfoundland. At the close of the year the harbor defences were brought into good condition, and capable of affording a tolerable defence in case of invasion. Two press warrants were issued this year by the Council; one on 31st January to Admiral Murray for twenty-four hours in the town, and another in October to Admiral Vandiput for two months through the province.

On the night of the 21st March a fire broke out in the range of houses opposite St. Paul's Church, in Barrington Street, which consumed the property of Dr. Greaves. The trees around the Church escaped uninjured.

The sudden death of James Michael Freke Bulkeley, the Secretary of the province, on the 12th November, threw a gloom over the community. He was a young man of pleasing address and highly esteemed. He had been for some time member for the county, which he held in conjunction with that of Provincial Secretary. He had succeeded his father, Richard Bulkeley, in the office but a short time before his death.

In November, the fleet, under Vice Admiral Vandiput, sailed from Halifax on a cruise. It consisted of the Resolution, 74, bearing the Admiral's flag, Capt. Ledmore; Assistance, 50 guns, Capt. Mowatt; Andromeda, 32 guns, Capt. Taylor; Ceres, 32, Capt. Otway; Lynx, 18, Capt. Hall, and the Hunter, 18, Capt. Tucker.

1797. During this summer the town was enlivened by the presence of four or five hundred embodied militia who did garrison duty. Several battalions were enrolled in the country with the intention of their being removed to Halifax for the protection of the town in the absence of the regular troops. They were, however, not required, and were discharged in the latter part of October by order of the Governor.

At this time Dr. Robert Stauser was rector of St. Paul's, Dr. Archibald Gray, minister of St. Matthew's, at the corner, Mr. Michael Bernard Houseal, missionary to the Germans and minister of St. George's, north suburbs. Chief Justice Strange resigned this year and was succeeded in the office by Mr. Sampson Salter Blowers, who remained Chief Justice until 1835, when he was succeeded by Sir Brenton Halliburton. Chief Justice Blowers died in 1842, at the age of 100 years. His monument is in the south-east corner of the east aisle of St. Paul's. He built the house at the corner of Barrington and Blowers Streets, lately occupied by Mr. Romans as a hotel, and known as the Waverley House, where he resided for about thirty-five years.

Mr. Shaw was Sheriff of Halifax this year; he was succeeded by Lewis M. Wilkins, afterwards a Judge of the Supreme Court, and father of the late Judge Wilkins of that Court.

Prince Edward, who was Commandant of the garrison, appears to have patronized almost all the public entertainments in the town. He dined with the national societies, and honored the balls given by Governor Wentworth with his presence. His manners were affable, and he was, in consequence, quite popular with all classes in the town. He was very much affected by the sudden death of Lieutenant Charles Thomas of his own regiment, the 7th Fusiliers, who was accidentally shot by a brother officer while on a hunting expedition in August of this year. Lieut. Thomas was the son of Nathaniel Ray Thomas, a magistrate and collector of the customs of Windsor, and a cousin of Governor Wentworth. He was a favourite and protegé of Prince Edward, who attended his funeral and erected a monument at his own expense over his grave.

On the 23rd November, this year, H. M. Ship La Tribune, Capt. Baker, was lost in coming into the harbor. The following authentic account of this disaster is from the newspaper of the day:

"La Tribune was one of the finest frigates in His Majesty's service, mounted 44 guns and had been lately captured by Captain Williams in the Unicorn frigate. She was commanded by Captain S. Barker, and sailed from Torbay the 22nd September, as convoy to the Quebec and Newfoundland fleets. In Lat. 49° 14' Long. 17° 29' she fell in with and spoke His Majesty's ship Experiment from this place, out 12 days. She lost sight of all her convoy October 19th, in Lat. 46° 16' Long. 32° 11'. On Thursday morning last, they discovered this Harbour about 8 o'clock. The wind being E. S. E they approached it very fast, when Captain Barker proposed to the master that they should lay the ship to till they could obtain a pilot; the master replied, 'he had beat a 44 gun ship into the harbour—that he had been frequently here and that there was no occasion for a pilot, as the wind was fair.' Confiding in these assurances Captain Barker went below and was for a time employed in arranging some papers he wished to take on shore with him. The master in the meantime taking upon himself the pilotage of the ship, and placing great dependence upon the judgment of a negro man by the name of John Casey, (who had formerly belonged here) whom he had placed forward to con the ship. About 12 o'clock the ship had approached so near the Thrum Cap Shoals, that the master became alarmed and sent for Mr Galvin the master's mate, who was sick below. On his coming on deck he heard the man in the chains sing out 'by the mark five,' the black man forward at the same time singing out 'steady.' Galvin got on one of the carronades to observe the situation of the ship, the master in much agitation at the same time taking the wheel from the man who was steering with an intent to wear ship, but before this could be effected or Galvin able to give an opinion, she struck. Captain Barker instantly came on deck and reproached the master with having lost the ship. Seeing Galvin also on deck, he addressed him and said (as he knew he had formerly sailed out of this harbour) that he was much surprised that he could stand by and see the master run the ship on shore. Galvin informed the Captain he had not been on deck long enough to give an opinion. Signals of distress were instantly made and answered by the military posts and the ships in the harbour. Boats from all the military posts, from His Majesty's ships and from the Dockyard, proceeded to the relief of La Tribune. The military boats and one of the boats from the Dockyard, with Mr. Rackum, boatswain of the Ordinary, reached the ship; but the other boats, though making the greatest exertions, were not able, the wind being so much against them, to get on board. The ship was immediately lightened by throwing all her guns, except one retained for signals, overboard, and every other heavy article, so that at about half-past eight o'clock in the evening the ship began to heave and about nine she got off from the shoals. She had before at about five or six o'clock lost her rudder, and on examination it was now found that she had seven feet of water in the hold. The chain pumps were immediately manned and such exertions made that they seemed to gain on the leaks, and by advice of Mr. Rackum the Captain ordered to let go the best bower anchor. This was done but it did not bring her up. The Captain then ordered them to cut the cable, and the jib and fore topmast stay sail were hoisted to steer by. All this time the violent gale, which had come on from the south east, kep: increasing and carrying them to the western shore. In a short time the small bower anchor was let go, at which time they found themselves in about thirteen fathoms water. The mizzen mast was then cut away. It was now about ten o'clock, the water gaining fast on the ship, little hope remained of saving the ship or their lives. At this critical period Lieut Campbell quitted the ship. Lieut. Nooth was taken into the boat out of one of the ports. Lieut. James of the Royal Nova Scotia Regiment, not being to be found was so unfortunate as to remain, and to the great distress of his worthy parents and friends shared the general fate. From the period when Lieut. Campbell quitted the ship all hopes of safety had vanished, the ship was sinking fast, the storm was increasing with redoubled violence, the rocky shore to which they were approaching resounding with the tremendous noise of the billows which rolled toward it, presented nothing to those who might survive the sinking of the ship, but the expectation of a more painful death from being dashed against those tremendous precipices, which even in the calmest day it is almost impossible to ascend.

Dunlap, one of the survivors, informs us that at about half-past ten, as nearly as he could conjecture, one of the men who had been below came to him on the forecastle and told him the ship was sinking; in a few minutes after, the ship took a lurch as a boat will do when nearly filled with water and going down; immediately on which Dunlap began to ascend the fore shroud, and at the same moment casting his eyes towards the quarter deck saw Capt Barker standing by the gangway and looking into the water, and directly after heard him call for the jolly-boat. At the same time he saw the Lieutenant of Marines running towards the taffrail, he supposed to look for the jolly-boat, as she had previously been let down with four men in her—but instantly the ship took a second lurch and sank to the bottom; after which neither the captain nor any other of the officers was seen. The scene, sufficiently distressing before, became now peculiarly awful—more than 240 men, besides several women and children were floating on the waves making their last efforts to preserve their existence. Dunlap, whom we have before mentioned, gained the fore top. Mr. Galvin, the master's mate, after incredible difficulty, got into the main top—he was below when the ship sank, directing the men at the chain pump. He was washed up the hatchway, thrown into the waist and from thence into the water, and his feet as he plunged, struck a rock. On ascending, he swam to gain the main shrouds when he was suddenly seized hold of by three men—he was now afraid he was lost. To disengage himself from them he made a dive into the water which induced them to quit their hold. On rising again he swam to the shrouds and arrived at the main top and seated himself on an arm-chest which was lashed to the mast.

From the observations of Mr. Galvin from the main-top and Mr. Dunlap in the fore-top, it appears that near one hundred persons were for a considerable time hanging to the shrouds, the tops and other parts of the wreck; but from the extreme length of the night and the ferocity of the storm nature became exhausted, and they kept at all periods of the night dropping off and disappearing. The cries and groans of the unhappy sufferers, from the bruises many of them had received and as their hopes of deliverance began to fail them, were continued through the night; though as morning appeared from the few that then survived they became feeble indeed. The whole number saved from the wreck amounted to eight persons and several of them so exhausted as to be indifferent whether they were taken off or not. Mr. Galvin mentions that about twelve o'clock the mainmast gave way; at that time he supposes there were on the main-top and on the shrouds upwards of forty persons. By the fall of the mast the whole were again plunged into the water, and of that number only nine besides himself regained the top. The top rested upon the main yard, and the whole remained fast to the ship by some of the rigging. Of the ten persons who regained the main-top four only were alive when morning appeared. Ten were at that time alive on the fore-top, but three of them had got so exhausted and had become so unable to help themselves that before any relief came they were finally washed away; three others perished, and four only were also finally left alive in the fore-top. The place where the ship went down was only about three times her length to the southward of the entrance into Herring Cove. The people came down in the night to the point opposite to which the ship sunk and kept large fires, and were so near as to converse with the people on the wreck.

The first exertion that was made for their relief was by a boy, thirteen years old, from Herring Cove, who ventured off in a small skiff by himself about eleven o'clock the next day; and this truly deserving young lad with great exertions and at extreme risk to himself, ventured to approach the wreck and backed in his little boat so near to the fore-top as to take off two of the men, for the boat could not with safety hold any more; and here a trait of generous magnanimity occurred which deserves to be noticed. Dunlap and Munroe had, throughout this disastrous night providentially preserved their strength and spirits beyond their unfortunate companions, and had endeavoured to cheer and encourage them as they found their spirits sinking; they were now both of them able to have stepped into the boat and put an end to their own sufferings, but their other two companions, though alive, were unable to help themselves. They lay exhausted on the top, wished not to be disturbed, and seemed desirous to perish as they lay. These generous fellows hesitated not a moment to remain themselves on the wreck and to save, though against their will, their unfortunate companions. They lifted them up and by the greatest exertions got them into the little skiff, and the manly boy rowed them triumphantly to the Cove and instantly had them conveyed to a comfortable habitation. After shinning, by his example, older persons who had larger boats, he put off again in his little skiff, but with all his efforts he could not then approach the wreck. His example, however, was soon followed by the men in the Tribune's jolly-boat and by some of the boats of the Cove, and by their joint exertions the eight men were preserved, who, with four that escaped in the jolly-boat make the whole number of survivors of this fine ship's company.

Some have been disposed to blame Capt Barker as exhibiting too much obstinacy in not abandoning the ship and preserving his crew, as a violent storm was evidently approaching, but on examining the men who have survived we find (though other officers in the same situation might have formed a different judgment) that the conduct of Capt. Barker was throughout the trying scene completely cool and collected. Though from the manner in which the ship had been run ashore, no blame could attach to him, yet he could not reconcile it to himself to lose so fine a ship without making every exertion to save her. Having by the greatest efforts considerably lightened her, he had reason to suppose she might get off before high water. She made no water while she lay aground, there was therefore great hopes, if she could not that night have been got up the harbour that she might with safety have been brought to anchor and have rode out the gale. When she finally got off, universal joy was diffused throughout the ship—every man thought the object of their joint efforts was attained—but the rapid manner in which the water poured into her, soon damped their joy and plunged them into despair. Had the ship been finally saved by the great exertions which were made to effect it, every man would have praised Capt. Barker, and, notwithstanding those exertions failed, we think we may justly say, in the language of Mr. Addison,

"'Tis not in mortals to command success
Barker did more; he did deserve it."

To his memory therefore and that of his brave fellow-sufferers, the commiseration of their countrymen is justly due. From every generous heart they will receive that commiseration; and while the mind runs over the whole trying scene the tears which must involuntarily flow will embalm their memory.

Having closed the general scene, we think it will not be unacceptable to our readers if we notice the conduct of some individuals. A quartermaster belonging to the ship, by the name of McGregor, had his wife on board; they were a respectable couple and greatly attached to each other. McGregor from his affectionate solicitations for her safety, endeavored to persuade her, while the ship lay on the shoals, to go ashore in one of the boats which came off from the Island, as his mind would be more at ease, could he put her in a place of safety. To his solicitations she replied, 'that she never would abandon him; if it was his lot to perish, she wished not to survive him.' Finding it in vain to urge her further, he desisted from the attempt and she afterwards shared the common fate. A considerable time after the ship had foundered a man was discovered swimming towards the wreck. On his pproaching near it was found to be McGregor; he informed his comrades who were hanging by the wreck, that he had swam towards the shore; that he had ventured as far as he could with safety into the surf, and found if he went further he should be dashed to pieces, and he cautioned them all to avoid making a like attempt, but if possible to hold by the wreck. He himself gained the main shrouds and remained there till the mast gave way, and then met the same fate as his unfortunate consort, whose death he was continually deploring while on the shrouds.

Dunlap relates another instance which occurred, which though it may appear ludicrous after the distressing scenes we have noticed, is so descriptive of that cool thoughtlessness of danger which so often distinguishes our British tars that it would be inexcusable to omit it. Daniel Munroe, one of the survivors had as well as Dunlap got into the fore-top. After a while he disappeared and it was concluded that he had been washed away with many others; after an absence from the top of about two hours, he suddenly popped his head up through the lubber hole to the surprise of Dunlap, who enquired where he had been; he said he had been cruising about for a better berth; and it appeared that, after swimming about the wreck for a considerable time, he had returned to the fore shrouds, and crawled in on the cat-harpins and had actually been to sleep there more than an hour, and he said he was and really appeared to be greatly refreshed.

Mr. Brennan of the Dockyard, who had gone aboard with Mr. Rackum, after the sinking of the ship, had got on the maintop and remained there till the mainmast gave way and was never after seen.

While noticing the immediate disasters of the ship, we forebore to mention the fate of one of the boats which had gone from George's Island. About nine o'clock as the ship went off, the boat got under the ship's bow and was upset; by this circumstance a part of the men, consisting of two sergeants and four privates of the Royal Nova Scotia Regiment were unfortunately drowned; the remainder were taken up by the boat belonging to the Eastern Battery. Too much praise cannot be given to the men who manned these boats, and particularly to Sergt. Bourke, and the boat's crew who persevered in following the ship, and finally brought off Lieuts. Campbell and Nooth of the Royal Fusiliers.

Great praise is also due to the dock-yard boat which carried Mr. Racknm on board. They followed the ship at a short distance till she foundered, and with extreme difficulty at length reached Herring Cove. We are sorry to mention that Mr. Rackum, whose exertions on board La Tribune to preserve the ship were gratefully acknowledged; perished with the unhappy ship's company.

Having mentioned all the disastrous circumstances which have attended this distressing scene, it is with pleasure we now notice the attention which has been paid to the widows and children of the unfortunate sufferers. His Royal Highness Prince Edward with that uniform generosity which has distinguished his Royal Highness during his residence in this province, directed immediate provision to be made for the bereaved families, and there is reason to hope through his Royal Highness' representations, that provision will be made as permanent as their sufferings. Actions like these dignify even kings and add splendour to the highest rank.

Besides the attention shown by his Royal Highness a liberal subscription has been made by the garrison and gentlemen of the town for the widows of the soldiers who were drowned and for the men who manned the boats.

There is another instance of generosity, which the occasion seems to require, and it seems to be the earnest wish of the men who were saved from the wreck; it is that some reward may be bestowed on the boy who first came off to them. They attribute in a great measure their deliverance to him, and they mention with the warmest gratitude, not only his exertions to save them from the wreck, but his kind and hospitable attention to relieve them after they had reached the Cove. Surely if a subscription were set on foot, there is not a man in the country who would not give something to reward and encourage so young an instance of humane and heroic magnanimity.

Mr. Club, the master of La Tribune, was master of the Active, frigate, when she was run ashore on the Island of Anticosti.

Mr. Fennel, first lieutenant, and Mr. Galvin, the master's mate, were both formerly prisoners at Guadeloupe with Colonel Wetherall, and were all for a considerable time chained by the legs together. Lieut. Fennell declared to Lieut Campbell that his only motive in coming out in La Tribune was to have the pleasure of seeing Colonel Wetherall; and such appears to have been the attachment of Galvin to Lieut. Fennel that, though he speaks with becoming feeling of the fate of the ship's company, the loss of Lieut. Fennell seems peculiarly to affect him. On enquiring of him if he saw Lieut. Fennel after the ship sunk, he replied, he did not, for if he had, though he was himself in a place of apparent security, he would again have risked his life to preserve him, and would have effected it or perished with him. A similiar attachment to each other appears among the men who have survived the wreck, and these circumstances unite to prove that the virtues which render human being the most pleasing are those they are taught in the trying school of adversity.

List of the officers lost in La Tribune:—Captain, Scory Barker; First Lieutenant, Thomas Fennel; Second do., Thomas Clarke; Third do., Thomas Sheirp; Master, James Clubb; Lieutenant Marines, James Cregg; Surgeon, ——Jones; Purser, ——Stanford; Carpenter, James Jurd; Boatswain, John Franklin; Master's Mate, William Stacey; Midshipmen, John Dennington, Charles Belcher, John Clowdsley, William Crofton, ——Nops; Captain's Clerk, William Foley; Surgeon's Mate, James Mulquinney; Gunner, William Thomas.

List of officers and men saved from La Tribune:—John Galvin, Master's Mate; Seamen, Abraham Wauhill, James Crawford, Robert Parker, Daniel Monroe, E. Knowles, Richard Bust, James Green, Henry Husley, Chris. Dowling, Robert Dunlap and John White.

We have been favored with the following extract of General Orders, dated Halifax, November 20, 1797:

Lieutenant General, His Royal Highness Prince Edward thinks it his duty to return his particular thanks to Lieutenants Halibur on, Campbell and Noath of the Royal Fusiliers, also to the several non-commissioned officers and privates of the Royal Nova Scotia Regiment, who manned the boats sent to give assistance on Thursday last to His Majesty's frigate Tribune, unfortunately wrecked by getting on shore at the mouth of this harbour.

His Royal Highness most sincerely laments the loss of Lieut. James and two non-commissioned officers with four privates of the Royal N. S. Regiment, who were unfortunately drowned in executing the first of all duties, that of giving succor to brother officers and men in distress.

His Royal Highness directs that the Commissary-General will serve free rations to the widows of the non-commissioned officers and privates lost, as follows:—

To the wife of Sergt. Baker, and two children, two rations.
To Sergt. Mullen's wife, one ration.
To the wife of John Bush and two children, two rations.

Tuesday last the body of Lieut. James was found and brought up to town to his disconsolate parents—and Wednesday was interred with military honors."

Michael Wallace was appointed Treasurer of the Province in October of this year on the resignation of Benning Wentworth. Mr. Wallace remained treasurer until 1827 or 1828, when he was succeeded by his son. Mr. Wallace administered the government as senior councillor several times during the absence of the Governor, Sir James Kempt.

The old playhouse lot in Argyle Street was granted, about this time, to James Putnam, from whom it came into possession of the trustees of the Acadian School. The grant from the Crown of part of the King's Stores for a fishmarket, before referred to, was, on 29th August, signed by the Governor and the Prince as commander in chief of the troops. This is what was called the new fishmarket. The old market had formerly been private property, and the rents of stalls at this time were received by Mr. Cochran, but it was subject to town regulations. Commissioners were about the same time appointed to purchase land and to erect buildings for the accommodation of the Legislature and Courts of Justice as soon as peace should occur and the price of labor should be lower. The Act formerly passed for erecting buildings for this purpose on the "lower parade" was repealed, and that of 1797 was amended in 1799 and the Commissioners were directed to purchase land in the south suburbs, and build a Government House.

The winter of 1797–8 was again very severe. The heavy falls of snow rendered the road from Halifax to Windsor impassable. The Prince ordered the troops to clear the road between the town and his residence on the Basin. The supply of fat cattle from the country for the troops was retarded for a long time by the state of the roads.

It was proposed to raise a fund in the town to be at the disposal of Government for the purposes of war. The inhabitants subscribed a sum approaching £4000 towards this fund; the officers of the Royal Nova Scotia Fencible Regiment, £200. The boys of the Grammar School contributed about £24, and the regiment in garrison and the officers in the public departments, including the contributions of the Nova Scotia Regiment, amounted to £2097. Much enthusiasm on the subject prevailed, and great loyalty was displayed by the people.

A general fast was proclaimed on 21st May, which was kept at Halifax with much solemnity.

A commission was issued in July to William Forsyth, Andrew Belcher, William Cochran, Lawrence Hartshorne, Charles Hill, Richard Kidston, John Bremner, William Sabatier and Michael Wallace, as directors for the Shubenacadie Canal. A survey and report was made by this committee which was printed and published.

There were several regular traders at this time between Halifax and Boston. The principal and most regular one was the Schooner Nancy, Captain Tufton.

In the month of January, 1798, a boat arrived in the harbor with Capt. Wyatt and several passengers of the Brig Princess Amelia, bound to Halifax, which had been wrecked on the south side of Sable Island on 9th November. The wreck had been reported by an American schooner, who saw signals of distress on the Island. Sir John Wentworth immediately sent a vessel to the Island with clothing and provisions for the relief of the sufferers. Capt. Wyatt equipped his long boat and, having got over to the north side of the Island, embarked with four of his crew and Lieut. Cochran of the Fusiliers, one of the passengers, intending to seek relief. He arrived safe in one of the harbors to the eastward of Halifax, where he obtained a pilot who brought him to Halifax. Capt. Parker, who had charge of the vessel sent to the Island, brought off the remainder of the crew and passengers in safety.

1798. On the 8th August, this year, Prince Edward received an injury by a fall from his horse while riding on one of the streets in the town. The horse broke through a defective wooden bridge over one of the street gutters. The horse rolled over him hurting one of his legs; it did not, however, prevent him from attending to his military duties. He was recommended by the physicians to go to England for further advice. An address subscribed by about four hundred of the inhabitants was presented to him on his departure, which took place on the 21st October, when he embarked in H. M. Ship Topaz, Captain Church. The House of Assembly had previously voted five hundred guineas to purchase a star of the order of the Garter to be presented to His Royal Highness.

Among the events of the year was the arrival in the harbor, in November, of the United States Squadron, consisting of the Sloop-of-War Herald, Capt. Stevens, and the Pickering, Capt. Chapman, with the Brig Commerce, Capt. Childs. Salutes were exchanged, and the captains landed and paid their respects to the Governor, Admiral and General, and were hospitably entertained. The United States was at this time at war with France.

On the 25th November news of Nelson's victory at the Nile arrived in Halifax. The town was illuminated in the evening. Salutes were fired and other demonstrations of joy occurred throughout the day. A number of prizes were brought into the port during this autumn.

Mr. James Stewart, afterwards Solicitor-General, was this year elected without opposition for the county.

On the 25th September a tremendous hurricane visited Halifax and continued through part of the night. Nearly all the wharves in the town were swept away, and most of the shipping in the harbor damaged. The tide rose to an unprecedented height, overflowed Water Street and did much damage to property. The water came up to the old market house where the city brick building now stands. The market wharf and King's wharf were partially destroyed, and the market slip or public landing swept away. The loss of property in the town, including the shipping, was estimated at above £100,000.

Among the names of persons engaged in business in the town this year we find, James Kidston, Wholesale and Retail Dealer, Matthew Richardson, at the foot of Prince Street, James Moody and James Tidmarsh just entered into co-partnership; Forman & Grassie, Fraser, Thom & Co., Shipping Merchants, Lyon & Butler, Shopkeepers, near the market house; Thomas Moody, Dry Goods, etc., corner of Marchington's wharf; James Leaver, opposite the

Dartmouth Mill Flour Store, in Water Street; John McMasters, Benjamin Etter, Watchmaker and Hardware Store at the corner of George and Barrington Streets, lower side of Grand Parade (Crosskill's corner); Phoebe Moody, Dry Goods, opposite the Parade, in Barrington Street. In the following year the names of Jonathan and John Tremain, Samuel Hart, Tremain & Boggs and William Annand appear.

The members of Assembly for the county were: Michael Wallace, Jonathan Sterns, Lawrence Hartshorne and Charles Morris. Mr. Sterns was replaced by James Stewart.* William Cochran and J. G. Pyke were still members for the town. Mr. Benning Wentworth was Provincial Secretary. The Hon. Richard Bulkeley, the senior councillor, was Grand Master of the Masons.

The papers of the day are filled with long advertisements about the Government Lottery.

1799. The chief event which occupied the attention of the good people of Halifax during the autumn of this year was the arrival and movements of His Royal Highness Prince Edward, who had now been created Duke of Kent. Having received the appointment of commander-in-chief of the troops in British North America on 6th September, he arrived in H. M. Ship Arethusa, Capt. Wooley, forty-three days from England. The Prince landed in state. A procession of boats was formed from the frigate to the King's Wharf under a royal salute from the ships, and on reaching the wharf, by a salute from the Citadel. A double line of soldiers, including the militia, lined the street from the King's Wharf to Government House, through which the procession passed. The Governor and Council, Admiral Vandiput, General Ogilvie, the officers of the staff and public departments and a number of the principal citizens, attended. On his arrival at Government House the bells of St. Paul's and the old Mather Meeting House rang out a merry peal, and a large number of the inhabitants crowded around to bid him welcome again to Halifax. In the evening, bonfires were lit on the Grand Parade in honor of his arrival. The Duke soon after removed to

---

*NOTE.— Mr. Stewart was the son of Anthony Stewart, before mentioned, a Loyalist gentleman from Maryland. He was Solicitor General and afterwards a Judge of the Supreme Court. He married a sister of the late Chief Justice, Sir B. Halliburton. Judge Stewart's residence was the yellow brick house at the corner of Pleasant Street and Morris Street, afterwards the residence of Mr. Alexander Stewart, Master of the Rolls, but not related to Judge James Stewart. The late Reverend James Stewart, of Dartmouth, was his grandson.

his villa on the Basin, six miles from town. This beautiful little retreat had been erected by Prince Edward on the land of the Governor, Sir John Wentworth. The grounds were laid out and improved at considerable expense under his direction. The Rotunda, or music room, on the opposite side of the road, next the water, surrounded by the rich foliage of the beech groves, and surmounted by a large gilded ball, flashing in the sunlight, presented a beautiful and picturesque appearance on the approach to the Lodge. The villa was built altogether of wood, consisting of a centre of two stories containing the hall and staircase, with a flat roof. There were two wings containing the Duke's apartments. In the rear was a narrow wooden building with pointed gothic windows, resembling a chapel, containing the kitchen and offices, which extended some distance southward beyond the main building. The grouping of the beech and birch trees in the lawn and around the house was well arranged. They were the original forest trees, selected and permitted to stand in clearing away the space for the buildings. The rooms were not spacious, and the ceilings low, which appears to have been the fashion of building in Halifax at the time. The woods around were very beautiful. They were traversed by walks, and in several places by a carriage road with vistas and resting places where little wooden seats and several imitation Chinese temples were erected. Several of these small summer houses were in existence in 1828, and probably later, and portions of them could be seen through the openings in the trees on passing the main road. The Duke erected a range of low buildings on the edge of the Basin, a little to the north of the Rotunda, which were occupied by two companies of his regiment, and contained the guard room and a mess room for the officers. This building was afterwards known as the Rockingham Inn, a favourite resort in summer, when tea and ginger beer were to be had under the piazza which ran along the edge of the water. This hotel acquired the name of the " Rockingham," having been for a long time after the Prince's departure the place of meeting of the Rockingham Club. This club was established either while the Duke was resident here, or very soon after his leaving for Canada. It was composed of Governor Wentworth, the members of His Majesty's Council, the Admiral of the station, several of the principal military officers, and a number of the leading citizens of Halifax. Dr. Stanser, rector of St. Paul's, was one of its members; also the Hon. Andrew Belcher, both of whom had villas on the Basin, the former at Sherwood, afterwards the property of the late Mr. Thos. Kenny, and the latter at Birch Cove, now in the occupation of the family of the late Peter Donaldson.

The Rockingham Club was partly literary and partly social. The members dined together at the hotel, which was styled the Rockingham House, in compliment to Sir John Wentworth, the head of whose family, the Marquis of Rockingham, was about that time in, or at the head of the British Ministry. The large room which extended along the south wing of the building, east and west, with the end to the water, was hung with the portraits of many of the members of the club painted by Field, a portrait painter of considerable talent who, at that time and for several years after, resided in Halifax, and from whose brush the portraits of many of the then principal citizens and their ladies still remain.*

In 1799 the prices of provisions in Halifax markets were as follows: Beef, by the quarter, from 4d. to 5d. per pound; pork, 6d., mutton, 7d. to 8d., veal, 8d. to 9d., fowls, from 3s. to 4s., oats, 2s. 6d. and 3s., butter, 1s. 3d. and 1s. 6d.

In 1798 the number of illegitimate children in the Halifax Poor House was fourteen, in 1799, seventeen, and in 1800, fifteen. The total cost of the establishment during the three years was £570 16s. 1d. Fines received at Halifax, 1798, £60; 1799 and 1800, £82 10s. Fresh Water Bridge was renewed and completed in 1798.

In 1799 the Legislature made some amendments to the Act for the erection of public buildings. The Commissioners appointed by the Governor and Council were authorized to purchase land for the site of a new Government House. The old House to

---

*Among Field's portraits remaining in Halifax, are those of the Hon. Michael Wallace, Hon Wm. Lawson, Hon. Andrew Belcher and Mrs. Belcher, Bishop Charles Inglis, Rev. Dr. Archibald Gray and Mrs Gray, the late Andrew Wright, of the firm of Belcher & Wright, and his sister Mary, the late Dr. W. J. Almon, and others. That of Sir John Wentworth, a full half length, the best performance of Field in this country, was removed from the Rockingham to Government House by Sir John after the club had been dissolved, and became Government property. It was afterwards removed to the Province Building, whence it was taken some years ago, and is said to have fallen into private hands, having been either lent or given away by order of one of the gentlemen who, some years ago, occupied the office of Provincial Secretary. It is to be hoped that ere long it will find its way back to its place in the Building.

That of Commissioner Inglefield, also a member of the club, hung for many years over the mantle piece of the committee room of the Legislative Council Chamber, but was afterwards presented to the late Admiral Inglefield, father of Sir Edward Inglefield, lately Admiral on this station.

be appropriated to the House of Assembly and Courts of Law. The Commissioners were Messrs. Wallace, Cochran, Hartshorne, and John Beckwith. The House of Assembly voted £10,500 for the building, etc. The old Government House having been found unfit for the accommodation of the Legislature, was sold and the block of buildings known as Cochran's, before mentioned, was leased this year for £300 per annum for the accommodation of the Law Courts, the Legislature, and the public offices connected with the Provincial Government. Commissioners were also appointed to build a new market house for the butchers and for a vegetable market. This was the wooden building which was removed during the administration of Governor LeMarchant, to make way for the present brick structure. A clerk of the market was appointed. There being then no convenient accommodation for the vegetable market, the country people were permitted to sell in the streets and the square in front of the market house.

This has once more become the custom; the portion of the new market appropriated to the country people having been lately taken for city offices. The want of sufficient space in the central parts of the town for the convenience of markets and the erection of public buildings, has been always an impediment to the improvement and embellishment of the city. The small dimensions of the lots as originally laid out, being only forty feet by sixty, and the short space between the streets, the narrow spaces allowed for the public landings, and the small size of the water grants for the erection of wharves in the old town, have been a continual drawback to the convenience of trade and the progress of improvement in front of the town. And it is a subject of regret that at the present day so little attention is paid by the public authorities to the future welfare of the city in respect to laying off building lots and streets by private owners and speculators.

The regular packet between Halifax and Boston, the Schooner Nancy, usually occupied three days in her trips. She was commanded by Capt. J. Huxford. He was afterwards known in Halifax as Crazy Huxford. He was on board the Shannon, frigate, in the engagement with the American ship Chesapeake, and had been wounded in the head, from which he never fully recovered. He was one of the best pilots on the coast and was, until his death, a naval branch pilot attached to the Dockyard. When under the influence of liquor he became frantic and was continually shouting through the streets of the town without hat or coat. This poor old man died about twenty-five or thirty years ago at a very advanced age.

In May the small pox made its appearance in the town and strict quarantine regulations were enforced. Dr. Gschwint (pronounced Swint) was appointed health officer.

The elections took place this autumn. Messrs. William Cochran and John George Pyke were again returned. The former polled 104 votes and the latter 346. At this time the electors were confined to freeholders only. The franchise was not altered till about the year 1836. Mr. Cotnam Tonge, Edward Mortimer, Messrs. Fulton and Morris were elected for the county. Only two resident in the town succeeded, Tonge and Morris; Wallace, Stewart and Hartshorne were rejected by the Pictou votes.

On Saturday, the 11th August, attempts were made by persons unknown to set fire to the Dockyard, Government house and the engine house. The Governor and Council offered a large reward for discovery. A night patrol of militia and inhabitants was ordered out under the superintendence of the magistrates.

The Rev. Bernard Michael Houseal, minister of St. George's, in the north suburbs, died on the 9th March, this year, in the seventy-second year of his age. He was a native of the Duchy of Wurtemberg, was educated at one of the German universities, and was esteemed a good scholar and a pious minister of religion. He had been chosen by the learned consistory of Stuttgart for the ministry of the Lutheran Church, and embarked for America in 1752. After being several years in the ministry he took charge of a congregation of Germans in New York, and came with the Loyalists to Halifax in 1783. He was buried in the old German burial ground attached to his church in Brunswick Street, and his tombstone remains there. Mr. Houseal was succeeded in the Church of St. George by the Rev. George Wright, who was also principal of the Halifax Grammar School and chaplain to the garrison. The Round Church, in Brunswick Street, was at this time only in process of erection and was not finished until the year 1811, or thereabouts.

On the 30th October, H. M. Ship Porcupine, Capt. Evans, arrived from New Providence, having on board the Duke of Orleans and his two brothers, the Duke of Montpensier and Count Beaujoile, attended by Count Montjoye. They had been waiting for a passage to England and had proceeded here in the Porcupine in hope of meeting with an opportunity of going to Europe. Finding no immediate opportunity to England, they both took their passage in a merchant ship for New York. Though considered as prisoners on parole, they dined with the Governor, and paid a visit to the Duke of Kent at the Lodge. They also attended a public ball at Government House on the 17th November. The Duke of Orleans was afterwards elected to the French throne as Louis Philippe, King of the French, and eventually died in exile in England. After he became king, on meeting with several persons from Nova Scotia, he very kindly enquired after several gentlemen of Halifax by name and spoke with much feeling of the kindness he experienced while in Halifax. On arrival he was found to be in very straitened circumstances and the Duke of Kent was believed to have given him pecuniary assistance to enable the party to proceed on their voyage.

CHAPTER VI.

1800. At the commencement of the century Halifax presented a prosperous condition. The population now approached 9,000. Trade was brisk, and the place was enlivened by a large garrison and the presence of a Prince of the Blood Royal. The harbor was the resort of the fleet and was the principal station of the naval commander. The war was at its height and the Prize Court in full operation. Several privateers had been fitted out by the merchants of the town and captures of French vessels were frequent, though the trade of the port occasionally suffered from the French cruisers on the coast. Among the captures from the enemy at the time, the most remarkable was that of two prizes, one French and one Danish, brought in by Captain William Pryor, commander of the Privateer Nymph, of Halifax.

Several public buildings were commenced this spring. On the 5th June the Prince laid the corner stone of the Masonic Hall. His Royal Highness was Grand Master of the Masons of Lower Canada, and acted for the Hon. Richard Bulkeley, Grand Master of Nova Scotia, when age and infirmities prevented him from attending. A masonic procession was formed and the ceremony is said to have been one of the finest which Halifax ever witnessed. The band of the Prince's own regiment, the 7th Fusiliers, performed under the direction of Mr Selby, organist of St. Paul's, one of the craft.

On the 10th April, Sir John Wentworth laid the corner stone of the Round Church (St. George's) in Brunswick Street. The Legislature this session voted £500 towards its completion. The land on which the church was erected had been purchased some time previously by the Committee of Superintendence. The design is said to have been the work of the late John Merrick and Mr. J. Fliegar of the Surveyor General's department, and for some years surveyor to Governor Wentworth while Surveyor General of Woods and Forests in Nova Scotia. St. George's old church, then known as the Dutch Church, was at this time occupied by the congregation of the north suburbs, many of whom were the descendants of the first German settlers. Though always an independent congregation, it had been considered part of the parish of St. Paul's, the whole Township of Halifax having been originally included in that parish, and it continued so until legally erected into a separate parish by the name of St. George's parish, under the Act of the Legislature passed for that purpose in 1827. The Rev. George Wright was at this time minister of St. George's congregation. He had lately succeeded Mr. Houseal, who was styled Missionary to the Germans.

A sum of money, as we have seen, had been voted by the Legislature for the erection of a Government House. Much discussion had arisen in the House of Assembly and with the Executive authorities, regarding the funds to be appropriated for this purpose, and some difference of opinion existed regarding the site for the building. It was finally arranged that it should be placed in the field between Hollis and Pleasant Streets, to include the site of the old hospital. The corner stone of this edifice was laid by the Duke of Kent on the 11th of September. A procession was formed which proceeded from the old Government House, accompanied by a band of music, and the ceremony was concluded by a prayer by the Rev. Doctor Robert Stanser, Rector of St. Paul's. Isaac Hildrith was the architect, and John Henderson chief mason. No building since erected in Halifax exceeds Government House in neatness of design and solidity of workmanship. Some of the old brick buildings now remaining in the city were erected by Mr. Henderson.

The old market house was taken down this year and the new one commenced. This old market occupied the site of the recent City Court House. The new one was erected in the open space opposite the King's wharf, where the new brick market house now stands. It was a flat-roofed wooden building intended to accommodate the butchers only. A pitched roof was afterwards put on this building. There was a small green market built at the same time next the north line of the fuel yard, which was afterwards removed. These buildings were erected at the expense of Government, the sum of £2,252 having been granted by the House of Assembly to be appropriated to the erection of this new meat market, also to the repair and extension of the market slip or public landing, and for the fish-market, and, at the same time, £250 was voted to the heirs of the late Joseph Gerrish who claimed some interest in a portion of the old market house lot. A small piece of ground at the corner of the military fuel yard, next to the new market house, was about the same time purchased from Mr. Kidston who then occupied it for weigh scales and other purposes. The Grand Jury refused to accept the grant from the Crown of the old market house lot in the way it had been drawn by the Secretary of the province. The Council declined to make the alterations in the grant required, and concluded that the old building and the lot should remain under the control of the Commissioners of Public Markets, and ordered the old buildings to be taken down and the ground leased.

In March the House of Assembly was in session. The elections of Mr. Tonge for the County and Mr. Pyke for the Town were declared void by the House in consequence of some defect in their qualifications. On the 9th April following, the new election for the town took place, and on the 14th, Andrew Belcher was returned by a majority of 65 votes. Mr. Michael Wallace was returned for the County. Mr. Tonge, having been also chosen by a country constituency, fell back on the double return and retained his seat. On the 12th March, the House attended at St. Paul's church in a body, when the Rev. Dr. Stanser, then chaplain, preached before them.

This summer His Royal Highness the Duke of Kent took his final departure from Halifax. The usual addresses were presented by the House of Assembly, His Majesty's Council and the people of the Town. He embarked in H. M. Ship Assistance on the 3rd August, and sailed on the 4th. His embarkation was attended with full military ceremony, the troops lining the streets. His Royal Highness, accompanied by the Governor and Council and the principal Naval and Military Officers, proceeded on foot through the avenue formed by the troops to the King's Wharf, whence he reached the ship under salutes from the batteries, the artillery corps and the ships of war. Several of the old inhabitants not many years since recollected the scene, and could describe the feelings evinced by the townspeople on the occasion. His tall commanding figure in full military uniform, his hat surmounted by the lofty white plume, then worn by the fusiliers, could be seen above the heads of the surrounding crowd as he walked down the line with a smile of recognition for his friends, on passing them, amidst the plaudits of the crowd.* Though the Duke exhibited on all occasions the most kind temper in civil life, and his manner and conversation with those he liked almost amounted to familiarity, yet his sternness in military affairs never forsook him. Eleven soldiers had been sentenced to death for mutiny and desertion, and had been left by the Duke for execution, which was carried into effect under his orders a few days after he left our shores. On the 7th August, those unfortunates were brought out on the Common, dressed in white, with their coffins, accompanied by the Revd. George Wright, the Garrison Chaplain, and Doctor Burke, the Roman Catholic clergyman, in the presence of the whole garrison. Eight of them were reprieved under the gallows, and the three who belonged to the Newfoundland Regiment were hanged. Public feeling was against the Duke in this affair. It was thought that on the eve of his departure he should have granted a remission of the death sentence, which, as General Commanding, he had power to do, until the King's pleasure should be known. Three executions only a day or two after his departure, produced a disagreeable impression of His Royal Highness in the minds of the people of Halifax, who had just taken leave of him with so much kind feeling.

The Quarter Sessions having authorized the establishment of a military exercising ground on the north end of the Common, an act for which they had no authority, laid the groundwork of much dispute and controversy with subsequent military commanders, who on several occasions later undertook to interfere with the City authorities in beautifying and improving the Common.

The death of the Hon. Richard Bulkeley, late Secretary of the Province, occurred this year; he was inh is 83rd year. Mr. Bulkeley came to Halifax as Aide-de-Camp to Governor Cornwallis in 1749, and had twice administered the Government as Senior Councillor. Also that of Anthony Henry, the King's printer. He published the Royal Gazette at Halifax for about 40 years. John Howe was his successor in the office of King's printer.

---

*NOTE.—After the Prince's departure Governor Wentworth occupied the Lodge on the Basin, which had been built on his land. He resided there for some time after retiring from the Government.

1801. Early this year it was proposed to establish a bank in Halifax by means of a joint stock company whose capital was to be £50,000 in shares of £100 each. A committee of management was named consisting of Edward B. Brenton, William Forsyth, Foster Hutchinson, Lawrence Hartshorne, James Forman, James Fraser and Captain John Beckwith. They required a monopoly, which was refused them by the House of Assembly, and the project fell through.

The winter of 1800-1801 had been very sickly. Smallpox had made its appearance in town early in the autumn, and 182 persons had died of it between September, 1800, and the month of February following.

Several fires occurred during the winter. Sir John Wentworth's stables at the lodge were burned down. The most disastrous fire which had occurred in the town for many years took place on the 5th February, when the block fronting the old Government House on Hollis Street was partially destroyed.

On the 13th February this year, the society known as the Sun Fire Company was established at Halifax. It was, perhaps, the first Fire Company ever instituted in the town. Those known as the Phœnix Fire Company, the Hand and Hand and the Heart and Hand were of a subsequent date. The Sun Fire Company in the year 1810, included most of the principal inhabitants of the town. Their names will be found in the Appendix.

1802. A considerable outlay of money appears to have been made on the streets of the town about this time. The commissioners appointed for this purpose were Charles Morris, J. G. Pyke, Lawrence Hartshorne, Michael Wallace and William Lyons. The expenditure this year on the streets amounted to £930, and in the two succeeding years to £696 and £808. The sum of £500 had been granted in 1801 towards the expense of paving some of the streets; the remainder probably was raised by assessment.

The names of the town magistrates in 1802, were John Newton, Custos, Jonathan Binney, Geo. W. Sherlock, J. G. Pyke, Dr. Michael Head, W. Taylor, Stephen H. Binney, Jas. Gantier, Wm. Cochran, Charles Morris, Junior, Daniel Wood, William Thompson, Michael Wallace, Charles Hill, Richard Kidston, P. Marchington, Jonathan Tremain, James Clarke, William Schwartz, Hibbert N. Binney and John Bremner. These are the Magistrates for the

County of Halifax. They all appear to have been residents in the town. Lewis M. Wilkins was Sheriff; John Newton and H. N. Binney were joint Collectors of the Customs; Daniel Wood, Inspector; John Cleveland, Collector of light duties; and John H. Fliegar, Gauger. The Firewards of the town were Mr. Pyke, Mr. Wallace, Mr. Hill, Mr. Cleveland, Mr. Clarke, William Millet, Elias Marshall, Thomas Fillis, Andrew Liddell, John Fillis, Wm. Lyons, Thomas Boggs, John Howe and Garret Miller.

The Royal Nova Scotia Regiment on being disbanded this year, presented an address to Sir John Wentworth, their Colonel, in August. The names of the officers of this Regiment were Lt. Cols. Francis Kearney and Samuel V. Bayard,* Major Geo. Thesiger, Capts. John Solomon, Jones Fawson, Alexander Howe,‡ John Allen, William Cox and Joshua W. Weeks, Capt. Lieutenant John G. Degreben; Lieutenants Thomas Morris, Otto W. Schwartz, Philip Kearney, Eric Sutherland, George H. Monk, Michael Pernette, Charles Rudolf, John C. Ritchie, John Emerson, Timothy Ruggles, Richard Green, Isaac Glennie, Hebbert Newton, Thomas A. C. Winslow, Alexander Hamilton, Charles W. Solomon and John Fraser; Ensigns James Moore, Robert Bayard, Henry Green, Thomas Wright, Richard Gibbons; Paymaster Beuning Wentworth, Surgeon John Fraser.

Governor Wentworth directed his reply to this address from " the Lodge."

The population of Halifax had again decreased towards the end of the year 1802. The returns of the number of inhabitants in the town and on the peninsula were as follows:—

	Men.	Women.	Boys.	Girls.	Total.
Whites	1924	2489	1790	1669	7872
Blacks	96	166	81	108	451
In Naval Yard	25	36	27	27	115
Dutch Village	15	16	30	33	94
Total					8532

---

*Col. Bayard retired from active service and settled in Annapolis County. He was the father of the late Dr. Bayard of St. John, and grandfather of the present Doctor William Bayard of that city.

‡Capt. Howe was a descendant of the Hon. Ed. Howe, one of Cornwallis' first councillors.

There were 1000 dwelling houses in the town and peninsula. In taking the census, the wards of the town were distinguished as follows: North Barracks Ward, Pontac Ward, Market House Ward, Governor's Ward, Meeting House Ward, South Barracks Ward, South Suburbs and North Suburbs.

The sum of £8,900 had been expended by the Commissioners on the building of Government House, and but the first story had been completed. Much dissatisfaction was expressed in the House of Assembly with the course pursued by the Commissioners. Belcher, Hutchinson, Cochran and Beckwith had kept no minutes of their proceedings. Wallace appears to have had the principal supervision. He was censured by the House for having acted without the concurrence of those associated with him, and for exceeding the limits prescribed him by law. But his zeal and ability were commended and no corrupt motives were attributed to him. In 1804 an additional sum of £2,500 was voted to complete the building, a considerable sum having been voted and expended the previous year.*

Several fires occurred in June which were supposed to be the work of incendiaries. It had been proved beyond all doubt that buildings in several parts of the town had been set on fire. A patrol of militia under Colonel Pyke was ordered to patrol the streets from sunset to sunrise, and all suspected persons who could not give a good account of themselves at night were ordered to be arrested. A reward of £100 was offered for discovery, and several arrests were made. A boy who confessed to having attempted to set fire to the Dockyard was sent out of the province.

On the 2nd September the 97th regiment arrived in the harbor and landed immediately at the King's Wharf. On the 14th the fleet arrived from Jamaica under the command of Commodore Baynton, consisting of the Cumberland, 74, Bellerophon, 74, Ganges, 74, Vanguard, 74, Goliah, 74, Thesis, 74, Elephant, 74 and the Pelican, Brig. The 7th regiment embarked shortly after, and the town people presented a farewell address to Col. Layard and Lieut.-Col. Edwards. In April the Governor and Council were prevailed on to grant a press warrant to Capt. Bradley of the Cambrian for

---

* The building cost about £15,000.

ten days in the town to enable him to fill up the number of his crew, it being 50 short of its complement.

The Rev. Dr. Burke was at this time Roman Catholic Vicar General of Nova Scotia under the Bishop of Quebec; he afterwards administered the Episcopal office in Halifax as Bishop of Zion. Dr. Burke was a gentleman of education and highly esteemed in the community.

The death of a very aged inhabitant, John Murphy, occurred this year. He was 90 years of age, and had been one of the first settlers of the town. He had acquired a large property in fields in the south suburbs, where he kept a large number of cows, and for a great many years supplied the principal inhabitants with milk and butter. The fields extending northward from Smith's tan yard to the corner house formerly occupied by the late Sheriff Sawyer, were known formerly as Murphy's fields.

1803. The following is an account of the butchers' meat sold in the Halifax market for six months commencing July 1st and ending December 31st, 1802.

	Sheep.	Calves.	Oxen.	Pigs.
July	785	264	157	—
Aug	964	147	186	—
Sept	1409	91	273	21
Oct	1017	85	224	76
Nov	928	78	465	407
Dec	883	—	614	692
Total	5986	665	1919	1196

The above is exclusive of the meat issued under contract for the Navy, but it is to be assumed it included the Army contract.

1804. This spring the House of Assembly recommended that the old market house should be taken down and a new building erected on the ground for the purpose of a County Court House and police office. This was the brick building lately used for city purposes. An Act was passed in 1804 with that object.

The trade of the port was much depressed this season by the number of captures made by the enemy, and from the low prices obtained for fish in the West India market, where the merchants of Halifax were undersold by U. S. fishermen.

Among the events of the year was the arrival of several distinguished prisoners, among whom was General Brunet and suite, who put into Halifax on their way to England, having been made prisoners at St. Domingo. Governor Wentworth assigned them the old Rockingham Inn, near the Prince's Lodge on the Basin, as a place of abode while here. They were shortly after removed to England.

In the autumn General Boyer, commandant of the garrison, undertook to try the metal of the Haligonians by causing a false alarm of invasion. The report was spread early in the morning that the French were off the harbor. Before 10 o'clock, A.M., about 1,000 militia men were embodied and at their respective posts. Two hundred of them were artillery men. The dress companies were all in uniform and fully equipped. Among the first who appeared on the parade ground with their guns were Parson Wright, head master of the grammar school, and the Solicitor General, James Stewart, better known as Judge Stewart.

1805. Press warrants were granted by the Council on the 6th May to Vice Admiral Sir Andrew Mitchell, then in command of the station, for fourteen days. He afterwards demanded an extension of his warrant for six months, which was refused by the Council at their meeting on the 18th. In their reply to the Admiral they mention that the number of seamen engaged in the West India trade, etc., had been so reduced by captures, imprisonment and other causes that there were not sufficient in the port to man the vessels, and that all the seamen to be found in the town would not now be enough to meet half the demand for one sloop-of-war in the fleet. Moreover, that there were many at the time in French prisons whose families were supported by charity in the town. This, together with the high rate of wages in the United States, had reduced the commerce of the port to the greatest necessity. Finally, that the execution of impress warrants on shore were attended with much disturbance and annoyance to the laboring poor and others not fit for service, and the Council were of opinion that it should only be resorted to on the most urgent occasions and when advantage from it was to be reasonably looked for.

Mitchell, finding he could not prevail on the Council, undertook, in the following October, to send press gangs through the town without warrant. An armed party of sailors and marines from the Cleopatra, frigate, under the command of one or more officers, were sent out. The citizens resisted and a riot ensued, which resulted in the death of one person and the wounding of several others. One of these encounters occurred in the store of Messrs. Forsyth & Co., where a number of merchant sailors had secreted themselves. General Wentworth called a meeting of the Council on 23rd November, and it was ordered that the Solicitor-General should proceed to prosecute all persons belonging to the ships of war who had been engaged in impressments. The Attorney General, R. J. Uniacke, Mitchell's father-in-law, was in England at the time, on leave of absence. The Admiral's gang had broken open the store of Forsyth & Co. under the pretense of looking for deserters, and Sir Andrew defended his conduct under the authority of a warrant from the Admiralty, but he was condemned in heavy damages for his illegal proceedings.

The town artillery at this time consisted of three companies commanded by Captains Charles Morris, Bremner and Fillis, and there was another under Capt. McIntosh of Spryfield, which did duty at York Redoubt, composed principally of market fisherman who were regularly trained to battery exercises. Governor Wentworth appears to have been assiduous in his efforts to keep up the local defences of the town, and to have placed much reliance on the volunteer companies for that purpose.

There was a plentiful harvest this year throughout the whole province. Provisions of all sorts were plentiful in the town, so much so that the arrival of the fleet and a large export to Bermuda and Newfoundland did not augment the prices. The importations of flour from the United States, both this and the following year, were very extensive.

In October an unfortunate French prisoner named Pierre Paulin was executed on the common for the murder of a fellow prisoner. The Governor and Council refused to reprieve him.

In December the town was illuminated and other joyful demonstrations made by the inhabitants on the news of the Battle of Trafalgar.

1806. In the month of February, Lieut.-General Gardner, the commandant of the garrison, died at Halifax; his funeral was attended with much military pomp and ceremony. He was buried under old St. Paul's Church.

A general election occurred in 1806, when Edward Mortimer of Pictou, Simon B. Robie, S. G. W. Archibald and William Lawson were returned for the county, and John George Pyke and Foster Hutchinson for the town. Cochran, the old member, petitioned against Lawson on the ground of qualification.

The Government House remained still unfinished. The sum of £4,292 had been expended on the building since the last session, which was £2,000 more than had been voted.

On the 29th April Halifax was thrown into alarm by the appearance of a number of large vessels in the offing. Signal guns were fired from the alarm posts in the harbor, and the military and militia were under arms. There was another alarm of French invasion on or about the 20th May, when several large vessels were again reported off the harbor. The militia of the town were again assembled, but the greater part of them were without arms. Governor Wentworth had previously made several applications to the Imperial Government for arms for the Halifax Militia, but it does not appear that much attention was paid to his solicitations.

Among the advertisements which appeared in the the Gazette this year was notice of a periodical publication to be called the " Nova Scotia and New Brunswick Magazine or Historical Library," which was offered for sale at the book stores of Messrs. Morrison, Bennet, Edmund Ward and William Minns. Morrison kept his book and stationer's shop at the corner of Duke and Granville Streets, afterwards known as Joseph Robinson's hat store, now owned by Mr. Kiezer. He was succeeded in his business by George Eaton, who was the principal book seller and stationer in the town for several years. This old building, with others along the upper side of Granville Street was destroyed by fire about 1827. At this time there was a law in existence to prevent persons building wooden houses in the town above a certain height. The present wooden building at the corner was then erected under this law and did not exceed what by measurement was deemed one story and a half. Several stone and brick buildings were erected in consequence of this law. That to the south of Kiezer's corner occupied by Mr. Simonds and others, another in the same block built by the late William Macara, druggist, and the large double three story stone building in Barrington Street, nearly opposite St. Paul's, were all erected about this time by Mr. Matthew Richardson on the site of the late Andrew Belcher's garden. Several old gamble roofed houses, the remnant of the first settlement, were destroyed by the above-mentioned fire.

On 22nd December, the American Government laid an embargo on all vessels within American ports bound to any foreign places, and the officers of the Customs throughout the States were directed to refuse clearances to all such vessels. This was a great check to trade, and Halifax felt the result in the scarcity of provisions and particularly of flour, which went up immediately to £5 per bbl., the inhabitants having been in a great measure dependent on the States for that article.

A sailor named John Wilson had been taken from the American Frigate Chesapeake on charges of mutiny and desertion. He was tried in Halifax by Court Martial on board the Flag Ship Belleisle on 26th August, condemned and executed on 31st. Two other seamen were in October following executed on board the Jason, Capt. Cochran, for mutiny.

The following list of town officers appointed by the Grand Jury for the Town in 1806, will be found interesting:

Halifax, Nova Scotia, } COURT OF QUARTER SESSIONS.
March Term.

The Grand Jury present to the Worshipful Court the following as proper persons to serve as Town Officers for the ensuing year, in the different offices to which they are named, viz:

William Lyon, County Treasurer; Henry Yeomans, Town Clerk; Samuel Muirhead, Stephen Oxley, Clerks of the Market; Richard Woodin, Michael Denny, William Hogg, Enoch Wiswell, Surveyors of Lumber and Fence Viewers; Joseph Hamilton, James Romans, Sealers of Leather; Nicholas Vass, Thomas Adams, Patrick Ryan, William Ford, John Knowdlie, Frederick Stormy, Surveyors of Pickled Fish; Thomas Adams, William Ford, Cullers of Dry Fish; Nicholas Vass, William Ford, Frederick Stormy, Gaugers of Oil; John H. Fleigher, Gauger; Henry Shiers, Richard Woodin, William Graham, Measurers of Wood; Francis Le'Guire, Measurer of Wood and Coals for the Fuel Yard; Richard Woodin. Henry Shiers.

William Graham, Measurers of Grain; Richard Woodin, Henry Shiers, William Graham, William Hogg, Measurers of Salt and Coal; John Brown, William Ford, Cullers of Hoops and Staves; James King, Edward King, Weighers of Hay; John Metchler, Surveyor of Bricks and Lime; W. G. Forsyth, Lawrence Hartshorne, John Sullivan, John William Morris, Hogreaves; John Phelan, Pound Keeper; Thomas Stone, John Atkins, John Mansfield, David Fletcher, William Shea, George Isles, Peter Laffen, Edward Herbert, John Clarke, Richard Munday, Henry Wright, Hugh Chisholm, Andrew Bowers, Francis Wade, Alexander Cummings, Patrick Tobin, Constables; Jacob Michael, Constable for Dutch Town; Peter Shaffro, Constable for Dutch Village; John Mc'Alpin, Overseer of Highways for Dutch Village and Pen.; Jacob Bower, George M'Intosh, Overseers for Harriot and Spryfields; William Adams, Constable for Harriot and Spryfields; Peter Vambolt, John Duffeney, Constables for Margaret's Bay; Christopher Boutteleer, Overseer of Highways for Margaret's Bay; Frederick Boutteleer, Measurer of Cordwood for Margaret's Bay; George Duffeney, Fence Viewer for Margaret's Bay; George Mc'Intosh, Overseer of Highways from Spryfield to Catch Harbour; William Keys, Overseer of Highways from Windsor Road to Gay's River; Robert Fletcher, Terence Canty, Constables for the Shubenacadie Fisheries; Edmund Bambrick, Jonathan Shelling, George Hiltz, Overseers of Roads from Sackville Bridge to the extremity of the County; Jacob Haverstock, Overseer of Roads from Nine Mile River to Hammond's Plain; George Dunn, George Hilts, Surveyors of Lumber for Nine Mile River to Hammond's Plain and Windsor Road; Colin Grant, Christopher Shultz, Robert Anderson, Fence Viewers; Christopher Haverstock, Joseph Fielding, Jacob Pentz, Constables for Windsor Road and Hammond Plains; Henry Bambrick, George Fultz, Hogreaves; John Shultz, George Hershman, Hugh Bambrick, Assessors of the County Rates; Henry Miller, Pound Keeper; Edward Foster, Surveyor of Highways from Dartmouth Town Plot to the Basin; Samuel Hamilton, Constable from Dartmouth Town Plot to the Basin; Jon. Tremain, Sr., William Penny, Surveyors of Highways, Dartmouth Town Plot; David Larnard, Constable, Dartmouth Town Plot; James Munn, Pound Keeper, Dartmouth Town Plot; Henry Wisdom, Surveyor of Highways from the Ferry up the Preston Road to Tanyard; Mark Jones, Constable; John Wisdom, Hogreave; Mark Jones, Pound Keeper; George Simpson, Surveyor of Highways and Fence Viewer from Tanyard to Simpson's; Hugh Ross, Constable; Thomas Settle, Surveyor of Highways and Fence Viewer from Simpson's eastward to the new bridge; Philip Molyneux, Constable; Timothy Crane, Surveyor of Highways for all Preston, and Fence Viewer; John Richardson, Constable; Thomas Settle, Surveyor of Lumber and Bark; George Horn, Hogreave; John Stewart, Surveyor of Highways from Cole Harbour to Turner's; Robert Collins, Surveyor of Highways from Turner's to Jones'; Robert Turner, Constable; Peter Mc'Nabb, Surveyor of Highways, Eastern Passage; Benjamin Horn, Constable; Adam Archibald, Musquodoboit, Surveyor of Roads; William Gould, Constable; George M'Leod, Robert Nelson, Fence Viewers; Hugh Archibald, Pound Keeper; Archibald Crawford, Overseer of Roads for Meagher's Grant; Alex. Grant, Constable for Meagher's Grant; Peter Ogilvie, Overseer of Roads from Meagher's Grant to George Anderson's; Peter Gordon, Constable for Meagher's Grant to George Anderson's; Jacob Bayer, Overseer of Roads from Musquodoboit Harbour; John Turple, Constable for Musquodoboit Harbour; George Bayer, Overseer of Roads for Pitpiswick; George Baker, Constable for Pitpiswick.

March 5, 1806.   WILLIAM LYON, *Foreman.*

On 11th May, 1807, it having been reported to His Majesty's Council that the Grand Jury and Sessions had refused to accept a grant of the piece of land on which the old Market House stood, upon the conditions which had been inserted in the grant, (probably on it being vested in Commissioners) the Governor and Council refused to alter the grant, and if not accepted by the Session it was ordered that the old building be taken down and the ground cleared and remain under the control of the Commissioners of Public Markets. This was the site on which the late City Court House was afterwards erected.

1808. In the month of April, 1808, the new Governor, Sir George Provost, arrived to take the place of Sir John Wentworth, who was allowed a retiring pension of £500 per annum. He brought with him the 7th, the 8th and the 23rd Regiments, consisting of about 3000 men, with Brigadier General Houghton. The Governor came in H. M. Ship Penelope. At six o'clock on the same evening of his arrival, he landed at the King's Wharf under a salute from the Batteries. Sir John Wentworth was at his villa on the Basin — the Prince's Lodge as it was called — when his successor arrived, and did not receive the official letter announcing his appointment until 18 days after the arrival of Sir George Provost. On the 13th April, Sir John came to town and the new Governor was sworn into office.

It was deemed advisable that some trusty person should be sent to the United States to obtain information as to warlike preparations then progressing in that country. Mr. John Howe, the postmaster at Halifax, was chosen. He proceeded to Boston and afterwards visited other parts of the Union. Mr. Howe was again dispatched on a second mission late in the fall, and on his return made a report to the Lieutenant Governor.

Mr. Samuel Hood George, afterwards Sir Samuel, came out with Sir George Provost. He was appointed Provincial Secretary, and afterwards represented the County of Halifax in General Assembly. He was the eldest son of Commodore Sir Denis George, who married Miss Cochran of Halifax, and succeeded his father in the Baronetcy. This young man died early of consumption, and was succeeded both in the Baronetcy and the office of Secretary by his youngest brother Sir Rupert D. George, who remained in office until responsible government was established in the province.

The ships Milan, Observateur and Conturian were stationed at Halifax during the winter. The Centurian was the ship in which Lord Anson circumnavigated the globe. She remained in the harbour as a receiving and store ship for many years, and was broken up at the Dockyard somewhere between the years 1820 and 1823.

Among the visitors to Halifax this year was the notorious Aaron Burr, late Vice-President of the United States. He passed under an assumed name.

1809. The winter of 1808–9 was remarkably severe. During the month of February the cold continued so long that the great expenditure of fuel was felt by all classes of the community. Much distress prevailed among the poor, and large sums of money were raised by subscription for their relief.

An expedition had been fitted out at Halifax, under the command of Sir George Provost, for the capture of the French Island of Martinique. It was composed of the 7th, 8th and 23rd Regiments with a Brigade of Artillery. Having succeeded in this enterprise they returned to Halifax on the 15th April. The gentlemen of the town gave a ball at Mason Hall in honor of their return. Three soldiers of the 7th Fusiliers were the only men killed in the expedition, the place having surrendered immediately on the attack being made. A tablet to the memory of these three soldiers may be seen in the gallery of the Round Church in Brunswick Street.

The Harbour was again this year the scene of another of those Naval executions, which were performed with so much severity during the time of war. A mutiny had occurred, or was supposed to have occurred, on board the Columbine on the 1st August, off St. Andrews. Four seamen and two marines were found guilty and executed on the 18th September. They were afterwards hung in chains on Meagher's Beach.

One of the most atrocious cases of piracy and murder on record occurred this autumn on the coast to the eastward of Halifax. The vessel was the Three Sisters, of Halifax, owned by Jonathan and John Tremain, merchants of the town, commanded by Captain John Stairs, brother of the late Honorable William Stairs, formerly president of the Union Bank. She was on her way from Gaspé Bay to Halifax with a cargo of fish. Edward Jordan, who had been formerly owner of this vessel or in some way concerned with her, took passage for himself and wife and four children with Capt. Stairs for Halifax. The following account is taken from a Halifax newspaper of 16th October, 1809:

"MONDAY, OCTOBER 16, 1809.—The following are the particulars received from Capt. Stairs, of the piracy and murder that took place on board the schooner Three Sisters, belonging to this place, some account of which we gave in our last.

"This most atrocious act of piracy and murder, of which none could be guilty but the most diabolical incendiaries in human shape, took place, as has been stated, on the 13th ult. off Cape Canso, on the coast of this province, on board the schooner Three Sisters, bound and belonging to this place from the Bay Chaleaur. Edward Jordan, who has been represented as a passenger, and who had some interest in the vessel, appears to have been the exciter of this act of barbarity. Jordan having corrupted the mate, Kelly, who joined him in effecting his wicked intention, they secured the arms, and availing themselves of that moment most likely to assist their horrid design, which was when Capt. Stairs was below with one of his men,* shot the other man who was on deck, and taking aim at Capt. Stairs through the sky-light with a pistol, wounded him in the face and shot the man who was near him in the breast. Capt. Stairs immediately ran on deck, where he met Jordan with a pistol in one hand and an ax in the other. Capt. Stairs then retreated into cabin and searched for his pistols but found them taken from his chest with a sword; finding himself destitute of arms he again ascended the deck and saw Jordan giving the fatal blow to the man who was on the deck, when he turned from him and presented another pistol at Capt. Stairs, which flashed when they closed and the pistol in the struggle was thrown overboard. The man who had received the wound below having reached the deck, made an effort to assist his captain, but in his attempt, from weakness, fell on his face, where he was shortly after dispatched with an ax by Jordan. In the scuffle Capt. Stairs called upon his mate (Kelly) for assistance, whom he perceived was in the act of loading another pistol, but who made him no answer. At which time Jordan's wife, a fit companion for so base a monster, attacked him with a boat hook which he parried with his arm, and after much exertion disengaged himself, and seizing one of the hatches, jumped into the sea. The wind blowing a strong breeze, the vessel soon left him to his precarious fate, where he remained about three hours, when he was taken up by the schooner Eliza Stoddard, of Hingham, in an almost lifeless condition from wet and cold."

The vessel was captured and brought into Halifax, and Jordan and his wife placed on their trial before a special commission for the trial of piracies on the high seas on 15th November. The Commission or Judges who sat on this occasion were Lieut.-Gen'l Sir Geo. Provost, Vice Admiral Sir John Borlase Warren, Chief Justice Blowers; Councillors, Butler, Wallace, Brenton, Hill, Uniacke and Morris; Capt. Lloyd, R. N., Capt. Lord James Townshend, R. N. and Capt. Simpson, R. N., Sir Samuel Hood George, Provincial Secretary, T. N. Jeffery, the Collector of Customs. Doctor Cooke, the Admiralty Judge, refused to attend because the Commissioners would not allow him precedence of the Governor with a veto on the proceedings of the Court. No jury was called under this commission. Jordan was found guilty and sentenced to be hanged, which sentence was carried into execution on the beach some distance below Fresh Water Bridge, and the body was afterwards gibbeted on the shore some distance further down. The wife was acquitted, and a subscription was raised in the town to send her to Ireland. Dr. Burke, the Roman Catholic clergyman, Dr. Archd. Gray, minister of St. Matthew's, and Dr. Stanser, Rector of St. Paul's, acted as a committee for the purpose.

---

* Thomas Heath, who left a wife and two children in this town.

The court assembled again a short time after, for the trial of the mate, Kelly, who was convicted, but afterwards pardoned.*

This being the 50th year of the reign of King George III, a jubilee was celebrated at Halifax on the 23rd October, with great ceremony.

The market slip, the new fish market and meat market were all repaired and improved this year at the cost of £571, £500 of which had been voted by the Assembly for the purpose. The taxes gathered in the town for liquor licenses in 1809 amounted to £1400.

The Fire Insurance Association of Halifax was established on 24th April, 1809. The first directors were Andrew Belcher, Charles Hill, Lawrence Hartshorne, Foster Hutchinson, James Fraser, George Grassie and H. H. Cogswell. Mr. J. H. Fliegar was secretary and the office was kept in his house in Hollis Street, where it continued to be kept for a great many years. He was succeeded by Mr. William Newton, at whose death Mr. Tremain was appointed.

Meetings of the Committee on Trade were held during the autumn. The Halifax Marine Insurance Company first opened their office for business in Water Street, opposite the fuel yard, this year. The committee of management were George Grassie, Jesse Woodward, Garret Miller, James Kerby, Lawrence Doyle, Lewis E. Piers, John Osborne, Thomas Deblois and John Albro'.

Among the merchants of Halifax at this time we find, in addition to the above, the names of Wm. Stairs, Wm. Bremner, Hartshorne & Boggs, at the old corner of George and Granville Streets, Kidston, Dobson & Co., Richard Kenefick, who had lately brought out Irish linen goods, Forman & Grassie, Shipping Merchants; William Bowie, afterwards a partner of Stephen W. Deblois, and who lost his life in a duel with the late Judge Richard Uniacke, Alexander Izat, Dry Goods, at corner opposite two pumps, corner of Hollis and Duke Streets, now occupied by the People's Bank; Martin Gay Black, Dry Goods; Geo. N. Russell, afterwards Wallace & Russell, Hardware Merchant, corner of Hollis and Prince Streets, now occupied by the Union Bank building; Temple and Lewis E. Piers, Ship Chandlery. This firm several years later

---

* A report of these trials was published in 1810 by Mr. Bagnall at the office of the newspaper called the "Novator," taken from the notes of two students at law, Charles R. Fairbanks, afterwards Master of the Rolls, and Andrew W. Cochran, who for many years was Secretary of the Province of Lower Canada and member of Council.

purchased the irregular shaped lot adjoining the City Court House lately occupied by Stairs, Son & Morrow, removed a range of one story buildings or sheds known as the Ratstail, and erected a building in which they carried on the ship chandlery business until the establishment was purchased by Mr. William Stairs. Henry Austin, afterwards a partner with William Stairs in ship chandlery, Water Street, south of the fuel yard, and John Owen, shop keeper and shipping merchant.

There was a small newspaper, quarto size, called the "Novator" established or published at Halifax in 1809 by one James Bagnall in Sackville Street. It was not of long continuance.

Jones Fawson was Sheriff of Halifax this year.

From the commencement of the year 1810 until the month of April, 1812, there was a constant apprehension of a rupture with the United States. The garrison and navy enlivened the town by their frequent balls and festivities. The Rockingham Club, before mentioned, continued to have their weekly dining on Saturday at the old Rockingham Hotel on the Basin. It was then customary for the merchants and other principal inhabitants, occasionally to give public dinners to the generals, admirals and principal officers of both army and navy. These dinners, as well as those of the National Societies, were held at the old Mason Hall, that building then containing the most spacious and convenient room in the city.

In January, 1811, the merchants of Halifax petitioned the King, through the Lieutenant-Governor, to permit the coal mines in Nova Scotia to be opened and worked under regulations. A proposal was made this year for the formation of a Joint Stock Bank. The books for subscription were opened at the office of Henry Yeomans, insurance broker, and were first signed on 13th February by the Committee of Trade, consisting of William Sabatier, Andrew Belcher, John Black, James Fraser, George Grassie, Charles R. Prescott and John Pryor. No further proceeding appears to have been taken towards this object.

Much suffering as usual among the poor prevailed this winter. A society for the relief of the poor had been formed, which distributed during the year ending 9th February, 1811 :

```
285 cords wood which cost ............ £994
860 lbs. sugar .......................     49 15 6
111  "   tea .........................
702  "   rice ........................
236  "   flour .......................
1560 loaves bread to 255 persons. ......     36
                                         ─────────
                                         £1079 15 6
```

Eighty-four persons in distress, with their families, and others, in Halifax, Preston, Dartmouth, Chezzetcook, Windsor Road and Lawrencetown, with several families in Digby and Shelburne, were relieved at the time from the same funds.

```
Subscriptions raised for the above purposes....  £255
Donations from individuals, &c..............      384
                                                 ─────
                                                 £639
```

The committee in charge of this fund and its distribution were Edwd. B. Brenton, Revd. Robert Stanser, Revd. Archibald Gray, W. J. Almon, M. D., Hibbert N. Binney, John Lawson, Treasurer.

On Wednesday the 19th February, a public fast was proclaimed throughout the Province, which was observed at Halifax, with due solemnity.

Two fires occurred this year, one at Commissary Buildings on Hollis Street, the spot on which the Bank of Nova Scotia stands, on 18th April, and the other at Bellemont, Mr. John Howe's residence at the North West Arm, on 6th May. Both buildings were saved.

The office of the Nova Scotia Marine Insurance Company was kept by Henry Yeomans, broker, of the Company. A new Marine Insurance Office had been started in February; George Grassie was Chairman of the Committee of Management, and John Bonnett was Secretary.

THE PROVINCE BUILDING.

Decisive measures were adopted this session by the Legislature for the erection of a building for the accommodation of the legislative bodies, the courts of law and the public offices, on the site of the old Government House on Hollis Street. . Commissioners were appointed and plans and elevations prepared or procured by Mr. John Merrick. Chief Justice Blowers, Mr. Speaker Wilkins and Judge Hutchinson had the planning of the interior arrangements, and George Grassie, Winkworth Allen and John Merrick were the commissioners to erect the building. Mr. Richard Scott was the builder employed to conduct the work. The building was fully completed and finished, ready for the sittings of the Courts and Legislature, in 1820, at the cost of £52,000.

A new steeple and an addition of 16 feet to the northern end was added to old St. Paul's Church this year, at the cost of £1000, granted by Government, £500 from a fund known as the Militia Arms Fund, and the remainder from funds arising out of the forfeited estate of óne Jonathan Clarke. Hibbert N. Binney and H. H. Cogswell were the churchwardens. Their advertizement for tenders for the work appears in the Gazette. The sum of £500 from the Arms Fund was at the same time granted to St. George's Church towards finishing the interior of that building. These works were commenced this year, but were not finished until late in 1812. But one capital criminal conviction is recorded in 1811, that of one Sarah Wilson for burglary. She was sentenced to death, but afterwards reprieved.

On the 27th May the sloop of war, Little Belt, Capt. Bingham, arrived from a cruise. She reported having fallen in with the United States frigate, President, by whom she was fired into, and had sixteen men killed and twenty-one wounded, and the rigging of the ship much cut up. The two nations being at peace at the time, the affair caused much excitement in Halifax. Explanations were offered on the part of the Captain and Officers of the U. S. frigate, which only tended to show the bitterness of feeling which shortly afterwards manifested itself in open hostilities. Early this season non-intercourse was established between the United States and Great Britain.

Sir George Provost was now appointed to the chief command in Canada. The inhabitants of Halifax presented a congratulatory address on his promotion on the 19th August. He sailed for Quebec on the 25th, and Sir John Cope Sherbroke, his successor, arrived with his family from England on 16th October following in the ship Manilla.

On 26th September a poll was opened by Capt. Jones Fawson, then Sheriff, for the election of two members for the town and four for the county. John Pryor, John Geo. Pyke and William H. Taylor were nominated; the latter retired and the two first were declared elected. The four old members for the county were returned. Mr. William Sabatier was nominated but afterwards retired from the contest.

The merchants of Halifax, on 20th July, petitioned the Governor respecting the state of trade, etc., stating that they were agreed to take gold and silver coins at the following values, viz: A Guinea, £1 3 4, Halifax currency; a Johannes, at £4; a Doubloon, at £3 17 6; an Eagle, at £2 10; the old French Guinea, at £1 2, and and all the other decimal parts of the same coins at a proportional value; English and old French Crowns, at 5s. 6d.; Spanish Dollars, (including those which heretofore passed current at 4s.) at the rate of 5s. At this time British silver was unknown at Halifax— Spanish silver was the current coin. It came up from the West Indies and Spanish America in the course of trade, and the British Government found it more convenient for various reasons to pay their troops stationed here in Spanish silver than to import British coin for that purpose.

The names attached to this petition were William Bowie, Garret Miller, Starr & Shannon, Charles Loveland, Moody & Sinclair, Alexander McDonald, William A. Black, Martin Gay Black, John Albro, Charles Boggs, Henry Ford & Co., Henry Austin, Michael Forrestall, Jonathan and John Tremaine, John W. Pyke, Matthew Richardson, Richard Tremain, Samuel Head, M. D., Kidston, Dobson & Telford, H. Taylor, John Liddell & Co., Capél Hines, Jas. Ewing, George W. Mitchell, Prescott Lawson & Co., James Fraser, Winkworth Allen, Smith & Thom, Scaiffe & Baine, R. Lyon, Sr., Andrew Belcher, Forsyth, Black & Co., Lawrence Hartshorne, Charles Hill, Forman Grassie & Co., John Lawson, James Leaver, William Minns, John Osborne and John Owen.

A proposition concerning some alteration in Water Street, near the Ordnance Yard, was made by Captain Gustavos Nichols of the Royal Engineers. It was understood that the town would not agree to the proposal unless the Military authorities surrendered a road in continuation of Hollis Street, southward. The subject had been mooted for a long period previous to this time, but no arrangement could be agreed on between the military and the town authorities. Captain Nichols' letter makes an offer according to the plans therein enclosed. This letter and plans are not now forthcoming among the City or Provincial Records, and therefore the particulars of the proposition made by the Engineer Department cannot now be understood. Copies of these plans may possibly exist at the Lumber Yard and Engineers' office.

On the 17th March, the Irish Society celebrated the anniversary of St. Patrick this year by a dinner at Mason Hall, which was attended by the Governor, General Balfour, Commissioner Inglefield, Judge Croke, the Captains of the Navy in port and the Staff of the Garrison, etc. The Hon. Charles Morris was President, and Samuel Hood George, afterwards Sir Samuel, was Vice. The dinner was at five o'clock, the fashionable hour in those days. The Governor and principal guests retired at nine. The rest of the company sat late, but the utmost harmony and good feeling prevailed. These national festivals were better attended in those days, when no political animosities existed to disturb the harmony of the good people of Halifax.

On the 11th May, there was a public examination of the Halifax Grammar School under old parson Wright—a ceremony in which the inhabitants at this period took much interest. On this occasion Mr. Edward Monk, son of Judge Monk, took the first prize; Lewis M. Wilkins, the late Judge, won the second, and the third was given to James Bailey, and the fourth to Edward Fairbanks, a brother of S. P. Fairbanks, Esq., and of the late Judge Charles R. Fairbanks, Master of the Rolls.

A Company was formed this year, in Halifax, for prosecuting the codfishery. The managers were John Lawson, Henry H. Cogswell, William Pryor, Garret Miller, John Brown, John William Morris and Charles Loveland. A large capital was raised in shares of £50 each.

On the 20th November, the fleet sailed for Bermuda, consisting of the Flag Ship of Admiral Sawyer, the Spartan and Melampus, Frigates; the Atalanta, Ratler and Indian, Sloops-of-War.

At the commencement of the year the following Ships of War, under the command of Sir John Borlase Warren, were on this station, viz.: Swiftsure, 74; Guerriere, 40; Melampus, 36; Æolus, 39; Cleopatra, 32; Euridice, 24; Little Belt, 22; Halifax, 18*; Indian, 18; Emulous, 18; Atalanta, 18; Colibre, 18; La

---

*This brig was the only vessel of war ever built at the Halifax Dockyard.

Fantome, 18; Plumper, 12 and the schooners Vesta, Juniper, Holly, Barbaro, Bream, Cuttle and Chub. The old Centurian was the receiving ship; she remained for many years off the dockyard. The Pyramus was afterwards used as a receiving ship for the fleet lately sold and broken up; she was an old-class 50 taken from the Danes at the capture of Copenhagen.

The Eighth and Ninety-eighth British regiments, the Nova Scotia Fencible Infantry, with a battery of Artillery and a company of Engineers composed the Garrison of Halifax. Captain Philip Van Cortlandt was Town Major, and Stephen Hall Binney, Barrack-master. The former was succeeded by Lieutenant John McColla as Town Major, who resided in Halifax for a number of years, and was Adjutant General of the Provincial Militia. Major-General Balfour* commanded the Garrison. Captain J. N. Inglefield, R. N.,† was Commissioner of the Dockyard, and Mr. P. F. Wallis, first clerk. Mr. W. was father of Admiral Sir Provo Wallis, who distinguished himself in the action of the Shannon and Chesapeake.

A Marine Humane Society existed at Halifax in 1811. Their drags, for the recovery of drowned persons, were advertised as being lodged in the respective stores of Hon. And. Belcher, John Pryor, John Brown, Samuel Muirhead and John Starr.

The 30th September was marked by a severe gale of wind from the S. E., by which many of the wharves in the town were ripped up and much damage done to the shipping in the harbour and along the coast.

The year terminated by a proclamation opening the Port of Halifax to vessels of neutrals. The proclamation bears date the 24th December.

Among the deaths recorded this year was that of James Gautier, Esq., for many years clerk of His Majesty's Council and keeper of the public records in the Secretary's office. He died poor. The Legislature voted £30 to defray the expenses of his funeral. He left no family.

The principal retail merchants in the town at this time were Martin Gay Black, Smith & Thom, Carret & Alfort at the corner

---

*General Balfour was this year removed to New Brunswick, where he died Lieutenant Governor of that Province.

†Commissioner Inglefield was grandfather of Vice Admiral Sir Edward A. Inglefield, lately in command of the Squadron at Halifax.

lately occupied by Messrs. Duffus; John Liddell & Co., H. Ford, McDonald & Co., Robert Lyon, W. Bremner, John Lawson, Kidston, Dobson & Telford, Scaiffe & Bain, Thomas Heaviside, James Fraser, Arthur Brymer, all Dry Goods—Moody & Sinclair, C. & R. Hill & Co., Red store, road leading to Dockyard, Thomas Leaver and William Remmington, all Auctioneers; William Minns and Geo. Eaton, Stationers. Mr. Minns occupied the old building in Barrington Street below the Parade, opposite Dalhousie College, where he died about 1825. He conducted a paper called the Weekly Chronicle for above 20 years. Windham Madden and William Conroy kept Livery Stables.

1812. Orders had been issued early this season to put the Forts in repair; the works on the Citadel Hill having again fallen into a dilapidated condition. Captain Nichols, commanding the Royal Engineers, made an elaborate report, and operations were commenced forthwith under his superintendence. The United States had now declared war. Commodore Rogers, in command of an American Squadron, had fallen in with the British Frigate Belvidere, 36 guns. She sustained the attack for two or three hours and at length got off with the loss of several of her crew killed, the Captain and 22 wounded. The Belvidere came into the harbor on the 27th June, and on the following evening a special dispatch arrived from the Governor of New Brunswick with intelligence of the Declaration of War. Sir John immediately made the necessary arrangements for calling out the militia. All able-bodied men between 18 and 50 were to be ballotted for service and a portion of them to be immediately embodied. This was arranged by Order in Council dated 28th June. The Belvidere, after she had escaped from the American Squadron, captured three American merchant vessels which she brought in with her. Halifax being the headquarters of the Naval force under Admiral Warren, who had upwards of 60 pendants under his command, prizes now began to be brought into port. The Court of Admiralty under Judge Croke was in active operation, and the newspapers of the day appear filled with advertizements of sales of prizes and prize goods. Cartels frequently came and went between Halifax and the American ports for the exchange of prisoners. With all this bustle of business money became plenty, and the foundations of small fortunes began to be laid by the Crown lawyers and the prize agents. The presence of a large army and navy caused much dissipation in the town. Festivities of all kinds prevailed. Subscription assemblies at Mason Hall were kept up during the winter under the management of Mr. Jeffery, Collector of the Customs, Capt. Brenton, of the navy, and Lieut.-Col. Robertson, of the garrison. Dinner parties at Government House, and balls and levies on state days, with the frequent rejoicings on the news from time to time of the success of the British Armies, both in Europe and America, completed the round of Halifax festivities.

The capture of the British ship Guerriere, a first class frigate commanded by Capt. Dacres, belonging to the Halifax squadron, by the Americans, in August, caused much talk and excitement throughout the community. Capt. Dacres, a young and inexperienced officer, it was thought had surrendered too early to the enemy. He had only left the harbor a short time when he lost his ship.

In July, a press warrant was granted to Rear Admiral Sawyer for 48 hours. Desertions from the navy were frequent and large offers were reported to have been made by the enemy for such able seamen as would come over to the American navy. The Commander-in-Chief, in consequence, found it necessary to publish a proclamation at Halifax offering the King's pardon to all who had deserted, on their returning to their duty. Letters of Marque against the Americans were ordered in Council on 31st July, and all vessels were prohibited from leaving the port without special license, for the space of one month.

The old Halifax Artillery Company was at this time a very popular corps, and included many of the young merchants as well as tradesmen of the town. It was at one time supposed that the property owned by those whose names were on its roll comprised no small part of the wealth of our town.

An Act of the Legislature was passed this year regarding that part of the public road or highway which leads from Fort Massey to the exercising ground on the Commons. His Majesty's service required that this piece of road should be enclosed for the purpose of enlarging the Artillery Park. It was therefore enacted that when the officers of His Majesty's Ordnance should have laid out a new road agreeable to the plan submitted to His Excellency Sir

John Cope Sherbrooke, and filed in the Surveyor General's office, measuring fifty feet in breadth, through the field of John George Pyke, and shall have procured a release from Mr. Pyke, and shall have completed said new road, that the Engineer should take in 310 feet in length of that part of said road which now leads from Fort Massey to the exercising ground on the Common, forever for the Ordnance Department at Halifax. The new road to be substituted therefor.

1813. The arrival of DeWatteville's regiment of Germans in May on their way to reinforce the army at Quebec, and of the American ship Volante with a valuable cargo and mounting 21 guns taken by H. M. Brig Curlew, Capt. Michael Head,* and the accession of the 64th Regiment to the strength of the garrison were the chief events during the spring of 1813.

On Sunday morning, the 6th June, the inhabitants of Halifax were surprised by the arrival of His Majesty's Ship Shannon, Capt. Broke, with her prize the United States Frigate Chesapeak, Capt. Lawrence. The engagement which was said to be the result of a challenge on the part of Capt. Broke, took place off Boston Harbor a very short time after the Shannon left Halifax. The enemy surrendered after about 20 minutes fighting. Capt. Broke ran his ship in upon the Chesapeak, and captured her with his boarding party who, "rushing upon the enemy's deck, carried away everything before them with irresistible fury." Capt. Lawrence, and his First Lieutenant, Ludlow, were killed; the latter died at Halifax on the 13th June. The engagement was one of the most bloody on record. The Shannon had 30 men killed and 57 wounded, and the Chesepeak 74 killed and above 100 wounded, all within the short space of little more than fifteen minutes. When the ships came up the harbor the decks were being swabbed and the scuppers ran quite red. Numbers of the inhabitants of the town put off in boats and visited the ships. Though the bodies of the slain had been nearly all removed from sight, yet the marks of the slaughter were terribly conspicuous. Mr. Provo Wallis, a Halifax man, one of the Lieutenants of the Shannon, brought in the prize. He received his promotion as Commander soon after, and later became a full Admiral and Knight Grand Cross of the Bath. On the 8th, the

---

* Brother of the late Dr. Samuel Head of Halifax.

funeral of Capt. Lawrence took place. The body was landed under minute guns from the ships and the procession proceeded from the King's Wharf to the old English Burial Ground attended by an immense concourse of people. The coffin was covered by the U. S. colours and six British Post Captains bore the pall. The 34th Regiment formed the firing party. The officers of the garrison, His Majesty's Council, the principal civil officers and heads of departments, and all the officers of the navy in port followed in procession, the American officers walking next the coffin.

On the 10th August, following, an American Brig with a flag of truce arrived for the bodies of Capt. Lawrence and Lieutenant Ludlow, which were taken up and carried to their native country. That of Capt. Lawrence lies in the yard of Trinity Church, Broadway, New York, where his tomb is to be seen on the left of the entrance.

A memorial of the merchants of Halifax, numerously signed, was presented to the Colonial Secretary through the Governor, complaining of the permission of American vessels to resort to the British West Indies, and of the right of fishery conceded to the Americans by the Treaty of 1783, and praying that the interests of Nova Scotia might be considered in any future negotiations. Among the principal signers were William Sabatier, John Black, John Pryor, Geo. Grassie and Enos Collins. At this time the English Government was very jealous of British Colonial rights, and was ready to fight in their defence.

The town and its vicinity had for the last two years abounded with French prisoners of war. Those taken from American prizes now increased the throng. A prison had been erected at Melville Island, at the head of the North West Arm, for their accommodation, and soon became crowded. Many of the French sailors were ingenious workers in wood and bone, and made articles of use as well as ornament, which they sold to the numerous visitors who were freely permitted access to Melville Island. It was the favorite resort of the young people on Sundays and holidays, where a pleasant hour could be passed in conversing with the French prisoners and examining their toys. The French naval officers were on parole of honor, and resided in Dartmouth and Preston. They spent their time chiefly in field sports, occasionally visiting Halifax, where they mixed freely in society. M. Danseville, the Governor of St. Pierre and Miquelon, resided in the house near Preston lately owned by the Hon. Michael Tobin, known as the Brook House, where he entertained his friends with great politeness and hospitality. Many of the French prisoners were permitted to come to town and work for the inhabitants. A number of our own Halifax people were at this time languishing in French prisons. The sum of £130 sterling was subscribed in Halifax for their relief, and remitted to England in the month of July of this year.

Great quantities of prize goods were sold at auction this year, taken principally from American vessels. The American trade was terribly cut up by the British cruisers. On one occasion we find advertised for sale at public auction by order of the Court of Vice-Admiralty, dated 19th March, twelve full-rigged ships, eight brigs, seven schooners and ten or twelve small vessels, with their cargoes.

On 7th September, the merchants of Halifax petitioned the Governor and Council for permission to export to the States portions of the prize goods as being particularly adapted to the American market. The following names, among others, appear attached to this petition: John Lawson, Temple F. & Lewis E. Piers,* Jas. Forman, Samuel Head, M. D., Hartshorne, Boggs & Co., James and Michael Tobin, James Hamilton, Roy Leslie & Co., Carrett & Alport, Scaiffe & Bain, G. Grassie, James Ewing, William Annand, Matthew Richardson, William Phillips, James Russell, Miles W. White, Smith & Thom, John Brown, W. H. Reynolds & Co., Harding & Hill, A. McDonald, Henry Ford, Stephen W. DeBlois & Co., Wm. Bremner, John Moody & Co., Collins & Allison,‡ Henry Austin, William Stairs, Richard Tremain & Co., G. N. Russell, Jonathan & John Tremain.

On the 7th September, Sir Borlase Warren with his fleet arrived in Halifax Harbor in eight days from the Chesapeake. The fleet consisted of the St. Domingo, 74 guns, Diadem, 64, Diomede, 50, Junon, 38, Romulus, 36, Success, 32, Fox, 32, Nemesis, 28, Loupcervier, 18, Mariner, 15, Highflyer, 10, and several transports.

---

* Messrs. Piers were the grandsons of Mr. L. Piers, who came with Cornwallis in 1749. Descendants of Temple F. Piers still reside in Halifax.

‡ This firm was Hon. Enos Collins and Joseph Allison, both of whom became members of His Majesty's Council. They succeeded to the business of Prescott & Lawson on the wharf afterwards known as Collins' wharf, where Mr. Collins, in 1825, built the range of stone stores, a part of which is occupied by the Halifax Banking Company.

The following passage from Murdoch's history affords a lively picture of the condition and aspect of Halifax at this period, drawn no doubt, in some measure from his personal recollection :

"The effects of the war upon the people of Halifax were very marked. Our harbor had become the temporary home of the ships of war, and the place where their prizes were brought and disposed of. Our youths were eager to participate in the path that seemed to lead by a few steps to honor, glory, and fortune ; and indeed when it is borne in mind that several Halifax lads rose to be admirals, we can hardly wonder at the school-boys' desire to wear the white stripe on his collar, and the ivory-handled dirk that indicated his authority to command men. The little capital, then occupying a restricted space, became crowded. Trade was active, prices rose. The fleet increasing, provisions were in great demand, and this acted as a large bounty in favor of the agriculturist and the fisherman. Rents of houses and buildings in the town were doubled and trebled. A constant bustle existed in our chief streets, cannon were forever noisy ; it was a salute of a man-of-war entering or leaving, practising with guns or celebrating something or somebody. There is another side to this picture which must not be omitted. The moral condition of the town had become dreadful in the extreme. Eight or ten thousand soldiers, sailors, and prisoners of war let loose in a little town of less than 10,000 inhabitants can well be imagined."

The upper streets were full of brothels ; grog shops and dancing houses were to be seen in almost every part of the town. A portion of Grafton Street was known under the appellation of Hogg Street from a house of ill-fame kept by a person of that name. The upper street along the base of Citadel Hill between the north and south barracks was known as "Knock him Down" Street in consequence of the number of affrays and even murders committed there. No person of any character ventured to reside there, nearly all the buildings being occupied as brothels for the soldiers and sailors. The streets of this part of the town presented continually the disgusting sight of abandoned females of the lowest class in a state of drunkenness, bare headed, without shoes, and in the most filthy and abominable condition.

The Acadian School was this year established by Walter Bromley, Esq., on the Lancaster system. It was intended chiefly for the instruction of the poor. Mr. Bromley had been paymaster of the 23rd Fusiliers, and having retired from the army while that regiment was in garrison at Halifax, devoted all the energy of his philanthropic mind to the amelioration of the condition of the poor. He first opened his school on 13th January, 1814 in the old building in Argyle Street, then lately used as a theatre for amateur performers, where he held Sunday school for poor children of all denominations and had a large class of blacks, both children and adults, to whom he devoted particular attention. Many colored men and women who afterwards became valuable servants, and some of whom entered into business in Halifax, owed their success and subsequent christian life to the exertions of Mr. Bromley. His labors to improve the condition of the Mic-mac Indians will be remembered by not a few individuals now living. His house was open to them at all times, where those who were not addicted to the habitual use of spirits were hospitably treated, clothed and furnished with means of following their hunting and other occupations. This continued until he left the country. The old play house having fallen into decay, the present stone building was erected on its site in 1816 and apartments for Mr. Bromley were therein provided. A printing press which had been established by him at the Acadian School became the means of disseminating his views regarding education throughout the province, and his little pamphlets, entitled Appeals to the People of Great Britain on behalf of the Indians of Nova Scotia, were very forcible and touching. The first edition of T. C. Halliburton's history of Nova Scotia was issued from Bromley's press in 1824. When Bromley left Halifax in 1828, the poor lost a true friend and the Indians their chief patron.

Halifax was visited by a great gale of wind in the autumn of 1813. The Gazette of the 19th November says:

"On Friday evening last, a most tremendous gale, or rather hurricane from the south-east, rushed up the harbor with such destructive violence as has not been witnessed since the tornado which happened in September, 1798. The lapse of little more than one short hour left but few vessels at their anchors and of those scarcely one that had not sustained material injury. Its utmost fury being felt about dead low water, less damage was sustained by the wharves and stores than might otherwise have been expected, but several shallops and small craft were sunk, and many others wrecked and torn by the sea. H. M. Ships St. Domingo, Hogue, Maidstone, two brigs and a schooner were driven on shore. Fourteen other men of war, including small ones, suffered by vessels being driven against them. The Barossa, Diadem and the old Centurian suffered least. There were forty-six merchant vessels, transports and prizes, all large vessels except about seventeen, stranded; most of them having been got off again. Twenty-four, including store ships and transports, suffered more or less injury, and a brig, a transport and one or two sloops sank and were totally lost. Several schooners were sunk at Prospect, and two large vessels were reported overset off the harbor. A number of lives were lost during the gale, and many seamen badly hurt on board the ships of war."

Among the deaths recorded this year was that of James Creighton, Esq.,* in his 81st year. He was the son of one of the settlers who came with Governor Cornwallis in 1749, and had acquired a large property in the neighborhood of the town which was inherited by his son who was the ancestor of the family of that name now in the city. The fields in the north suburbs adjoining the common were for many years known as Creighton's fields; long since laid off into building lots, including the streets known as Maynard Street, Creighton Street and Bauer Street, etc.

The death of Sir Samuel Hood George, Provincial Secretary of the Province, took place this year in England, where he went for the benefit of his health. He died of consumption in the 24th year of his age.

In the month of January, 1813, a murder was committed on the Market Wharf, which caused considerable excitement in the town. About 7 o'clock on Monday evening, January 25th, five soldiers, having had some dispute with the shallop men on the wharf, attacked them with their bayonets and badly wounded four men, Frederick and Henry Publicover, Cornelius Uhlman and George Teele. The main guard from the King's Wharf being called out, three of the soldiers were secured. Henry Publicover died of his wounds and the Coroner's Jury brought in a verdict of wilful murder against some persons unknown. One of those who had been apprehended, a young soldier named Oliver Hart, was tried and convicted of the murder at the Easter term of the Supreme Court, but was afterwards pardoned by the Governor. Much dissatisfaction existed in the community in consequence of the termination of this affair.

In the month of March the crew of a Spanish schooner, the Serifina, was brought into Halifax. They had killed six of their fellow-sufferers upon the alleged necessity of saving their own lives by subsisting on the flesh of those they killed. Investigations were entered into, the result of which does not appear.

The Commissioners of Streets for the town were appointed on the 12th May. They consisted of James Forman, John Albro, Michael

---

* Mr. Creighton was not related to Lieutenant Creighton, who afterwards settled in Lunenburg and was known as Col. Creighton. He came out, however, in company with him in the same vessel, being friends; they were both from the same part of England.

Tobin, Frederick Major, James Fraser and John Allen. The three former remained in office until about 1829 or 1830, when a new system was inaugurated under the management of H. H. Cogswell and others. Matthew Forrester was the Overseer and Superintendent of Streets under the Commissioners for many years. The old Commissioners, a short time before their retirement, undertook to remove all obstructions to side paths; many old houses stood on banks with cellar doors projecting into what was supposed to be part of the street. Others again were approached by flights of steps, all of which were removed to the detriment of many buildings in the suburbs. At this time the town was adorned in many places by ranges of trees in the sides of the streets. St. Paul's Church was surrounded by large old willow trees; a range of fine old willows extended from William Pryor's corner down the eastern side of Hollis Street past the Lumber Yard Gate. A fine range of willows of less dimensions also ran along that part of Argyle Street between the late H. H. Cogswell's stone house and the residence of the late R. J. Uniacke, since sold for a country market. Again in Poplar Grove, and the old Grenadier fort house which stood on the site of the present Trinity Chapel in Jacob Street, on both sides of Brunswick Street, particularly on the east side, there were several fine clusters of Lombardy poplar trees of gigantic size, several being in front of the residence of James Kirby. There were also some fine trees in other parts of the town. These were all cut down without mercy by Mr. Forrester, under the directions of the Commissioners before the year 1830, and the lower stairs of a number of buildings were buried in levelling the streets. Albermarle and Grafton Streets were at this time in a very rough condition, particularly the former, where banks of earth and stones were to be seen in the centre of the street, sufficient in some places to obstruct carriages. These were removed by the new Commissioners.

The town was at this time supplied with water by public wells and pumps in various parts of the town. A pump stood at the north end of the Province Building Square, in George Street, known as Black's pump; another at the south end of the square; another, known as the White pump, stood in the centre of Prince Street, where it is crossed by Albermarle Street; this was one of the last to be removed. There were two known as the Sisters at the corner of Duke and Hollis Streets, near the site of the building occupied by the People's Bank. There were four or five along the east side of Brunswick Street, one at the foot of Cornwallis Street, and a number in the south suburbs and other parts of the town; also two in Barrington Street in front of the Parade.

1814. During the winter of 1813-14 some distress existed among the poor in the upper streets. This part of the town was chiefly occupied by people of the lower order, and in consequence of the war had become a resort for soldiers and sailors. Barrack Street, before mentioned, was known as "The Hill" and was as well known through His Majesty's dominions for its evil reputation as the worst haunts of Plymouth or Portsmouth in England.

On the 25th February a public fast was proclaimed by the Governor, after which we do not find any further proclamations of this kind for many years.

A press warrant was granted to Rear Admiral Griffiths on 28th February, when many of the idle and worthless vagabonds of the town were happily secured for His Majesty's service, where they would be brought under wholesome restraint.

It had been arranged this spring that a residence for the Admiral of the station should be erected. The British Parliament had granted the sum of £3000 for this purpose, which being found insufficient, the House of Assembly of this province voted £1500 towards its completion. A site was selected in the field between the Naval Hospital grounds and Gottingen Street, and the present building known as Admiralty House was commenced this year, but not finished until some time after. Why the local funds of the province should have been devoted to this purpose does not clearly appear.

The arrival of the English packet on 21st May furnished news of the fall of Napoleon Bonaparte and the entry of the allied armies into Paris. It being Sunday, the event was celebrated on Monday by a military review with salutes, and the whole town was illuminated in the evening. A military band performed during the evening on the flat roof of the old market house, long since removed to make way for the present brick structure, and the streets were crowded to a very late hour. The merchants and many of the places, where hot suppers were consumed in honor of the occasion.

Among the captures this year was that of the American privateer, Snap Dragon, six guns and 70 men, brought in by H. M. Sloop, Martin on 5th July, taken off Sambro Light, and on the 13th, the United States Sloop Rattlesnake, 18 guns, by the Leander frigate, taken near Shelburne Harbor. About the same time 340 British prisoners were brought to Halifax in Cartels from Salem in Massachusetts. The Rattlesnake was afterwards sold and fitted out as a privateer by merchants in Liverpool, Queens County.

The British forces having captured Washington in August, 1814, a large number of black slaves, of both sexes, from the plantations along the Potomac and Chesapeake Rivers, who had deserted their masters, took refuge on board the British men-of-war while they laid in Chesapeake Bay. Sir George Cochran, the naval commander, sent them on to Halifax, where many of them arrived in September, following in a transport ship and the Brig Jasper. They were afterwards located at Preston and Hammond's Plains. Many of the domestic slaves remained in the town as servants, attaching themselves to the inhabitants. Those who went to the country, being unused to cold and hard labor, were unable even with the assistance of the Government allowance to make their living; soon became paupers and a burden to the community, a condition in which their children and grand-children largely remain. At the close of the war a quantity of American soldiers' uniforms, taken at Castine, in Maine, were served out to the Chesapeake negroes. Their grotesque appearance in the blue and yellow coats, occasionally intermixed with the green and red facings of the corps called the York Rangers, (at the peace disbanded in Halifax,) must be within the recollection of many of our old inhabitants.

The grand event of this year for Halifax was the fitting out of the expedition for the invasion of the State of Maine. This expedition consisted of the 29th, 60th, 62nd and 98th British Regiments, with artillery and some militia. The two brigades were commanded by Major Goslin and Colonel Douglas; the whole being under the command of Lieutenant-General Sir John Cope Sherbrooke. Rear Admiral Griffiths commanded the squadron, which was composed of 3 seventy-four gun ships, the Bulwark, Dragon and the Spencer, with two brigs, a schooner and ten transports.

Castine was taken on 1st September, and the town of Michias by Lieut.-Col. Pilkington, on the 11th. Thus all the State or District of Maine fell into the hands of the British as far west as the old bounds of Acadia. This territory was originally part of Nova Scotia, and at the peace of 1783 had been conceded to the Americans through the ignorance and imbecility of Lord Gambier, who had been intrusted by the British Ministry with the settlement of our lines. The British Government was erroneously induced to relinquish this conquest at the close of the war, a policy which has deprived this Dominion of the fairest timber lands of New Brunswick, and caused the loss of the most direct line of communication between the Canadian provinces through British territory, a loss which the whole expense incurred by the British Government during the war could not now repay. Sir John, having left a garrison to take care of his conquest, soon returned with his little army to Halifax. Several Halifax merchants availed themselves of the opening afforded to make money, sent agents with supplies of goods to establish shops at Castine, etc. The British authorities collected the Revenue of Maine while in occupation, which amounted to a considerable sum of money. This fund was placed by the colonial minister in the hands of the Lieutenant-Governor of Nova Scotia, who appropriated it in various ways as he thought most for the benefit of the country. It was from this fund that Dalhousie College was afterwards built and endowed by the Earl of Dalhousie, who succeeded Sir John Cope Sherbrooke in the government, the Legislature of the Province having been induced to vote the sum of £5,000 currency towards the same object.

In the autumn the small pox made its appearance in Dartmouth and Preston and was very fatal among the Chesapeake negroes.

The old Rockingham Club, which in the days of Prince Edward and Sir John Wentworth dined periodically at the Rockingham Hotel on the Basin, had ceased to exist, but it appears to have revived about this time under the name of the Wellington Club. A dinner at the Rockingham by the Wellington Club was announced in the papers of 26th August to take place on the 30th instant at half past four o'clock. Five o'clock was the fashionable dinner hour. The Governor's dinner cards of this date were all for that hour.

The old Rockingham was destroyed by fire nearly half a century ago. It stood on the shore of the Basin, a short distance north of the Rotunda. After the departure of the Prince it became a house of entertainment, kept successively by Graves, Paine and others. It was a favorite resort being a convenient distance from town. The approach from the post road was by a carriage drive next to the Rotunda, between two beech trees, from which hung suspended a sign with the Wentworth Arms. When destroyed it was the property of the estate of David Muirhead.

In September the body of General Ross, who had been killed before Baltimore, was brought to Halifax for interment. He was buried in the old English burial ground with all military honors. No monument to his memory appears in St. Paul's Church.

On the 24th November, the Man-of-War Brig Fantome, 18 guns, went on shore at Prospect. She soon went to pieces, as also a schooner which accompanied her. No lives were lost.

The merchants presented several petitions to the Governor this year relative to the trade of the port. The following names appear appended to these petitions, among which we will find those of many of our principal citizens whose faces were once familiar to many now living:

James Forman,[1] Belcher & Wright,[2] John Clarke, William Rudolf, John Stayner, Rufus G. Taylor, William Strachan, William Young, Jr., Austin & Stairs,[3] Jessie Woodward, Richard Kidston, Lawrence Doyle, John Carrol, Henry Yeomans, Francis Stevens, Benjamin Etter, John Merrick, W. C. Wilkie, Charles Boggs, And. Smith, William Duffus, James Kerby, Charles Tropolet. Again, Thomas Wallace, Bowie & DeBlois,[4] Hosterman & Etter, John & David Howe,[5] W. A. & S. Black,[6] James Baine, Martin Gay Black, Duncan McColl, Thomas Cleary, Robert Phelon, Levi Moses & Co., and John A. Barry.[7]

The Province Building and the Admiralty House were both slowly progressing during the summer and autumn.

NOTE.—1. For many years Custos of the County. 2. Hon. Andrew Belcher, son of the first Chief Justice and member of Council. His partner, William Wright, was son of old Parson Wright of the Grammar School. Neither left male descendants in Nova Scotia. 3. Hon. Wm. Stairs, Sr., afterwards in Council. 4. William Bowie, killed in a duel with R. J. Uniacke. 5. Both brothers of the late Hon. Joseph Howe. Provincial Secretary, etc. 6. Hon. William A. Black of the Legislative Council. 7. Mr. Barry was afterwards in the House of Assembly for Shelburne; died at LaHave aged 80 years.

Halifax did a brisk trade during the period of the American War. The following list of exports for the year 1813 is given by Murdoch in one of his notes: Vessels, 412; Tons, 54,457; men, 2,868; Boards and Plank, 1,881,722 feet; Staves, 232,562; Dry Fish, 82,059 quintals; Pickled Fish in tierces, 408; Barrels, 29,829; Smoked Herring in barrels, 142; Boxes, 6,425; Fish Oil, 49,668 gallons.

1815. The winter of 1814-15 was more severe than the previous one. The small pox had broken out in the town and many persons died of it. A number of the black refugee negroes had been, about the month of May, after the removal of the prisoners, placed on Melville Island. They were all vaccinated to prevent the spread of the disease among them. They remained here for a short time until they could be located in the country.

The treaty of peace between Great Britain and the United States was ratified in February 1815, and executed at Ghent on the 24th December following. An immediate exchange of prisoners took place after the ratification, and many seafearing men belonging to Halifax, who had been confined in American prisons, were restored to their homes. Peace was proclaimed at Halifax on 3rd March. This spring an Act of the Legislature passed for establishing a Bridewell or House of Correction in Halifax. It was placed under the control of the sessions, and the old gamble-roofed building formerly used as a poor house, then situated at the western end of the space known as the old poor house grounds, was taken for the purpose and fitted up with cells, etc., for the prisoners. This building was taken down, having ceased to be used after the erection of Rock Head Prison and the Provincial Penitentiary on the North West Arm. It was one of the oldest buildings in the town afterwards, and was in early days the residence of Mr. Wenman, the keeper of the Asylum. When it was first built is uncertain, but being situate within the lines of the old forts, was probably a military residence of some sort during the first five or six years of the settlement.

A regular police court was this summer established in the brick Court House. John George Pyke, John Howe and John Liddell were appointed police magistrates. Mr. Pyke had long been custos of the county, and he and subsequently Mr. Liddell gave regular attendance at the office. Mr. Pyke was allowed eleven shillings and eight pence per day, and had three police constables at his command, with the additional assistance of Hawkins, a colored gentleman, who dressed in an old military uniform with cap and feathers, usually escorted the criminals to and from the workhouse, and when occasion required inflicted his 39 lashes on juvenile offenders at the old whipping post, which stood at the south-west corner of the building opposite Messrs. Stairs' office—a system of punishment less expensive than paying their board and lodging for eight or ten weeks from the taxes of the citizens.

The Spring of 1815 was very backward. The Basin had been frozen up all winter, and was not free from ice until the month of June. On the first of June the harbor was full of ice so as for an hour or two to impede the progress of the ferry boats. It was partially collected from loose ice which came down the Narrows from the Basin, and some drift ice which was brought in in the night previously from the sea by the tide and southerly wind.

There were two ferries at this time. The upper ferry was conducted by John Skerry, whose memory is still cherished by many, both in Dartmouth and Halifax, as one of the most obliging and civil men of his day. Skerry's wharf in Dartmouth was a short distance south of the steam boat wharf. The other ferry was the property of Mr. James Creighton, known as the Lower Ferry, situate to the south of Mott's Factory. It was conducted for Mr. Creighton by deputy and was afterwards held under lease by Joseph Findlay, the last man who ran a ferry boat with sails and oars in Halifax Harbor. These ferry boats were furnished with a lug sail and two and sometimes four oars. They were large clumsy boats, and occupied some thirty or forty minutes in making the passage across the harbor. There were no regular trips at appointed hours. When the boat arrived at either side the ferryman blew his horn (a conch shell) and would not start again until he had a full freight of passengers. The sound of the conch and the cry of "Over! Over!" was the signal to go on board. The boats for both ferries landed at the Market Slip at Halifax. An act of the Legislature had been obtained this session to incorporate a Steamboat Company with an exclusive privilege of the ferry between Halifax and Dartmouth for 25 years. They could not succeed in getting up a company, steam navigation being then in its infancy, and in the following year had the act amended to permit them to run a boat by horses to be called the Teamboat. This boat consisted of two boats or hulls united by a platform with a paddle between the boats. The deck was surmounted by a round house which contained a large cogwheel, arranged horizontally inside the round house, to which were attached 8 or 9 horses harnessed to iron stanchions coming down from the wheel. As the horses moved round, the wheel turned a crank which moved the paddle. It required about twenty minutes for this boat to reach Dartmouth from Halifax. It was considered an immense improvement on the old ferry boat arrangement, and the additional accommodation for cattle, carriages and horses was a great boon to the country people as well as to the citizens of Halifax, who heretofore had been compelled to employ Skerry's scow when it was found necessary to carry cattle or carriages from one side of the harbor to the other. The first trip of the Teamboat was made on the 8th November, 1816. The following year an outrage was committed which caused much excitement and feeling in the town. All the eight horses in the boat were stabbed by a young man named Hurst. No motive for this cruel act could be assigned, drunkenness alone appearing to be the cause. The culprit was tried for the offence and suffered a lengthy imprisonment. Mr. Skerry kept up a contest with the Company for several years, until all differences were arranged by his becoming united with the Company, and after a short time old age and a small fortune, accumulated by honest industry, removed him from the scene of his labors. The teamboat after a year or two received an addition to her speed by the erection of a mast in the centre of the round house, on which was hoisted a square sail when the wind was fair, and afterwards a topsail above, which gave her a most picturesque appearance on the water. This addition considerably facilitated her motion and relieved the horses from their hard labor. As traffic increased several small paddle boats were added by the Company, which received the appellation of Grinders. They had paddles at the sides like a steamboat, which were moved by a crank turned by two men. In 1818 the proprietors of the old ferries petitioned the House of Assembly against the Teamboat Company suing these small boats as contrary to the privilege given them by the Act of Incorporation. It afterwards became a subject of litigation until the question was put an end to by Mr. Skerry becoming connected with the Company. Jos. Findlay continued to run his old boats from the south or lower ferry until about the year 1835.

On the 3rd August, the Man-of-War Brig Vesta arrived from England with the news of the Battle of Waterloo. The town was illuminated in honor of the victory, and the inhabitants kept up their rejoicings till a late hour in the evening. Preparations were made for a public dinner on the occasion, which took place at Mason Hall on the 15th. The Attorney General, R. J. Uniacke, took the chair and James Forman was Vice-President. The committee of management were Doctor William B. Almon, John Pyke, eldest son of old John Geo. Pyke, the custos. David Shaw Clarke, G. Lewis and John Howe, junior, John Albro, Thomas Heaviside, Edward Alport, Joseph Allison and William Bowie were the Stewards. Subscriptions had been opened throughout Great Britain and the Colonies for the families of those soldiers who were killed and wounded in the action. The Town of Halifax including the garrison and public officers contributed the large sum of £3,800.

This year an Act of the Legislature passed for regulating the appointment of Trustees and Master for the Grammar School of Halifax. The first Act establishing this school bears date 1780.

The refugee Negroes brought to Halifax by Admiral Cockburn had been in a great measure a burden upon the community. A proposition was made this year by the British Government to remove them to a warmer climate, but no steps appear to have been taken to effect the object. Had this suggestion been carried out at the time much suffering would have been spared to these poor people, and the inhabitants of Halifax relieved from a burden.

On 26th February a resolution passed the House of Assembly directing the commissioners of the poor to cause an account to be taken of the number of black persons in the Town and the environs, who were brought to this country from the United States of America. The following return, dated March 6th, was signed by Richard Tremaine, Chairman of the Committee :

	Men.	Women.	Children.	Total.
In the Town of Halifax	179	56	101	336
Windsor Road..........	11	14	26	51
Dartmouth and Preston	...	..	...	270
Mr. Fairbanks' Estate at Lake Porter				27
				684

The men and women with families were generally in need; none appear to have been located at Hammonds Plains at this time.

James Archibald was tried for the murder of Captain Benjamin Ellenwood of Liverpool, N. S., before Chief Justice Blowers, in Easter term of the Supreme Court at Halifax this year. He was convicted and executed soon after on the Common.

Another attempt to incorporate Halifax was now made. It will be seen that in 1785 the merchants of the town suggested the subject for the consideration of the Governor and Council, but they disapproved of the measure; again in 1790, the Speaker of the House of Assembly, in consequence of complaints regarding the settlement of the poor and the necessity of a police force, etc., drew up the following resolution, which was passed: "Resolved, that it "be recommended to this House to present a humble address to His "Excellency the Lieutenant Governor, to request that he will be "pleased to grant a charter to the Town of Halifax for incorpor- "ating the same, and enabling the inhabitants thereof to make such "by-laws as shall be sufficient to regulate the police of said town." No step, however, was taken by the Governor and Council relative to this resolution.

The merchants of the town had a meeting on the subject in 1816, which resulted in a definite proposition being made, in which all the details of the proposed charter were fully set out in a pamphlet of some length.

The following preface or introduction to this pamphlet affords a sketch of the plan proposed:

INTRODUCTION.

The following plan for regulating the municipal affairs of this town has been drawn up in the form of a charter, as the clearest and best method to express the extent of the proposed improvements. The objects have been pointed out by a thorough investigation into the various modes of conducting the public business; which was entered into in consequence of a presentment made by the Grand Jury to the Court of Quarter Sessions in the December Term of 1812. The Court having appointed six different investigating committees of the Magistrates to meet the various objects contemplated by the grand Jury, their several reports combined clearly prove the necessity of some reform; but as it would now become an invidious as well as a useless task, to point out the *prevailing errors* of the present practice, which are but too evident to admit of a doubt, the gentlemen who have undertaken the task of sketching out the *means of improvement*, have left it to the Public to compare the one with the other.

It will be perceived by a perusal of the following sheets, that the Charter has but two leading objects:—to establish regularity in business, and to define and extend the powers of the Magistrates and Grand Jury (acting as a Common Council) to the same limits as (and not a step beyond) the powers granted to all corporations within the King's Dominions.

The only novelty introduced is that of preserving a gradual change of the ruling members of the corporation, without incurring the unpleasant duty of the electing system. This is done by the appointment of ten magistrates to act as trustees, two of whom will go out and two others come in annually, and the appointment of the Grand Jury of the existing year, (or if it is preferred that of the last year, or a draft from the whole list until it is gone through), to act as a Common Council.

By these means the whole of the leading members of the community (likely to take an active part in the affairs of the town) will, in turn, partake of the duties of a respectable office, and become intimate, and thereby feel interested in its affairs. The various articles of consumption and of commerce will be better inspected than they are at present; the revenues will be regularly attended to, and every desirable improvement in possession of other similar communities in His Majesty's Dominions will in time, no doubt be adopted.

The provisions of the Charter have been selected and drawn up with the utmost care to avoid objections by an attentive reference to the London, Philadelphia, New York and New Brunswick Charters, and the East Company's by-laws; and the whole is arranged and worded agreeably to the most approved forms, in order to obviate any difficulties on the part of Government, or from local partialities.

In debating the merits of the following pages, these three queries will naturally occur to and guide every reflecting mind:

1st. Whether the present management requires any improvement?

2nd. If so—is this an effectual plan?

3rd. If not—what is better?

N. B. When the terms of the Charter are agreed on and assented to by His Excellency the Lieutenant-Governor, it is proposed to apply to His Excellency to grant it for a term of three or five years by way of trial; during which period such amendments may be made to it as experience shall point out to be necessary;—after which, if it proves acceptable to the inhabitants, application may be made to renew it for another term of a few years, for the purpose of improving it still further, as its deficiencies may appear; then the Charter may be made perpetual if the inhabitants approve of it. It will be necessary to have an Act of the General Assembly to confirm the Charter when first granted, and on every renewal of it.

Mr. Sabatier and a few others were principally concerned in endeavoring to forward the object, but the Governor and Council appear to have been still influenced by the belief that their own supervision of local affairs was preferable and better suited to the circumstances of the town at that time.

It will be seen that in the plan proposed the idea of a popular election of members of the corporation was not even thought of either by the Government or the people of the town.

CHAPTER VII.

1816. Soon after the peace the prosperity of Halifax began to wane. The price of provisions and all the necessaries of life, the value of real estate and the high rents of houses in the town all became more or less affected by the scarcity of money arising from the withdrawal of the troops and navy and the sudden alterations in trade. The reaction was not fully realized until about two years after peace was proclaimed, when the rapid fall off in the value of real estate and the sudden check given to commercial pursuits was found to have reduced many speculators to poverty.

Sir John Cope Sherbrooke having been appointed Governor General of Canada, the principal inhabitants of the town gave him a farewell dinner on 25th June. It was presided over by Chief Justice Blowers and the vice chair was occupied by Michael Wallace, the treasurer of the province. An address, largely signed by the inhabitants, was presented to the Governor on his departure. Sir John had rendered himself very popular in Halifax by his affable manners and his prompt and decisive way of treating all matters brought to his notice by the citizens. He embarked at the King's wharf on Thursday, 27th June, under a salute from the batteries and the cheers of the inhabitants.

The rough condition of the streets of the town at this period rendered immediate and extensive improvements necessary. Those in the least frequented parts of the town had been so much neglected that in many places they were impassable from the accumulation of rubbish and the broken condition of the wooden platforms or bridges at the gutters and crossings. In many places the streets were overgrown with grass except in the centre. Brunswick Street, though one of the principal highways of the town, was overgrown at each side with grass. Many of the old Dutch houses then still remaining in this street stood on banks a few feet above the sidewalk and where there were no buildings rough stone walls or fences marked the line of the street. Water Street, from the continual traffic and wear during the period of the war, had been worn into holes and was in wet weather almost impassable from the accumulation of mud, particularly between the Ordnance Yard and the foot of Prince Street. The market square at this time, as also that portion of Water Street between Collins' Wharf and the King's Wharf, was much lower than at present. It was found necessary to pave this portion of Water Street, which was accordingly accomplished during the years 1816 and 1817. The pavement, which was with round stones, extended from the Ordnance to Black and Forsyth's Wharf, (later Mitchell's) at the foot of Prince Street. The Provincial Legislature contributed the sum of £1,200 towards the work, and the expense of flagging the sidewalks was charged to the owners of property fronting on the street. About the year 1835 this pavement had so sunk down as to be no protection from the accumulation of mud. The lower part of the market square bordering on Water Street and the way leading to the market slip or public landing were raised about five feet. Between 1820 and 1824 new Street Commissioners were appointed. The Macadamizing system began to be introduced and extensive improvements in the way of levelling the streets and filling up hollow places were proceeded with.

The Acadian School, conducted by Walter Bromley, had now been under way for about three years. It was inspected on 31st July. There were 400 children in attendance. On this occasion Mr. Bromley stated that since the opening of the school in 1813, eight hundred and ninety-three children had received instruction there, and about one hundred apprentices and colored children in the Sunday schools. The latter were under the special superintendence of Mr. Bromley himself, who devoted all his leisure to the instruction of the black children and others who could not attend school throughout the week. The small sum of £200 was voted annually by the Legislature in aid of this school. Subsequently a grant of money was made by the Assembly to the National School, which was about this time set on foot on the Madras system, under the auspices of the Bishop and members of the Church of England in Halifax, who had lately erected the large three-story building in Argyle Street, opposite the parade, for the purpose. In 1818 this school had 117 children in attendance. The daily attendance at these two schools exceeded 500, which was a large number considering the extent of the population at this period.

The appointment of Dr. Robert Stanser, Rector of St. Paul's, to the Bishopric of Nova Scotia, vacant by the death of Bishop Charles Inglis, took place in 1817. Interest had been made with Lord Bathurst, the Colonial Secretary, and the Archbishop of Canterbury to have Dr. John Inglis, son of the late Bishop, appointed to the See. The appointment was said to have been arranged in favor of Dr. Inglis, but a recommendation from both branches of the Legislature then in session in favor of Dr. Stanser, their Chaplain, prevailed, and Dr. Inglis was appointed Rector of St. Paul's, vacant by the elevation of Stanser to to the Bishopric. Dr. John Inglis proved a highly popular Rector; his bland manners and kind disposition rendered him a favorite with all classes and denominations, and when he afterwards, in 1825, obtained the Bishopric he carried with him to England addresses in his favor not only from his own parishioners, but largely signed by his friends among other denominations.

The remains of the old Bishop were brought to town from Aylesford, where he died, and buried under St. Paul's Church on the 29th February. The funeral was attended by the Governor, Sir J. C. Sherbroke, Sir John Wentworth, the retired Governor, His Majesty's Council and a large assemblage of the citizens. A monument to his memory is on the west side of the chancel of the church.

On the morning of the 18th April great excitement prevailed throughout the town in consequence of a murder which had been committed in one of the streets during the previous night. Capt. Westmacott of the Royal Engineers who, as officer of the night, was going his rounds on horseback to visit the guards, met two men in Sackville Street whom he challenged in consequence of their suspicious appearance. They immediately attacked him and by a sudden effort threw him from his horse, having first wounded him fatally with a bayonet. He lingered until the 4th day of May, when he died. The murderers were soon after discovered and proved to be two soldiers, deserters from one of the regiments in garrison. They had been stealing fish through the night from a store on one of the wharves. They were identified by the Captain and, being tried and convicted of the murder, were executed on the Common.

The Nova Scotia Fensible Regiment, after the close of the war, remained in Canada for some time. Early in June of this year they embarked at Quebec for Halifax. The transport in approaching Halifax ran upon a reef of rocks known as Jeddore ledges, which lies off the harbour of that name eastward from Halifax. The weather was calm and the troops were landed in safety, with the exception of four private soldiers, two women and several children, but with the loss of considerable part of the baggage. It was found on landing the men that the tide was rising, and that in all probability the greater part of the ledge would be covered at high water. It was proposed that the women and children should be first landed and placed on the higher part of the rock. But on the soldiers perceiving that Colonel Darling, who commanded the Regiment, and several of the officers were intending to avail themselves of the higher parts of the ledge, immediately declared that all officers should be compelled to remain with their respective companies and share the fate of their men. One officer, a captain, is said to have shown symptoms of impatience or something worse on the occasion, and abandoned his wife and family and his men, seeking shelter for himself on the rocks amidst the reproaches and jeers of his comrades. The Regiment was, however, successfully landed on the ledges, chiefly through the heroic exertions of the Adjutant-Lieutenant Stewart, who volunteered to carry a cable from the bowsprit of the ship to the rock, when having there made it fast the sailors were enabled to construct means for landing the men in safety. Part of the Regiment was brought to Halifax in coasting vessels about the first July, and others found their way by land, having been brought on shore from the rocks by the fishermen of the neighbourhood. Col. Darling and some others being displeased at all the credit of the exploit being attached to Lt. Stewart, who was probably not a favorite of the Colonel, brought him to a Court-Martial for some trifling offence supposed to have been a breach of orders, and it is said he was compelled to leave the Regiment.

Two very extensive fires occurred at Halifax this year. One on the 8th October, remembered as the "Haliburton" fire in consequence of the brick building at the corner of Hollis and Sackville Streets owned by Mr. George Haliburton, having been the first house consumed. The fire destroyed nearly the whole block from Haliburton's corner to where Mrs. Howard's new stone building stands, on the east or lower side of Hollis street. All the buildings on Sackville Street down to the corner known as Reynolds' corner, and the whole of the buildings on the upper or Western side of Bedford Row were consumed. The fire commenced at ten o'clock in the evening and continued to rage until six o'clock next morning. It was considered the most disastrous fire that had ever occurred in Halifax. The old buildings were all of wood except Haliburton's corner house. The block was soon rebuilt with a better description of buildings. Mr. W. K. Reynolds erected a fine stone store at the corner of Sackville Street and Bedford Row, which still remains; this was far the finest store in Halifax at the time. A range of brick buildings along Bedford Row were at the same time erected by the late Nicholas Vass. Haliburton's corner was also rebuilt of brick, and the buildings on Hollis street, the property of Mr. LeNoir and others, were built about the same time by the late Judge William Hill and his brother T. T. Hill, then both at the Halifax Bar. Several old wooden houses were pulled down during the fire by order of the firewards to prevent the spread of the fire. The town was assessed to pay the damage. The other fire was on Water Street at Creighton and Grassie's wharf. It occurred in the night of 17th December, during very cold weather. All the stores at and near the head of the wharf were consumed, and the fire extended to buildings on the opposite side of the street. Mr. Grassie rebuilt with brick and stone, and afterwards lined the shutters of his new store with sheet iron.

The Earl of Dalhousie, a Scotch nobleman, who had distinguished himself in the Spanish campaign as a general of Division under Lord Wellington, had been appointed to succeed Sir J. Cope Sherbrooke in the Government. He arrived in Halifax on 24th October, 1816, in the Frigate Forthe. Lord and Lady Dalhousie, immediately after their arrival, landed in state and proceeded to the Council Chamber under a salute from the Citadel attended by the heads of Departments, civil and military, when the Earl was sworn into office in presence of His Majesty's Council. The troops lined the way from the King's wharf to Cochran's building where the Council Chamber was then situated.

There had been no theatrical performances worthy of mention in the town since the Duke of Kent's old theatre in Argyle Street had been appropriated to the school under Mr. Bromley. In the autumn of this year a company of players, Messrs. Price, Charnock, Placide, etc., fitted up an old store on Fairbank's wharf as a theatre. Placide, Price and Mrs. Young were considered good performers and attracted large audiences. At the close of their career the manager got into jail for debt, when Placide, the best comic actor of the company, distinguished himself by escaping from prison and passing the sentry at the jail gate in the night, who supposed it was a Newfoundland dog, Mr. Placide being famous for imitating the bark and whine of the canine species.

1817. The winter of 1816-17 was much more severe than that of the preceding year. The south-east passage was closed with ice all winter, and the ice remained until late in April. Great distress prevailed in the town as usual among the laboring classes during this winter, which was also the case throughout the whole Province. The sum of £600 was contributed this winter by the inhabitants of Halifax for the support of destitute emigrants who had been brought up from Newfoundland.

An attempt was made by the Legislature in their session of 1817 to relieve the pressing necessities of the county by an Act authorizing the Governor and Council to procure copper coin to the value of £2,000 to be issued from the provincial treasury. The Act was disallowed by the Colonial Secretary in England. No good reason appears to have been assigned for its rejection. The circulating medium at this time in the town and throughout the country was Spanish doubloons, old Spanish dollars, pistareens and other small Spanish coins, with a mixed collection of copper coinage, English and Spanish, with all kinds of half-penny tokens issued by private individuals in the town. No British coinage ever reached Halifax except the old English Guinea. The troops were paid in old Spanish money, which was brought from South America and the West Indies by the merchants in exchange for their cargoes of fish with occasional importations of Spanish silver by the British

Government for the troops, etc. An issue of paper money was at this time made under an Act of the province.

It was in the year 1817 that the project was first broached for the establishment and erection of a college on the Grand Parade. The sum of £9,750 was then remaining in the hands of the Governor from the revenues collected at Castine while the State of Maine was in the hands of the British troops. This sum Lord Dalhousie obtained the permission of the Colonial Secretary to appropriate towards the erection of a college in Halifax on the model of the Scotch Universities. The professors were to receive moderate salaries. The students were not to reside in the college building, but only to attend courses of lectures which were to be open to all students and all else who might feel disposed to purchase tickets for the courses.

This winter the theatre on Fairbanks' wharf was again in operation and as attractive as ever. Miss Powell was at this time giving lessons in dancing. She gave her spring ball at Mason Hall on 21st May. This lady, who was patronized by the fashionable part of the community, was the daughter of Mr. Powell who conducted the theatre in Argyle Street when under the patronage of the Duke of Kent. She lived many years in Halifax and died at an advanced age, having been dependent on the charity of her friends for several years before her death.

The naval force on the station had now been reduced to a few ships under the command of Rear Admiral Sir David Milne, father of Vice-Admiral Sir Alexander Milne, who some time since commanded on the North American Station. Sir David's flagship was the Leopard, Frigate.

It may here be noticed that the British and Foreign Bible Society had lately organized a branch in Halifax. The second annual meeting of the branch society took place on the 5th May. It was attended by the Earl of Dalhousie, who occupied the chair, and a number of officials. The chief speakers on the occasion were Judge James Stewart, the Rev. Dr. Archibald Gray, of St. Matthew's, and Judge Wilkins. Martin Gay Black was treasurer and Walter Bromley, secretary. Mr. Black continued to act as treasurer of this society to the year of his death. The Speaker of the House of

Assembly and a number of the members of the House were also present on this occasion.

The great destitution of the laboring part of the population during the winter, as usual, rendered it necessary on behalf of the Commissioners of the Poor for the town to call on the inhabitants for contributions in addition to the annual poor rate assessed. The poor house at Halifax was then, as has been the case frequently since, the receptacle for transient paupers from the country, and the sum of £300 was voted this year by the House of Assembly towards the expenses of the establishment.

The charitable societies of St. Patrick and St. Andrew dined together on the respective anniversaries of their patron saints. Richard J. Uniacke, the Attorney General, occupied the chair at the St. Patrick's dinner, and Dr. Samuel Head the Vice. The Governor, Mr. Philip Woodhouse, the Commissioner of the Dockyard, the Bishop of Nova Scotia, the Commanding Officers of the Garrison and other distinguished guests were present at both dinners.

A fire occurred in the southern part of Granville Street this winter, which destroyed the chocolate manufactory of Mr. John Ferguson and his dwelling house. The fire companies of Halifax at this time were, perhaps, the most useful institutions in the community. These companies consisted of several hundred gentlemen each, who formed themselves into a company for the purpose of rendering assistance at fires. Each member provided himself with a leather cap, two or three buckets, canvas bags, etc., on which were painted the name of the owner and device of the company. The members were elected by ballot. They held quarterly meetings and occasionally dined together, and gave annual balls at Mason Hall. The Heart and Hand and the Hand in Hand Companies were the oldest, but the Sunfire Company was the most exclusive. The Phœnix Company was also very efficient, being composed chiefly of young tradesmen of the town. The Engine Company was a very ancient institution, and tolerably efficient, considering the kind of machinery they had to work with. The Axe Company, as now, was composed of carpenters and others suitable for such work at fires. It was customary for the soldiers in garrison to turn out at fires and form lines with the inhabitants for the conveyance of water by buckets, handed through the lines from the harbor or the wells and tanks of the town. One feature which is now never seen at fires was the guard which was furnished by the military to take charge of the property removed to the streets from the burning houses. Scarcely a pile of furniture or goods could be observed without a sentry over it with fixed bayonet pacing up and down. The supply of water was principally drawn from the wells and pumps which were kept in order by the Magistrates of the town. These pumps have been before noticed. The inhabitants of the suburbs, however, depended for good water on their private wells. Almost every house in Brunswick and Lockman Streets had a good well in the garden or near the house. The north suburb lots were of very large dimensions; fruit gardens were numerous; the plum, the Dutch cherry and red and black currants were raised in abundance. The caterpillar and other vermin which now infest the fruit gardens had then not been imported.

Among the names of merchants who were carrying on business this year in Halifax we notice those of John Pryor, father of the late City Judge, Henry Pryor, William Strachan, White, Creighton & Co., Ironware Merchants, Wallace & Russell, Hardware and Wines, at the corner of Hollis and Prince Streets, now occupied by the Union Bank; Prescott & Calkin, Fruits, etc., in Granville Street; James Leishman & Co., Woolen Ware, lately from Glasgow; Hartshorne, Boggs & Co., Hardware, etc., at the old stand, corner of Granville and George Streets, and S. & W. DeBlois at the opposite corner. The firm of Hartshorne & Boggs existed for many years. The head of the firm, the Hon. Lawrence Hartshorne, retiring from business, the name was altered to Boggs & Hartshorne; the late Thomas Boggs became head of the business and Lawrence Hartshorne, Jr., afterwards County Treasurer, was junior partner. The business continued until the old corner building was taken down, about the year 184–, and replaced by the fine stone edifice erected by Mr. George E. Morton on the site.

Scarff & Bain, afterwards James Bain[*] & Co., carried on an extensive importing business at the corner now occupied by W. & C. Silver. James Romans, Boots and Shoes, who succeeded Mr.

---

[*] Mr. Bain married a daughter of the late Benjamin Salter and grand daughter of Malachi Salter, one of the first Members of Assembly for Halifax, the ancestor of Mr. Benjamin Salter of this city.

McNab at the old corner of Granville and Prince Streets, lately owned by Mr. Robert Romans, who succeeded his father in the business; John Witham and Thomas Donaldson, the former Groceries and Wines, the latter Confectionery, were fashionable resorts on the lower side of Granville Street. Mrs. Jane Donaldson carried on the business after the death of her husband and finally retired to her residence at Birch Cove on the Basin, which had been purchased from the late Andrew Belcher on his leaving the province for England. Sherwood, which was built by Bishop Stanser, was also the property of Mrs. Donaldson. The late William Donaldson afterwards sold it to Thomas Kenny, Esq. James Donaldson, the brother of Donaldson of Granville Street, was also a Confectioner and carried on business at the corner of George and Barrington Streets, now occupied by Cragg Bros., opposite the Parade, and was afterwards succeeded by the late Adam Esson. The principal auctioneers were Bowie & DeBlois, Moody & Boyle, Fillis & Perkins, and Charles Hill & Co. The latter carried on business in Bedford Row near the corner of Sackville Street. Among the dry goods stores were Israel Allison & Co., Carnot & Alport, where Mr. Duffus afterwards erected his stone building; Thomas Cleary, M. G. Black, Winkworth Allen & Co., in Cochran's Buildings near the market. Among the importing and West India merchants, Abram Cunard & Co., Lawrence Doyle, Collins & Allison, Collins' Wharf; James Forman, Sr., James and Michael Tobin, Tobin's Wharf; Thom, Salter & Co., Ship Chandlery.

A court for the summary trial of actions in the town was established this year. The Commissioners named by the Governor and Council were James Forman, Richard Tremain, William Minns, Charles Boggs and James Tobin. The Commission bears date in April of this year.

In addition to the public schools before mentioned, Mr. Thomas Crosskill kept a good school for young men in rear of the Acadian School, entrance from Barrington Street; his classes were more advanced than those of Mr. Bromley. Mr. Addison kept his classical academy in Marchington's Lane. There were several schools for young girls. Miss Wenman kept a school for small children in Granville Street; she was one of those who were burned out in the great fire before mentioned. Mrs. Henry in Barrington

Street and Mrs. McCage, for young ladies, also in Barrington Street, in the brick house lately the property of Mrs. Doctor Slayter.

On the 25th April, 1818, a public meeting was called to petition the British Government to make Halifax a free port so that foreigners might have access and take cargoes of the produce of the country or merchandise imported into it; accordingly, on the 27th May, an order of the Prince Regent in Council was obtained making Halifax and St. John, New Brunswick, free ports. Halifax was declared by proclamation of the Governor bearing date August 13th.

At the request of the inhabitants of the town an Act of the Legislature was obtained this year authorizing the leasing of 25 acres of the Common for a period of 999 years at a small ground rent. The lots were each 60 feet in front by 330 feet deep. These lots were gradually disposed of and the broad street known as Spring Garden Road was laid out with the lots fronting on it. Very few of these lots were built on at first, and not until many years after was there any appearance of improvement in this part of the town. The only residence westward of the General's quarters was the house of old Colonel Pyke, the Police Magistrate, which stood in the field next his brewery.

About this time the late John Stayner, of Water Street, commenced to erect the building known as Brookside, afterwards the residence of the late Hon. Joseph Allison. Many years afterwards John Spry Morris, the Surveyor General, erected the building, and planted the trees, lately occupied by D. Cronan. The fields on the west side of Queen Street, opposite the General's quarters, known as Pedley's Fields, or Smidtville, were not then built upon and the whole space from the present line of Queen Street to the Tower Road was occupied as pasture for cattle. Queen Street led up to Fort Massey military burial ground; it was covered with grass and seldom used except for military funerals.

Owing to the frequent alarms of fire and other disturbances in the town this winter, the Magistrates made application to the Legislature for an Act to establish a night watch, and accordingly, on the 5th May, a nightly watch was established by order of the Governor and Council for three months.

During the spring of 1818 and the previous autumn, several vessels arrived in this port with emigrants from Europe, many of whom were found to be in a most destitute condition. They could not be permitted to remain a burden on the town and the Governor and Council advanced funds to assist their removal to the country, and Mr. Samuel Cunard and Mr. Michael Tobin were intrusted with the funds for the purpose.

"On the 9th February there remained of these emigrants in "town only 20 families and 30 single men. Their distress and "that of the humbler classes in the town this winter induced "the Governor to place £100 more in the hands of Messrs. Tobin "and Cunard to be used by them to mitigate the suffering of the "poor in general. They, in consequence, established for a time "a public soup house, beginning with 50 gallons of soup a day; "but in three days they were obliged to double the quantity, "finding that 50 pounds beef and vegetables, producing 100 "gallons a day, did not more than answer the demand. The "fitting up of the place and eight days' issue cost over £50, and "they supposed the money would be all gone in a fortnight more. "They attended constantly in person at the daily issues and say "that 500 daily partook of the gift. They estimated that £200 "more would be required to keep up the establishment until the "pressure of want should be alleviated in some other way. The "first £50 was paid out of the Arms Fund, £100 from the Treasury, "and the House voted £200 on 10th February for temporary relief "of the poor at Halifax."—[Murdoch.]

Eight armed fishing vessels were seized this summer by the ships of war on the station, and brought into the Harbor of Halifax. Five were released and three condemned in the Court of Vice-Admiralty.

A general election occurred this year. The poll for the County and Town of Halifax was opened at the County Court House on Monday, 15th June, and continued until Wednesday, when one of the candidates, Mr. Richard Kidston, having withdrawn, the other two, Mr. John Albro' and Mr. H. H. Cogswell were returned. Capt. Thomas Maynard, R. N., was Sheriff this year. He resided in the old house in Jacob Street formerly known as the Grenadier

Fort, which stood on the spot where the Trinity Church has since been erected.

Among the events of the year worthy of notice was the appearance of Anthony H. Holland, proprietor of the Acadian Recorder newspaper, (which had been established in 1813) at the Bar of the Assembly to answer charges of having published severe animadversions on public affairs, particularly from some remarks relative to Edward Mortimer, one of the County members, for which Mr. Holland suffered a short imprisonment. This affair, with the letters of Agricola, which now began to appear in the same paper brought that paper into public notice.

A Bill was introduced into the House of Assembly this session by Mr. Shaw, who resided near the Three Mile House, for lighting Water Street, but it does not appear that the object was effected.

Paper money, issued from the Provincial Treasury, had been for some time in circulation and had to some extent taken the place of the Spanish Silver, which had been, heretofore, the only circulating medium in the town.

During the month of February this year, the harbor was blocked up with float ice as far down as George's Island. Between 13th and 20th, persons crossed from Dartmouth on the ice at the Narrows.

In the "good old days when George the Third was king," his birthday, the 4th June, was celebrated with great enthusiasm at Halifax. A levy at Government House, a review of the troops, and sometimes the militia on the common, and a royal salute from the Battery and shipping in harbor, terminating with a ball in the evening.

This year the officers of the 3rd Halifax militia regiment gave a dinner at the Exchange Coffee House in the large room lately occupied by the Corporation as a Council Chamber. The North British Society also dined together on St. Andrew's day at Masons' hall. Lord Dalhousie, and all the heads of departments, civil and military, and Bishop Burke attended. Judge Brenton Halliburton was President, and Geo. Mitchell Vice-president.

Dr. Burke had been officiating priest at St. Peter's, the old Roman Catholic church which stood on the present St. Mary's grounds at the head of Salter Street. He was this year appointed Bishop for this province under the title of Bishop of Zion. He was consecrated at Quebec on the 5th July. Dr. Burke was a very popular clergyman, was highly thought of in the town and was very remarkable for his hospitality, great benevolence, and Christian self-denial and care for the poor. Though on several occasions engaged in theological controversies with Dr. McCulloch of Picton and others, he never permitted those differences of opinion to interfere with that kindly and gentlemanly intercourse with his friends for which he was so remarkable.

On the 15th December this year the Agricultural Society of Nova Scotia was inaugurated at a public meeting held at Masons' Hall. The Earl of Dalhousie presided, the Hon. S. B. Robie, Judge Brenton Halliburton, Rev. Dr. Inglis, afterwards Bishop, and S. G. W. Archibald addressed the meeting. Resolutions were passed for the organization of the society, Lord Dalhousie appointed President, and John Young, the author of the letters of Agricola, was appointed Secretary with a good salary. Chief Justice Blowers was named as Vice-president, and a Committee of twenty named to manage the business.

Mr. Placide's theatre at Fairbanks' wharf was again in full operation this winter; Mrs. Young was the favorite actress, and young Mr. William Blake, a native of the town who joined the Company, acquired much popularity. Mr. Blake afterwards visited Halifax as manager of a company of play actors, about 1830 or '31.

Mr. John Black* and James Fraser, two wealthy Halifax merchants, were this year appointed to His Majesty's Council. Mr. Black was senior member of the firm of Black, Forsythe & Co., afterwards known as Fiddis, May & Robinson. This business was carried on for many years on the wharf at the foot of Prince Street, lately the property of George Mitchell. Mr. Fraser† carried on business near Commercial wharf. His residence was on the upper side of Water Street nearly opposite his place of business. His

---

*Mr. Black's daughter was the wife of the late Hon. Jas. B. Uniacke. Mr. B. built the handsome stone mansion near Government House in Hollis Street, afterwards the residence of Bishop Binney. The granite with which this house was built was brought from Aberdeenshire. Mr. William Black, his son, removed to Scotland.

†The Hon. James Fraser married a daughter of Mr. DeWolf of Windsor, his eldest son James D. Fraser, was for many years member of Assembly for Windsor, and his second son was Dr. Benjamin D. Fraser, of Windsor. His eldest daughter married Hon. Chas. Gore, afterwards Gen. Sir Chas. Gore, G. C. B., and her daughter married the Earl of Errol, a Scotch peer. Another daughter became the wife of the Right Rev. Dr. Suther, Bishop of Aberdeen.

garden extended into Argyle Street, and occupied the space on which the Salem Chapel stood.

CENSUS OF THE TOWN OF HALIFAX, TAKEN 1816-17.

Men, 3114, males under 16 years of age, 2120, Total males	5234
Females, total	5177
	10411
Colored population, males 391, females 354	745
Total population of the town	11156

MEMO :—Population in 1752,—4249.
" " 1791,—4897.

In the spring of 1819 the excavations at the north end of the Grand Parade were commenced for the erection of Dalhousie College. A grant under the great seal of the province, of a part of the parade ground had been made to Trustees as a site for the college in August 1818. The Legislature at their sitting in February, voted £2000 towards the erection of the building and a sum of £3000, part of the Castine fund before mentioned, was also appropriated to the building, the balance together with an additional vote of £2000 from the province being invested for the support of the college.

The space known as the Grand Parade had been reserved for military and other necessary purposes on laying out the town in 1749. It had never been military property or claimed by the military authorities, but was originally reserved as a place of muster for the militia of the town, though used also by the King's troops for mounting guard. An old building originally erected on the upper side of the space next Argyle Street for an Artillery barrack, was remaining there as late as 1777, and ranges of cannon appear in front of it in the old pictures of the town about that date. Prince Edward when General Commanding at Halifax had the parade ground walled up and a new rail or fence erected. The surface was levelled and the wall built at the north end bringing the surface high above Duke and Barrington streets; ice houses were built under this wall which were occupied by Mrs. Jane Donaldson, Confectioner of Granville street. This wall was removed to make way for the foundation of the college building. It had always been asserted as a right on the part of the inhabitants of the town, that a free, unobstructed way for foot passengers should be kept open across the centre of the old parade from one part of George street to the other, and wooden steps had been provided soon after the wall along the upper side had been erected and a gate and turn stile at the town side for the accommodation of the public.* There was a high wooden rail around the parade painted red.

The Province Building being now finished, the Courts of Justice and the Public Offices were removed from Cochran's building, and the Legislature, which met on the 11th February, took possession of the chambers appropriated to the Council and Assembly with all due ceremony.

The reduction of the Dockyard establishment this year was a great loss to the town. A large force of workmen were discharged, many of whom were thrown out of employ without any provision from government.

The project for the removal of the Dockyard to Bermuda was found in many respects not to have realized the advantages contemplated by the change. It was removed at the time that one of the Admirals on the Station had taken offence at some occurrences in the town and had used his influence to effect the change.

A few years afterwards the Shears, a gigantic apparatus at the Dockyard, for throwing down vessels, was demolished. The Shears

---

* The Grand Parade as it is called, like other spaces reserved in 1749 for public purpose, such as the old burial ground, public landing, the common, etc., had been used for the purpose to which it was originally appropriated but the title had been supposed not to have passed out of the Crown. Towards the close of the last century it was thought advisable to vest all the public property in Trustees under several grants from the Crown for that purpose; accordingly a grant was made of the parade ground to certain public officials and their successors in office, to be held by them for the public purposes for which it had been originally reserved. This grant with all the others had been constructed under the supervision of old Attorney General Unlacke and of Chief Justice Blowers, but it having been afterwards discovered that none of the public officials to whom it was granted possessed the corporate powers and therefore had no succession in law, and the original incumbents at the time of the grant being all dead, it was concluded that the title had lapsed to the Crown. Lord Dalhousie, Mr. Wallace and a few others, in their exuberant zeal for the erection of a college on the Scotch model, undertook to have another grant from the Crown passed of the whole or part of the parade ground to the Governors of the College, reserving, it is understood, certain privileges over a portion of the ground to the public.

The Governors of Dalhousie College claimed under this grant. The City contends that the old grant was not forfeited and that this space among other public property appertaining to the town was under the Act of Incorporation turned over to the city. That in order to create a legal forfeiture there must be process of Escheat gone through, and further, that though the public functionaries to whom it was granted were not possessed of corporate rights or had any succession of their offices in law, yet the fact of their having been by Royal patent constituted trustees of the property, by inference of law the Crown intended to make them a corporation for that particular purpose, and that their successors in the various offices they held, or the successor of any one of them, would possess the power of supporting the grant. Otherwise the object of the Crown in making the grant would be defeated, and as Crown grants are always constituted in law most favorably for the Crown, it might be inferred that the Crown intended to support its grant by constituting those public officers and their successors in office a corporation with succession for that special purpose. Later the dispute was settled by private arrangement.

was a very conspicuous object, and stood so high that it could be seen from most parts of the town. It is still in the recollection of many of our older citizens. The Royal Standard floated from the staff which surmounted the Shears on the King's and Queen's birthdays and other public holidays. The Dockyard of Halifax, as mentioned in a previous chapter, was first established in the year 1758. The present wall was first erected in 1769 and bears the date of 1770 over the gate, but it has been improved and some portions rebuilt since that time.

Anthony H. Holland, built a paper mill at the head of the Basin this year, on the stream near the opening of the Hammonds Plains Road. The paper made here was used for his newspaper, and the various pamphlets which issued from Holland's press and occasionally by other newspapers. It was of a very inferior quality. The brown paper, however, used for shop purposes, was of a tolerably good description. It was the first paper manufactory set on foot in Nova Scotia. It was kept up for many years after the death of Holland.

On the night of the 11th of November a fire broke out in the Naval Hospital adjoining the Dockyard, which destroyed several buildings. In consequence of the removal of the Naval Station the space remained unbuilt on for many years.

The Magistrates of the town, in session in December, voted a portrait of Chief Justice Blowers. It was painted by a Mr. Drake in full dress, wig, and scarlet gown. This picture occupies a place in the Legislative Chamber, with that of Chief Justice Sir Thomas Strange, by Benjamin West, late President of the Royal Academy.

Among the promotions which appeared in the Royal Gazette this year we find the appointment of Mr. Hibbert N. Binney[*] to His Majesty's Council.

An event occurred in the month of July which cast a gloom over the whole community. Mr. Richard J. Uniacke, junior son of the Attorney-General of that name, a member of the Bar, in his address to the jury at a trial before the Supreme Court, made some observations offensive to Mr. William Bowie, of the firm of Bowie and

---

[*] Mr. Binney was a native of the town. He was the father of the late Edward Binney and Grandfather of the late Bishop of Nova Scotia. His residence was at the corner of Hollis and Salter Streets, opposite that of the late Honorable William Lawson. The old house was removed some years since to make way for a range of wooden three-story buildings, erected by Henry G. Hill, along the east side of Hollis Street. Mr. Binney was many years Collector of Imports and Excise at Halifax.

DeBlois; a challenge from Mr. Bowie was the consequence, and on the morning of Wednesday, following the 21st July, the community was startled by the announcement that Mr. Bowie had been mortally wounded. The duel was fought in the grove at the Governor's north farm, near the Lady Hammond Road. Mr. Bowie was carried to the house at the corner, then or afterwards occupied by Mrs. McNeil as a tea house, where he died in a few hours, the bullet having entered his right side below the rib. Mr. Uniacke and the two seconds, Stephen W. DeBlois and Edward McSweeny, were indicted for murder and tried the same term, and were acquitted by the jury of the capital offence. This was the first criminal trial of importance which took place in the Province Building. The Court Room at the time, now the Legislative Library, comprised the three rooms overhead, lately used by the keeper of the building. A large gallery then surrounded the Court Room on three sides. This gallery was removed in 1827 or 1828, the height of the Court Room reduced, and the upper space made into three room, which were appropriated to the Law Library, Admirality Records, etc. This unfortunate duel excited much feeling in the town, and some blame was attached to the seconds who promoted or advised the parties to fire a second time, when a reconciliation might have been effected. The combatants were both gentlemen highly esteemed for their amiable qualities. Bowie was a handsome young man and very popular for his social qualities. He was buried from his lodgings in town, and his funeral was said to have been more numerously attended than any within the recollection of the oldest inhabitants. Mr. Uniacke afterwards became a Judge of the Supreme Court. The recollection of the sad event is supposed to have shortened his life. He died at the early age of 45. Judge Uniacke was one of the handsomest men Halifax ever produced, and was more popular than any other of his family, several of whom were in public positions.

1820. On 7th April, King George IV. was proclaimed at Halifax. The ceremony was performed by the Governor, Council, and such Members of the House of Assembly as remained in town, together with the Magistrates, the Grand Jury, and a number of private citizens, proceeding to the Council Chamber, where the proclamation was signed by the Governor, Councillors, and others. David Shaw

Clarke, the Clerk of the Peace, acted as Herald, accompanied by the High Sheriff in a carriage, escorted by a body of troops. The proclamation was read by the Herald in the Market Square, at St. Paul's Church, and on the Military Parade in Brunswick Street in front of the officers' old barracks. A royal salute was fired and the procession then returned to the Province Building, where the proclamation was again read. The Royal Standard, which had been flying on the citadel, was then lowered to half-mast and minute guns fired from George's Island, there being none mounted on the hill at the time on account of the decease of the late King George III. Sermons were preached in all the places of worship and the inhabitants of the town went into mourning.

The House of Assembly being dissolved by the death of the Sovereign, a public meeting of the freeholders of the Township was held at the Exchange* Coffee House on the 3rd May for the nomination of the candidates to represent the town. Richard Tremaine, Esq., was called to the chair. Mr. Stephen W. DeBlois nominated John Pryor and George Grassie. Mr. Cogswell, the former member, retired, as also Mr. James Forman and Mr. John Young, both of whom had been suggested. John Albro', one of the former members, led the poll at the close of the election, Pryor and Grassie stood even. Captain Maynard, the Sheriff, made a special return of the facts. It was said that the last vote polled was that of the Sheriff, who first declared the poll closed and then voted for Mr. Grassie, which placed the candidates even. On the validity of his vote rested the question of the majority. The election lasted three days and closed on Saturday evening. At the close the poll stood, Albro, 453; Grassie and Pryor, each 395. Freeholders or owners of real estate only had the privilege of voting at this period. The new House met on 12th November following, and Mr. Pryor having died in the interim the House ordered the return of Mr. Grassie.

William Lawson, Simon B. Robie, Samuel G. W. Archibald, and George Smith were returned for the County. Mr. Robie was elected Speaker of the new House. Mr. Smith resided in Pictou, the other three in Halifax. Pictou and Colchester then formed part of the County of Halifax.

---

*The building afterwards used as the City Hall was then called the Exchange.

The walls of the new College had now been built up even with the surface of the parade ground, and it was arranged that the corner stone should be laid with proper ceremony by Lord Dalhousie, the patron and originator of the scheme. Accordingly, on the 22nd May, 1820, the troops in the garrison were turned out and formed a double line from the Province Building to the Grand Parade. The Freemasons, under the Grand Master, John George Pyke, proceeded from Mason Hall along Barrington Street and formed a square on the Parade. About 2 o'clock, Governor Dalhousie, the Admiral, the officers of the Governor's Staff, with the Members of His Majesty's Council, the Magistrates of the town, and a number of leading inhabitants, proceeded through the line of troops to the south-east corner of the building. Dr. J. T. Twining, the Grand Chaplain, offered a prayer, after which a brass plate containing the necessary inscriptions and a quantity of coins, were placed under the stone, after which the Earl addressed the meeting and explained the objects contemplated in erecting the college. The stone was then laid with all due Masonic ceremony. A royal salute was fired from the forts and the whole was concluded by a ball and supper at Government House.

On the 24th May, the corner stone of St. Mary's Roman Catholic Church was laid with full religious ceremonies by Bishop Burke. The old church of St. Peter, usually known as " the chapel " was a small wooden building painted red. It stood opposite the head of Salter Street, inside a rail, and was approached by a gate and turn stile. This old building was the first Roman Catholic place of worship in Halifax. It was built some time between 1785 and 1790. It was removed soon after the new building was ready for occupation.

On the 29th November, Bishop Burke died in the 78th year of his age. He was laid out in state in his Episcopal robes and mitre for several days. Bishop Burke was succeeded by Dr. Fraser, Bishop of Tanen in partibus. He resided at Antigonish. Mr. Miniot was parish priest at this time; he was succeeded by Mr. O'Brien and afterwards by Mr. Lochnan, etc., until the appointment of Bishop Walsh. The St. Mary's Cathedral crept on slowly for many years for want of funds, but was finished according to the original plan about the time of the appointment of Bishop Walsh.

The Earl of Dalhousie having been appointed Governor General of Canada on the death of the Duke of Richmond, a farewell ball was given to him and his Countess by the officers of the garrison on 28th May, and on 31st the inhabitants presented him with an address. On the first of June, his successor in the Government, Sir James Kempt, arrived at Halifax in the Phæton, frigate, Capt. Montague, 42 days from England. He landed at the King's Wharf, and was driven to Government House. At 3 o'clock the same day he went to the Council Chamber, where he was sworn into office.

On the 5th, Lord Dalhousie embarked for Canada. The flank companies of the First Halifax Regiment of Militia, under the command of Capts. John Liddell and John Pyke, attended on the wharf as a guard of honor. Sir James Kempt brought with him as A. D. C., Major Charles Gore, afterwards General Sir C. Gore, G. C. B., Lord Frederick Lenox, a younger son of the Duke of Richmond, who lately died in Canada, and Major Couper, afterwards Sir George Couper, Comptroller of the Household of the Duchess of Kent, the Queen's mother. Sir James Kempt was one of Lord Wellington's Officers in the peninsular war. He commanded a brigade at the Battle of Waterloo, and after the death of Sir Thomas Picton, the General of Division, who was killed early in the action, the command of the division fell to him.

The only other occurences worthy of notice during this year were the dinner given to Governor Dalhousie by the inhabitants of the town, which took place at Masons' Hall on 17th June, the Hon. Michael Wallace in the chair, and John George Pyke, Vice. Sir John Wentworth, Baronet, the former Governor, died this year at his residence, Mrs. Flieger's, Hollis Street. His death took place on 8th April. He was in his 84th year. He was succeeded in his Baronetcy by his son, Charles Mary Wentworth, a native of Halifax, who had retired to England, where he held some subordinate office under Government. At his death, unmarried, the title became extinct. By his will, he gave the old villa and grounds on the Basin, built by the Duke of Kent, to Mrs. Gore, the novelist, who was a distant relative of his family.

A Fair and Cattle show was held by the Agricultural Society on 6th September on Camp Hill. The Governor distributed the prizes.

John Young, John Albro', William Young, John Starr, Peter McNab and Frederick Major, Esquires, were Judges of the cattle.

1820-21. This winter was, if anything, more severe than the three preceding. Early in January the harbor became frozen over, and by the 20th the ice extended to Meagher's Beach and was sufficiently strong to bear sleighs. By the 27th the ice formed a firm bridge between Halifax and Dartmouth, over which a continuous line of sleighs, teams and foot passengers might be seen on market days. Skating and sleighing parties were numerous. The Governor, Sir James Kempt, drove tandem almost to McNab's Island, and the double sleigh of Judge Brenton Halliburton, in passing over a weak spot in the ice, fell through but was rescued without damage to the horses or the ladies in the sleigh. The navigation was completely stopped for several weeks. A passage was, however, cut from Cunard's wharf to the mouth of the harbor with much labor and expense, to permit the Government Brig Chebucto to proceed on her cruise. This little brig was owned by A. Cunard & Sons, and was employed by the Imperial Government in cruising along the shores of the province to protect the fishery, and at the same time to enable the officers of Government to visit the outposts, and was occasionally employed on special service to proceed to Quebec and other places with despatches, etc. The channel through the ice by which this vessel was taken out, and which ran along close to the wharves, was afterwards kept open while the ice remained, and a boat and two rafts were used to convey over passengers and sleighs.

On the 17th September, a fire occurred in the town, which destroyed nearly all the buildings on the eastern side of Barrington Street, between Sackville Street and Blowers Street and extended back into Granville Street, where several houses were consumed. Most of the buildings destroyed were old and delapidaated except those at the corner of Granville and Sackville Streets occupied by Mr. Liswell's Bakery, etc. There were in all about 24 houses consumed. A large portion of the burned district remained for many years after unbuilt upon.

It was customary at this time for the dress companies of the militia to give balls. On 23rd January the Grenadier and Light Companies of the 1st Halifax Regiment gave a ball at Mason Hall at which 300 persons were present. The regiment was commanded by Hon. T. N. Jeffery, the Collector of the Customs, who had only lately succeeded old Col. J. G. Pyke in the command. John Liddell commanded the Grenadiers and Brevet Major John Pyke, the Light Company. Lieut.-Col. Richard Tremain commanded the Town Artillery.

The condition of the transient poor of the town was very sad this winter. An organized system of relief known as the Poor Man's Friend Society, was instituted. The town was divided into wards, and three or four gentlemen volunteered in each ward to visit the poor throughout the winter months. A soup house was established, and other arrangements made to meet the objects intended. This society continued for about six or seven years. In 1824 Beamish Murdoch was its secretary. The following year William Young (the late Chief Justice) was acting secretary.

A large issue of paper money by the province took place in 1820. Silver change was almost driven out of circulation by the issue of small notes, many at one dollar, at 2s. 6d., and even at 1s. 3d. These notes were issued by private individuals upon their own credit and responsibility. Those of William Lawson and Adam Esson were the most numerous. The doubloon was at this time established at £4 currency, and the Spanish dollar at five shillings. The price of flour had fallen to twenty-seven shillings and six pence per barrel.

An anonymous pamphlet was published from the press of A. H. Holland, charging the magistrates of the town with malpractices, which caused much excitement. It was discovered to have been written by Mr. William Wilkie, of Halifax. He was indicted for libel, tried at the Easter term of the Supreme Court, found guilty and sentenced to two years imprisonment with hard labor in the House of Correction. This was esteemed a most tyrannical and cruel proceeding on the part of the government. The pamphlet was a very paltry offence, such as at the present day would be passed over with contempt. Wilkie, though not a person of much esteem, yet being a member of a respectable family in the community, should have been spared the indignities thrown upon him by Chief Justice Blowers and the other Judges of the Supreme

Court. After the sentence was known, the sympathy in his favor was very general throughout the town.

The reaction after the peace had reduced the price of agricultural produce, not only in Halifax but throughout the province. The West India trade, then the chief branch of commerce, had begun again to be prosperous, and the merchants were looking forward to profitable voyages. But the value of real estate had so fallen that sales were made in the body of the town for much less than half the cost of the buildings. This state of things continued for several years, and very few new buildings were erected between 1819 and 1823. The population was about 15,000, but the number of houses did not exceed 1,600.

The market square at this period presented a very different appearance from what it does at present. A low wooden building stood on the site of the present brick market house. The roof was originally flat and afterwards a pitched roof was added. The butchers' stalls in this old building were very convenient, perhaps more so than those in the new market house. The cellars of this building fronting on Water Street were let for the benefit of the town, and the south end was, some time after this, occupied by Mr. Alexander McLeod as a liquor store and grocery for many years. The ground in front of the market wharf and market slip was much lower than at present, and also that part of Water Street between the old City Court House and Stayner's Wharf, all which was filled up about 1830 or, perhaps, a year or two later. A range of shops under the Court House before this alteration in the streets afforded a large revenue to the town, but their value as places of business was destroyed when the street was raised, and though partially occupied afterwards, they proved damp and unfit for storage of goods. The truckmen, who were then very numerous, ranged their trucks and carts in lines in the square fronting the meat market (there being no other stand allowed) and in cold weather they might be seen, in the afternoons, when not engaged in trucking, amusing themselves with the game of football. Two liquor stores, one at the head of the market, on Beamish's Wharf, and the other at the opposite corner, now known as Laidlaw's corner, kept by Samuel and David Muirhead, were the chief places where spirits and beer were retailed to the truckmen and fishermen. In front of these shops were ranges of apple and cake stalls kept by old women, where also gull eggs and lobsters boiled hard could be had by the fishermen and shallop men from the wharves. The red woollen night cap was generally worn in those days by the market fishermen and the people from the coasting vessels.

The sidewalks throughout the town with the exception of part of Water Street, were all of wood. The old platform on George Street, between Granville and Hollis Streets, was known as Hartshorne's platform. Messrs. Hartshorne & Boggs occupied a range of wooden buildings at the corner of Granville Street, since replaced by the stone building erected by George E. Morton and now occupied by Knowles' Bookstore. On the lower corner, known as Martin Gay Black's corner, there stood an old gamble-roofed house on a high green bank occupied by Mrs. Hart as a dry goods store, and afterwards by T. & S. Greenwood, watchmakers. This old building was about this time replaced by another which afterwards made way for the handsome free stone building erected by the late Martin Gay Black.* This platform was the resort of merchants and others who congregated there in the mornings for a short walk and to talk over the news. A large ship gun did duty as a post at Hartshorne & Boggs' corner, and another at Black's, and formed a neucleus for loungers—not smokers, for smoking was strictly prohibited in the streets of Halifax at this time by the Magistrates of the town. Opposite, near the Province Building rail, was the old town pump mentioned above, known as Black's pump, remarkable for its good water, where dozens of boys and girls might be seen towards evening getting water for tea. The old wooden range known as Cochran's building, which occupied the site of the present Dominion building, had been only lately evacuated by the Legislative Assemblies and the Courts of Law, and was now being fitted up for shops. Among those who first occupied shops in this building were Winkworth Allen, who afterwards went to England, Mr. David Hare, who afterwards became the purchaser of the property; W. A. Mackinlay, on the north side, and Clement H. Belcher, at the north-west corner, both well known stationers and

---

* This fine stone building has been since pulled down and a new building for the accommodation of the Merchants' Bank now occupies the corner.

booksellers, occupied their respective shops a long time, the latter for more than twenty years. At the opposite corner, to the south, on Hollis Street, stood a large three story building erected by the late James Hamilton, who carried on an extensive dry goods business. It was afterwards sold to Burns & Murray, who erected the present handsome freestone edifice on the corner. Mr. William A. Black kept his watchmaker's establishment at the corner below, now occupied by the P. Walsh Hardware Co. The old Halifax Journal office occupied a wooden building at the corner of George and Granville Streets, where the stone store of T. & E. Kenny now is. Mr. Benjamin Etter had his watchmaker's shop at the corner of George and Barrington Streets, now known as Crosskill's corner, in the same old wooden building which has since undergone extensive alterations. Mrs. Donaldson carried on the confectionery business at the corner opposite and was succeeded by Adam Esson. There were two Donaldsons, both confectioners, whose wives carried on the business after the death of their husbands and accumulated large properties, usually known as upper and lower Donaldson's; the latter was in Granville Street and was the most fashionable, being patronized by the military and navy officers during the war. The parade ground was surrounded by a high wooden rail painted red and had a gate and two turn stiles opposite George Street; the latter for foot passengers who claimed the right to pass across the ground to the steps which led up into Argyle Street, and which still remain. John Howe kept the Post Office in the old building opposite the parade later occupied by Mr. Brander, Cabinet Maker. The late Matthew Richardson a year or two later erected the three story stone building next to Mrs. Donaldson on the site of the Hon. Andrew Belcher's garden, which occupied an open space south of Donaldson's or Esson's corner. Mr. Belcher had, a few years before this, left Halifax to reside in England. His residence was in Granville Street, the same building formerly owned and occupied by the late Doctor Hoffman a short distance south of Kenny's buildings, and his garden extended in rear fronting on Barrington Street. No part of the city has undergone greater changes since this time than Granville Street. From George Street northward all the old houses on both sides have been replaced by lofty buildings with some rare exceptions. Between

Romans' corner and the Ordnance Square, the street at this time was elevated about 20 or 25 feet above the present level. It was cut down about the year 1830 or 31, (perhaps a little earlier) and the old shabby buildings on the upper side removed, and those on the lower side had an additional story added to them below in consequence of the street being lowered. The whole of this part of Granville Street has been since twice destroyed by fire and replaced by the present buildings, at a cost and in a style far beyond the requirements of the city. Proceeding southward along Hollis Street from the Province Building, both sides as far as Sackville Street were occupied by a range of small low buildings. At the corner now occupied by the Queen stone building, there stood an old gamble roofed house of one story with a little shop at the corner occupied by a worthy old man, James Smith, who held the office of Deacon of St. Matthew's Presbyterian Church, opposite. The other deacon was James Dechman, senior, who was for many years keeper of the town clock, and resided in the clock building. These two old worthies have long since gone to their rest. The latter was father of the late James Dechman, of Halifax, master carpenter, who died at an advanced age some years ago at his residence in Bishop Street. The Rev. Dr. Archibald Gray* was minister of St. Matthew's at this time. His place of residence was the old house in Granville Street, opposite the Province Building, now known as the Acadian Hotel. Several buildings both in Hollis and Granville Streets, remnants of the first settlement, stood on high grassy banks with porches and steps outside and cellar doors on the side of the bank with plank platforms over the gutters; the porches and steps frequently projecting out on the side path.

The Hon. John Black, a short time previous to the year 1821, built the fine granite building in Hollis Street north of Government House, afterwards the property of his son-in-law, Hon. James B. Uniacke, since the residence of the Bishop of Nova Scotia. The old house within the railing at the upper corner of Hollis & Salter Streets, lately owned by Mr. Esson, was then the residence of Hon. William Lawson. It was originally built by Malachi Salter about 1760, perhaps before. At the opposite corner stood the residence

---

* Dr. Gray married a daughter of Dr. Michael Head and was father of the late James F. Gray, of the Halifax Bar, many years Clerk of the House of Assembly.

of the Hon. Hibbert N. Binney, since removed. At the other corner Mr. Charles R. Fairbanks, some time Solicitor-General, afterwards Master of the Rolls in Chancery, son-in-law of Mr. Lawson, had just erected the fine brick building since occupied as a boarding school for young ladies. The late Samuel Lydiard Brewer built the iron stone house of three stories south of Mr. Binney's residence about the same time. The residence of the Hon. Michael Wallace, Treasurer of the Province, was in Hollis Street immediately opposite the Government House. It was a wooden building and considered a first class residence in its time; now altered into two separate dwelling houses. Trees were common in the streets of Halifax at this period as has been before mentioned. The stone building in Morris Street, the residence of Chief Justice Sir Brenton Halliburton, then Judge Halliburton, had been erected some years before this. Judge Stewart, his brother-in-law, built the yellow brick building at the north-west corner of Hollis & Morris Streets, now the residence of a gentleman of the same name, son of Hon. Alexander Stewart, late Master of the Rolls and Judge of Admiralty. The Hon. Thos. N. Jeffery, Collector of the Customs, built and resided in the building later occupied by Mrs. James Donaldson. The late Bishop Inglis, then Rector of St. Paul's, owned and occupied the low wooden building nearly opposite Mr. Jeffery's, since the residence of Mr. Hagarty. At the corner, opposite Judge Stewart's, was the old gamble roofed house, the residence of James B. Franklin, son of Governor Franklin. This old fashioned house still remains as one of the few relics of the early town. The Hon. Charles Morris built a handsome wooden dwelling house on the south side of Morris Street, between Hollis and Water Streets, afterwards the property of Hon. S. G. W. Archibald, Attorney-General and Speaker of the House of Assembly; since his death occupied as a boarding house. The late John Trider about the same time built his rough stone house at Freshwater Bridge. The late John Tremain had a Ropewalk adjoining his residence on the south side of the road leading up from Freshwater Bridge, now known as Inglis Street. This property was afterwards purchased by James Forman, Junior, and the old ropewalk building removed. The residence of Major Bazelgette at the head of this street had been originally constructed by John Trider from the materials of the old

Government House which had been removed and the materials sold to make way for the foundation of the Province Building. It afterwards became the property of the late John Moody, a merchant in the town, who sold it to Major Bazelgette about the year 1817 or 1818, who added to the building and improved the grounds. Mr. Moody purchased the adjoining grounds and erected a new house; after his failure his residence was purchased by Hon. Enos Collins, who improved the property and beautified the surrounding grounds.

Old Fresh Water Bridge, so well known in former times, crossed the stream from Smith's Tanyard nearly in the same place as the present abutment. It was a rickety old wooden structure with a rough curb or rail. It was a favorite resort of the young of both sexes on Sundays and summer evenings, and the old wooden rail was covered with names and initial letters carved with the pen knife by visitors. The walk down Pleasant Street and up the road now known as Inglis Street and round the new road, as the Tower Road was then called to Pyke's Bridge, and thence down Spring Garden Road to Government House, was the fashionable promenade for all classes on Sundays and holidays. The old English Burial ground was then surrounded by a high, rough stone wall, built without mortar, which was removed some years after the new cemetery on Camp Hill was consecrated. The Governor's garden up Spring Garden Road adjoining the burial ground extended as far as the General's quarters. A portion of this field was taken for the site of the new Court House and County Jail. The new Poor House in the opposite space, then lately erected, was a rough stone building whitewashed on the outside, but the Work House or House of Correction was the old gamble roof building probably originally erected as a soldiers' barracks in the days of the forts, and afterwards used as a Poor House. All these buildings have been since removed and the ground sold to private speculators, a step much to be regretted, as the space was very extensive and the most eligible situation for a public building in the whole city.

The Poor House Burial Ground, at the corner opposite the present new Court House, was at this time a standing nuisance in consequence of the want of drainage and the careless manner in which bodies of paupers were interred. After the law for closing all places of burial in the city had been carried into operation, this open space was planted with trees and ground carted in to fill up hollow places, and a substantial wall built around it. The old tan Yard of Andrew and John Smith was then one of the most picturesque and secluded spots in the neighborhood of the town. The stream which turned their mill passed down from the south common through Smith's Fields, where it formed a pond near the town road, known as the mill dam, for many years the resort of skaters in winter, continuing south-eastward to Freshwater Bridge and passing through a range of willow trees, some of which may still be seen above the present bridge. Southward from old bridge the road was at this time but a footpath winding along the shore to Steele's Pond, beyond which it was passable for carriages. At a very early period, however, there had been a broad carriage road all along the shore to Point Pleasant, but the earth had fallen in or been washed away by the tide. Black Rock, a point running out south from Trider's old lime kiln, was then, and for many years after, the resort of bathers. There was a fine gravel beach outside the old Freshwater Bridge leaving a large expanse of gravel when the tide was out. It was customary for gentlemen's servants, truckmen and others who came morning and evening to water their horses in the stream above the bridge to ride their horses in the surf at low water.

That part of the city known as Schmidtville, or Pedley's Fields, west from Queen Street and the General's quarters, was not laid out into building lots until many years after the period we are now describing.

The stone house at the corner of Prince and Argyle Streets, opposite the south-west angle of St. Paul's Church, was originally the mansion of the Hon. Richard Bulkeley, and is, perhaps, now the oldest stone building in Halifax; it was purchased about 1818 by H. H. Cogswell, who improved the old house and resided there until his death in 1854. The stone house at the opposite corner was built after the close of the war by Dr. William J. Almon. It afterwards became the residence of his son, Matthew Byles Almon, who sold it to Dr. Daniel McN. Parker. Proceeding southward along Argyle Street at the next corner was the handsome residence of Hon. Richard John Uniacke, who held the office of Attorney General for a great number of years. This was a wooden building of three stories originally with a flat roof and a parapet all around with ornaments in the shape of urns at the corners and in the centre. A roof was put on this building about the time of the death of old Mr. Uniacke, and the parapet removed. At the south termination of Argyle Street stood the residence of Mr. Alexander Creighton, a small low house, and along Blowers Street, to the west, was a low range of wooden buildings which had been a soldiers' barracks or guard house. The late Chief Justice Blowers, about the commencement of the present century, erected the large wooden building at the corner of Barrington Street, adjoining the Roman Catholic property, as a residence. After his death it was sold and became a hotel under the name of the Waverley House. It has since been purchased and attached to the Roman Catholic church property.

In the year 1821 there were no houses in Gottingen Street, north suburbs, except the stone house at the corner of the lane leading westward, some years before built by Major McCola, Town Major of Halifax, since owned by Mr. R. Duport. A wooden house, a short distance north of it, built by Peter Hay, Mason, and the old hipped roofed building at the corner of Gerrish Street, known as the North Pole, still standing. Mr. Lewis Demolitor had then lately built a large house at the northern extremity of Brunswick Street, which at that time was considered a very wild speculation. This is the same house lately the residence of the Hon. Senator Northup. The late Benjamin Etter also, about this time, built himself a residence at the corner of North Street, afterwards the mansion of the late Hon. William A. Black. Captain Michael Head, R. N., occupied the two story house to the westward of W. A. Black's property, which a few years before had been built by the late William Rudolf, of Halifax, and was afterwards the residence of Commissary General, W. H. Snelling, and afterwards by John Northup; now or lately known as Belle-Air. Lockman Street then could boast of very few buildings and was so grown up with grass as in some places only to afford a narrow path in the centre for pedestrians and occasionally a stray carriage. The original Lockman Street extended only from North Street to Gerrish Street, in the rear of what was called the Dutch Lots; it was afterwards continued southward by consent of the north suburb lots, as far as Cornwallis Street. The old house, formerly the residence of Major Leonard Lockman, a German officer, one of the original settlers, for whom the street was called, stood on the western side near the northern extremity of the street. It became very delapidated and was removed some years ago.

In the year 1818, or perhaps as late as 1820, that part of the north common known as Camp Hill, since appropriated as a public cemetery, as also all the swampy space westward of the drill ground, was in a state of nature, covered with cradle hills, laurel bushes and ground juniper. The butchers' boys kept their sheep there, and in autumn the swampy portions afforded to the sportsmen good ground for snipe, plover and curlew. An old building, known as the St. Andrew's Cross, stood on the hill at the corner where Quinpool Road, so-called, now meets the common. On the opposite side an old two story house called Quinpool, which had been the residence of a Mr. O'Brien, stood in a field to the north of the road. This old house became uninhabited and was afterward taken down by Dr. Cogswell, the proprietor of the property, when he divided the fields into building lots. There were two main roads leading from town to the Basin, both meeting at what was called the Three Mile House, a building erected by Mr. Shaw, a member of Assembly, as a hotel, afterwards known as Increase Ward's country house. The Wistermount Road was known as the Blue Bell Road from a very old house with a swinging sign which stood at the corner before you arrive at the Willow Park property. Mr. John Young, known as the author of the letters of Agricola, had then lately purchased this latter place, had improved the house and gardens, and was commencing to work it as a model farm. Further north were the old Dutch farms of Philip Bayer and Jacob Shefforth on either side of the road, surrounded by groups of old willow trees. The Bayer's house has disappeared, but that of the Shefforth family fell to the late Mr. Henry Vieth, who repaired the old buildings. The other road, known as the Fort Needham or Lady Hammond Road, was a prolongation of Gottingen Street. After passing the farms of the late John and James Merkel, it turned to the westward down the hill to the shore of the Basin at the Three Mile House. The Kempt Road had not yet been opened though for some time in contemplation. Two block houses, the remnant of the old fortifications of Halifax, overlooked these roads. The first or nearest blockhouse, was at Fort Needham on the hill south of the Governor's north farm. The other surmounted the hill just above the cottage of the late John Steel, called Three Mile Cottage, at the termination of the Blue Bell Road, near the present Three Mile Church. The old house at the Governor's north farm known as Lady Hammond's house was then in good repair, since fallen down. This house was erected by Lieut. Governor Hammond as a country residence for his family. The north farm, as it was called, extended eastward to the shores of the narrows and included the beech grove near the old railway station. This beautiful grove has been lately cut up by one of the Government Railway Superintendents who caused building lots to be laid off and sold in the grove. This fine collection of trees had been carefully preserved for nearly a century, and had been the scene of many festivities, and was associated with very many pleasing events in the minds of the older citizens.

The common was the usual resort of a large portion of the inhabitants on a Sunday afternoon during the summer months. It had been the custom for many years, and had continued to be so until discontinued by Governor Maitland, for the whole garrison, which usually consisted of service companies of three regiments, a part of artillery, and a company of sappers and marines, to parade on the common every Sunday afternoon at three o'clock during the summer season. The Governor and his staff attended and the whole brigade, with their regimental colors, and the artillery, with their field pieces, formed a line and were inspected by the Governor or Commander-in-chief, after which they marched around the drill ground, passing before him at slow time, saluting him in open column of companies. No booths, however, were allowed on the common for the sale of refreshments except on the King's and Queen's birthdays, when grand reviews came off.

Sunday presented a gay scene at Halifax in those days. There being then no garrison chapel for the troops, the regiments in garrison, preceded by their brass bands playing, marched in full dress to St. Paul's and St. George's churches amid the ringing of bells and the sound of martial music. The carriage of the Governor (who was then always a general officer) in full military costume, with his aids-de-camp, drove up to the south door of

St. Paul's, the whole staff having first assembled under the portico which then ran along the southern end of the church. His Excellency, followed by a brilliant display of gold lace and feathers, the clank of sabres and spurs, and the shaking of plumed hats of so many officers, many of whom were accompanied by their ladies, on entering the church, presented a most brilliant spectacle. All this was followed by the old Chief Justice Blowers in his coach and livery, the carriage of the Admiral, and those of several members of Council. All being seated and the body of the church full of fashion and dress, the peal of the organ began to be heard and the clergy in surplice and hood (he who was about to preach, however, always in the black gown) proceeded from the vestry up the east side aisle to the pulpit, preceded by a beadle in drab and gold lace, carrying a large silver headed mace, who, after the clergy had taken their seats, deliberately walked down the aisle again to the vestry with his mace over his shoulder. The Rector, Dr. John Inglis, usually preached in the morning, and the Curate, Mr. J. T. Twining, performed the service. They were frequently accompanied by other church clergymen on a visit to town, and in Lord Dalhousie's time, his Chaplain, the Rev. Isaac Temple, always took part in the service, frequently preaching in the afternoon at 3 o'clock. On the sermon in the morning being concluded, the troops marched back to barracks and the general and staff returned to Government House, where they partook of luncheon, and were again in requisition by 3 o'clock for the grand review of the troops on the common. There were no evening services in the churches and meeting houses in those days, except with the Methodists, who were quietly doing their work in the old Argyle Street meeting house, under the Rev. Wm. Black.

The police of the town were conducted by one paid magistrate and one unpaid assistant, together with the clerk of the peace and three police constables, afterwards increased to four. Old Colonel Pyke presided as Chief Magistrate for many years, and was usually to be seen sitting in the little police office in drab knee breeches with gray yarn stockings and snuff colored coat. Age and infirmity having at last compelled him to retire, Mr. John Liddell, the second in command, was appointed Chief Police Magistrate by Sir James

Kempt.* David Shaw Clarke had been for some years Clerk of the Peace. He was a member of the Bar and particularly well qualified for the office he held, the duties of which he performed with much satisfaction to the public. He was very remarkable as being the most corpulent man in town. The late Samuel Muirhead, who kept a liquor shop at the head of the Market Wharf, was next in size to Mr. Clarke. Muirhead died in 1820, and Clarke, from that time to the day of his death, had no competitor. No man was better known or more popular for about thirty years in Halifax than David Shaw Clarke. He was succeeded in his office by his son James Stewart Clarke.

Drunken people were frequently to be seen in the streets in those days, yet the peace of the town was tolerably well preserved by the three or four police constables. Old Jock Henderson was very corpulent, but his great knowledge of his profession rendered him an exceedingly useful officer. Jack Mahar was celebrated as a detective, but king alcohol at last put an end to his usefulness. The practice of publicly whipping thieves had almost altogether gone out of fashion by this time, though occasionally resorted to at the work house. Among the town oddities was Constable Hawkins. He was a negro, one of those who were brought from the Chesapeake by Admiral Cockburn. He had been for some years employed at the work house to do the whipping. He was usually dressed in an old military green uniform, epaulets, plumed cap, with red sash, and on state occasions, a sword. With constable's staff in hand, this worthy might be seen in the morning at the opening of the police office, escorting prisoners down George Street to the office for examination, accompanied by a mob of boys. Among the other curiosities of the town was old Ben Myers, usually known as Major Ben. This old fellow, an idiot, was dressed in a long tailed red coat of a fashion then long obsolete, a cocked hat and long white feathers hanging over his shoulder, and on particular occasions, a star on his breast and a sword and sash. He was the messenger of the poor house and Bridewell and came down to the market every morning with his wheelbarrow in which he brought back supplies for the establishments.

The troops mounted guard every morning on the Grand Parade and went through the salute and troop before relieving guard. This formed a great attraction to strangers and people from the country. The band usually played for half an hour before the ceremony of inspecting the guards commenced. At sunset and at gun fire, at eight o'clock in the evening, the drum and fife proceeded from the town clock, in Barrack Street, to Government House or the General's quarters, and back again to the barracks. This had been an ancient custom in the Halifax garrison and was partly kept up until about the year 1845. Guard mounting on the parade at 10 o'clock in the morning during summer continued until Governor Le Marchant left Halifax in 1856.

One feature of the town which frequently afforded amusement to visitors must not be omitted. The negro population of Hammonds Plains and Preston, the latter particularly, had been, after the peace, supplied with the American uniform coats taken at Castine or somewhere in Maine in the year 1813. The sky blue coats with red and sometimes yellow facings, in conjunction with old torn and patched trousers of every description, presented the most grotesque appearance. A short time before this a fensible regiment known as the York Rangers, having been disbanded in the town, their old green uniforms, faced red, and the sugar loaf shaped caps, were given to the negroes, who presented the most ridiculous appearance on market days.

M. Geneui kept dancing school at Mason Hall and gave many pleasant school balls in the winter season to the great delight of the young people. M. Perro, a polite old French naval officer, was most popular as a teacher of French and was much esteemed in the community. M. Chenalette was the most famous confectioner ever known in Halifax. In his latter days he kept his establishment in Sackville Street, opposite Bedford Row, and was celebrated for his French cordials and fancy confectionery. Such was Halifax in 1821 and thereabouts.

CHAPTER VIII.

FORTIFICATIONS AND DEFENCES OF THE TOWN—PUBLIC BUILDINGS, ETC.

From the year 1749 to '54 or '5, the defences of the town consisted of palisades or pickets placed upright, with block houses built of logs at convenient distances. This fence extended from where the Roman Catholic Cathedral now stands to the beach south of Fairbanks' wharf, and on the north along the line of Jacob Street to the harbor. These palisades were in existence in 1753, but were removed at a very early period, not being within the recollection of the oldest natives of the town living in the year 1825.

A large portion of the front of the present Citadel Hill was originally private property; a small redoubt stood near the summit with a flag staff and guard house, but no traces of any regular or permanent fortification appear until the commencement of the American Revolution. There were several block houses south of the town—at Point Pleasant, Fort Massey and other places. A line of block houses was built at a very early period of the settlement, extending from the head of the North West Arm to the Basin, as a defence against the Indians. The foundation of the centre block house was still to be seen in 1848 in the hollow below Philip Bayers' pasture. During Governor Lawrence's time, the Indians made an attack upon the saw mills at the head of the North West Arm, which stood near the site of the present mills, and murdered three men; their bodies were buried by the soldiers near one of the block houses, and were three times dug up by the Indians in defiance of the guard, for the purpose of securing the scalps. These block houses were built of square timber, with loop-holes for musketry,—they were of great thickness, and had parapets around the top and a platform at the base, with a well for the use of the guard.

In 1755, four batteries were erected along the beach—the centre one, called the middle or Governor's Battery, stood where the Queen's Wharf now is, being then directly in front of Government House; another where the Ordnance Yard was afterwards built, called the Five or Nine-gun Battery; the third was situated north of the present Fairbanks' wharf; and the fourth called the South or Grand Battery, still in existence at the Lumber Yard. They were composed of stone and gravel, supported by cross logs, covered with earth and planted with grass, having battlements in front and the two ends, elevated about twenty or twenty-five feet above the water. These fortifications were removed about the year 1783, and the grounds appropriated to their present purposes. The Ordnance Yard, then a swamp around the battery, and the King's Wharf, were both filled up and levelled by stone and rubbish removed from the five-acre lots of the peninsula which were beginning to be cleared about this time.

There were block houses along the beach, near the Dock Yard wall, built by Col. Spry about 1775. The drawings of the town, published about the year 1774 or '6, show a strong fortification on George's Island.[*] It was not until the commencement of the revolutionary war that regular works appear to have been constructed for the defence of the town and harbor. About the year 1778, the Citadel Hill appears to have been, for the first time, regularly fortified; the summit was then about eighty feet higher than at present; the works consisted of an octangular tower of wood of the block-house kind, having a parapet and small tower on top with port holes for cannon—the whole encompassed by a ditch and ramparts of earth and wood, with pickets placed close together, slanting outwards. Below this there were several outworks of the same description extending down the sides of the hill a considerable distance.

Fort Massey, George's Island and the East Battery exhibit the same kind of fortifications in the pictures of the town made about 1780. At the latter place there was a barrack, afterwards rebuilt by the Duke of Kent about 1800.

---

[*] We have seen that Governor Cornwallis, at the very commencement of the settlement, selected George's Island as the most eligible position for fortification. Prisoners were sent here at a very early period.

During the American Revolutionary War, Colonel Spry, the chief engineer, erected a battery and several small block houses near the old Dutch Church in Brunswick Street. Several fields on the north and east sides of the Citadel were then taken by government and equivalents given to the owners. There was another block house at the extremity of Brunswick Street, in the field adjoining the present Admiralty grounds; the first were demolished about 1783, and part of the land granted by the Crown as a parsonage lot for the minister of the Germans, but the latter remained many years after till it fell into decay.

The Lumber Yard, Ordnance Yard and King's Wharf were all commenced about the same time, (1784 or '5) but the present buildings were put up at a much later date. The north barracks were built soon after the settlement. The buildings known as the south barracks were erected under the directions of the Duke of Kent, as also the north barracks, destroyed by fire some years ago.

During the revolutionary war the main guard house stood on the spot now occupied by the Mason Hall. It was used as a military post at a very early period, as the French prisoners from Annapolis, etc., were lodged there. The guard house was removed over ninety years ago, and the present building afterwards erected.

A building called the Military Office stood at the south corner of the market wharf, near where the main guard house now is. It was used as a military office until 1790, or perhaps later. At this time a guard was kept at the Prince's old playhouse, where the Acadian School now stands.

The house lately owned by Capt. Maynard, where the Trinity Chapel now stands, in Jacob Street, was a barrack as early as 1769. It was the site of one of the old block-house forts erected at the first settlement. It continued to bear the name of the Grenadier Fort until removed to make room for the present brick edifice known as Trinity Church.

The old woooden fortifications were removed from Citadel Hill about the time Prince Edward was Commander-in-Chief.

The hill had been cut down and ramparts of earth constructed mounting five or six guns at each angle, with a deep ditch. There were also covered ways and passages leading into the fort; willow trees were planted round the ramparts, and the whole was surrounded by a picket fence. The remains of this work were removed at the commencement of the present fortifications. Much of the old work was performed by the militia drafts from the country, embodied at Halifax at the close of the last century, particularly in 1793, during Sir John Wentworth's administration, and at subsequent periods. The Maroon negroes from Jamaica were for a short time engaged on these works.

The towers on George's Island,* Point Pleasant, the East Battery, Meager's Beach and York Redoubt were built at the commencement of the present century. The Prince established signal stations between Halifax and Annapolis, the first post being on the hill behind his residence on Bedford Basin. He levelled the ground called the Grand Parade, and it is said, built the walls at the north-east and south-west angles. The Chain Battery at Point Pleasant was first constructed, it is said, by Lord Colville, in or about 1761. The present ring bolts were put down the war of 1812–15. The old block house at Fort Needham and that on the hill above Philip Bayers' farm on the road leading to the Basin, called the Blue Bell Road, were built during the American Revolution, and re-constructed during the Prince's time. They were there in 1820, but soon after fell into decay, being composed of square timber only. All the other block houses had disappeared many years previous to that date. The building used as an army hospital, which stood on the north slope of Citadel Hill, in rear of the north barracks, since destroyed by fire, was erected as the town residence of Edward, Duke of Kent, when commander of the forces. The low range of buildings since used as barrack stores and as a military library, were his stables and offices. His residence was a very elegant building with a portico supported by Corinthian pillars in front, all which remained for many years after it became an hospital. About the same time he built his villa on the Basin, the ruins of which were to be seen a few years ago. The Rotunda, or band room, still remains. The lands where the buildings stood were the property of Sir John Wentworth, the Governor, to whom he left it on his removal from the garrison. The old Rockingham Inn was his guard house, since burned down.

---

* Lately removed.

In the year 1765 there were two hospitals in the north suburbs, near the beach at the foot of Cornwallis Street, called the Red and Green Hospitals. They were there in 1785. One stood on the site of the present North Country or Keating's Market, the other on property now owned by the heirs of late H. H. Cogswell.

Until the year 1780 the streets of the town were in a very rough condition, and some of them least frequented were impassable for carriages, from stumps of trees and rocks. As early as 1761, there was a good road to Point Pleasant;—it was a continuation of Water Street, and said to have passed through or near the present Lumber Yard grounds, following the shore of the harbor.

In 1764 the people of the north suburbs applied to the Governor and Council to call their settlement Gottingen. The name soon fell into disuse; the main street obtained the name of Brunswick Street, the rear street only retaining that of Gottingen.

The first Government House was erected soon after the town was laid out; the frame and materials were brought from Boston, and the apartments prepared for the reception of the Governor early in October. He held a council there on the 14th of that month. It was a small low building of one story, surrounded by hogsheads of gravel and sand, on which small pieces of ordnance were mounted for its defence. It stood in the centre of the square now occupied by the Province Building. About the year 1757 or '8, this little cottage was removed to give place to a more spacious and convenient residence. It was sold and drawn down to the corner of George Street and Bedford Row, opposite the south-west angle of the City Court House, and again, about 1775, removed to the beach and placed at the corner of the street leading to the steam boat landing, where it remained until 1832, when the present building, occupied lately by Thomas Laidlaw, was erected on the site. The new Government House was built during the time of Governor Lawrence. Lord William Campbell built a ball room at one end, and several other improvements were made to the building by subsequent governors. It was surrounded by a terrace neatly sodded and ornamented. The building was of wood, two stories high. The office of Capt. Bulkeley, the Secretary, stood at the north-east angle of the square inside the rails. Prince Edward resided in this house with Governor Wentworth in 1798. This old house was pulled down about the commencement of the present century and the materials sold to Mr. John Trider, Sr., who used them in the construction of the building on the road leading to the tower at the head of Inglis Street, formerly owned by Colonel Bazelgette, and afterwards the residence of the late Mr. George Whidden.

St. Paul's Church is now, perhaps, the oldest building remaining in Halifax. It was erected at the expense of government in the year 1749, and was esteemed one of the best constructed wooden buildings in America. The oak frame and materials were brought from Boston, and the building was ready for divine service by the autumn of 1750. It received an addition to the north end with a new steeple somewhat similar to the old one in the year 1812. The first sermon was preached in this building by the Rev. Mr. Tutty* on 2nd September, 1750. It remained in nearly all respects as at its first erection until certain late alterations have changed its appearance, particularly an addition to the south end from which the fine old altar window, with its Doric pillars and small panes has been removed to make way for a large Gothic window full of painted glass, altogether incompatible with the architecture of the building itself. The old escutcheons in the galleries have been permitted to remain. The walls below are covered with monuments and tablets recording the deaths of governors, military commanders, who fell during the old American and French wars, and not a few of our leading citizens. The most conspicuous are those of Governors Sir John Wentworth, Wilmot, Lawrence, and Sir John Harvey, Capt. Evans of the ship Charleston, who was killed off the coast of Cape Breton in defence of a convoy against a superior French force, Lord Charles Montague, late Governor of Georgia, who died of fatigue after a journey in winter from Quebec to Halifax by land, the Right Rev. Charles Inglis, first Bishop of Nova Scotia, and his son Dr. John Inglis, third Bishop of the Diocese, Baron De Seitz, who commanded the Hessian troops in the old war, General McLean, the Hon. Richard Bulkeley, Attorney General Uniacke, with a number of others of lesser note. The first organ was purchased, partly by private subscription, during the

---

* Mr. Tutty usually officiated on the parade in the open air until the church was sufficiently advanced to enable him to hold service in it.

incumbency of Dr. Breynton, about 1765. It was replaced by a new one about 1829, but the old case of Spanish walnut was preserved.*

The old German church of St. George, in Brunswick Street, bears the date 1760 on its spire. It was originally erected by private subscription among the German settlers of the north suburbs in or about the year 1752 or '3. After the removal of the Germans to Lunenburg there were but fifteen families of Germans remaining in the north suburbs. This small congregation, not knowing any English, erected the building on the German burial ground as a school house and chapel. The present steeple was erected in 1760, and the following year the building was dedicated as a church by Dr. Breynton of St. Paul's, after which the congregation followed the forms of the Church of England. Dr. Breynton on that occasion preached in German and in French, after which he addressed the congregation in English. In 1783 Rev. Bernard Houzeal, a Lutheran minister, came to Halifax among the Loyalists from New York and, having been ordained a minister of the Church of England by the Bishop of London, became the minister of St. George's, receiving a stipend from the Society for the Propagation of the Gospel in Foreign parts. He died about the close of the last century, a few years after the present round church, known as St. George's, was erected, and Mr. Gray was appointed to the charge, after which service in the old church was discontinued. It was then appropriated as a school house. About the year 1833 or '4 it underwent a thorough repair which was superintended by several persons in the parish who were descendants of the original German settlers.

Old St. Matthew's was coeval with the first settlement of Halifax. Governor Cornwallis assigned a lot at the south-west corner of Prince and Hollis Streets for a dissenting meeting house in 1749. It was built soon after at the expense of government, and was called Mather's Church in compliment to the memory of Dr. Cotton Mather, the celebrated New England Congregationalist divine, by the dissenters then in the town, who were principally from New England and of that denomination. The Rev. Aaron Cleveland, from New England, was the first minister who officiated in this

---

* This organ has been lately removed to Trinity Chapel, in Jacob Street.

building. The Presbyterians from Scotland and the North of Ireland, having become numerous in the town, soon amalgamated with the American dissenters, and gradually obtained exclusive possession of the building, after which it received the appellation of St. Matthew's Church. The late Rev. Mr. Russell, father of the late George N. Russell, of Halifax, officiated there for some time after it became Presbyterian. Dr. Archibald Gray was the officiating minister there for about twenty years; he was succeeded by Rev. Ebenezer Renny, Rev. Mr. Knox, and finally by Rev. John Scott, the last minister who preached in the old building which was burned in the great fire which destroyed a considerable portion of Hollis Street, on New Year's day, 1859. The lot of land on which it stood was, some years after, sold to Doull & Miller, who erected there a large stone warehouse, which is one of the neatest and most substantial buildings in the city.

The first market house occupied the site of the brick building lately used for the City Courts and offices. It was built soon after the settlement. A balcony ran along the lower side which was used by merchants, etc., as a public promenade. About the commencement of the present century the remains of this old building were removed to make way for the brick edifice. The upper portion of the new building was let as a public coffee house; the large room now used as a City Council Chamber was appropriated for public meetings, festivals, etc., and the south end, above the police office, was occupied for many years as the Exchange or Merchants' Reading Room.

The first court house in Halifax, as before mentioned, stood at the corner of Buckingham and Argyle Streets, where Northup's store and country market stood later. Chief Justice Belcher held his court there in 1755, and the first Representative Assembly held their session there in 1758. It was destroyed by fire about the year 1783. Chief Justice Belcher resided in the old house in Argyle Street to the north of the old Methodist meeting house, formerly owned by the Rev. William Black, Methodist minister. This building, at the time of its removal, was one of the very few old buildings then remaining in the town. It was taken down some years ago and a range of shops and a market house now occupy its site. The old Zoar chapel, the cradle of Methodism in Halifax, has been lately turned into shops.

The stone house at the corner of Prince and Argyle Streets, opposite the south-west angle of St. Paul's Church, was originally built by the Hon. Richard Bulkeley, the first Provincial Secretary, and was his residence for many years. It was purchased by the Hon. H. H. Cogswell about 1818, and since his death has undergone extensive alterations to render it suitable for a public hotel. It is now known as the Carlton House. There is an old house still standing on the western side of Grafton Street, in Letter——, Forman's Division, which was the residence of William Nesbitt, the Attorney General of Nova Scotia and Speaker of the Assembly, in 1760. After the death of Mr. Nesbitt, towards the end of the last century, it fell to his daughter, Mrs. Swann. This old lady died there nearly 80 years ago and the property was afterwards sold. The street was cut down about 50 years since and a story or breast work was erected on the street under this little old cottage which may yet be seen projecting from the main building, presenting the appearance of a balcony. The residence of Richard Gibbons, formerly Attorney General, stood at the corner of Buckingham and Grafton Streets, formerly known as George Isles' corner; it was lately taken down and replaced by a range of brick buildings now owned by Mr. Maloney. This was also one of the remnants of the first settlement of the town. The building at the corner of Barrington and Sackville Streets, formerly occupied as the Halifax Grammar School, is also a very old building. The House of Assembly held its sittings there in 1765, perhaps earlier. After the court house was burned down the Supreme Court met there for several years. It was also used at one time for a guard house. It was devoted to the purpose of a school on the establishment of the Halifax Grammar School in 1785.

Houses of entertainment were numerous and well kept at an early period. The Great Pontack was a large three-story building, erected by the Hon. John Butler, uncle to the late John Butler Dight, previous to 1757, at the corner of Duke and Water Streets, afterwards known as Michael Bennett's corner, now Cunningham's corner. It was the principal hotel in 1764. In 1769 it was kept by John Willis. The town assemblies and other public entertainments were held at the Pontack in 1758.*

The Crown Coffee House, frequented by country people, was kept by William Fury in 1769 on the beach near the Dockyard. Jerusalem Coffee House occupied the northern extremity of the block near the Ordnance Yard, opposite Collins' wharf, between Hollis Street and Collins' stone stores. It was built by the Hon. Thomas Saul as a private residence about 1753 and afterwards occupied by the Hon. Alexander Brymer; some of the rooms were highly finished and ornamented with carved work, and the whole establishment was on a scale beyond any other private residence in the place. It was let out for a coffee house about 1789, or perhaps earlier. This old building was destroyed by fire in 1837. The present stone stork known as the Jerusalem Warehouse occupies the site of the old mansion.

Public Gardens were much in fashion between 1753 and '80. Adlam's garden was an extensive enclosure south of the Citadel, near the present Artillery Park and south barracks. It was opened to the public, contained a pavilion and a great variety of fruit trees and shrubs. The Artillery Park was then kept on the Grand Parade; the Artillery Barracks stood in a line with the late engine house; the Parade was not levelled at that time; a foot path from George Street passed through the centre, and the descent at the north-east corner was very abrupt.† Spring Garden was another place of public resort in 1768. At this time there was a Provincial Gardener, who received an allowance of £32 10s. per annum.‡ About 1764, Mr. Joseph Gerrish, of His Majesty's Dockyard, laid out an extensive garden in the north suburbs and imported fruit

---

*Among the annual festivals of the old times, now lost sight of, was the celebration of St Aspinquid's Day, known as the Indian Saint. St. Aspinquid appeared in the Nova Scotia almanacks from 1774 to 1780. The festival was celebrated on or immediately after the last quarter of the moon in the month of May. The tide being low at that time, many of the principal inhabitants of the town, on these occasions, assembled on the shore of the North West Arm and partook of a dish of clam soup, the clams being collected on the spot at low water. There is a tradition that during the American troubles when agents of the revolted colonies were active to gain over the good people of Halifax, in the year 1780, were celebrating St. Aspinquid, the wine having been circulated freely, the Union Jack was suddenly hauled down and replaced by the Stars and Stripes. This was soon reversed, but all those persons who held public offices immediately left the grounds, and St. Aspinquid was never after celebrated at Halifax.

† Whether there was a passage for carriages across the Parade does not appear; probably not, as it was used for a public parade ground in 1749.

‡ Probably employed at the Governor's gardens.

trees at great expense. This was a private enclosure, extending from Lockman Street to the beach, south of the Dockyard; his dwelling house stood in the centre and faced the harbor. Part of the old wall, a year or two since, was to be seen in Lockman Street. The old Governor's gardens, west of the English burying ground, were well kept up for about 30 years. There was a large summer house in the centre.

Mr. Grant, the victualling agent, had a large fruit garden south of Government House, where St. Matthew's Manse now stands, extending from Hollis to Pleasant Streets. It was surrounded by a stone wall. Ornamental trees were, at an early period, very numerous in the suburbs, particularly in the south, and tended much to the beauty and comfort of the town. The poplar trees which stood in front of the residence of the late James Kerby and others, in Brunswick Street, and the willows on the eastern side of the street, near the round church, are within the recollection of many of the old inhabitants. The fine old willow trees which occupied both sides of Argyle Street near the residence of the late Attorney General Uniacke, those at the south end of Hollis Street, near the Lumber Yard, and those around St. Paul's Church, are also still within the recollection of many. These trees were all cut down by the Commissioners of Streets in 1829 and 1830, because they grew on the side paths and were therefore deemed an encroachment on the public highway. Halifax was thus denuded of its shady walks by the gentlemen of taste who constituted the Commissioners of Streets at that period. Within the last few years several attempts have been made to re-produce trees on the sidewalks, but with partial success, there being no protection afforded to them by the city authorities.

Before the year 1760, the houses were generally built of square and round timber, some with small pickets placed upright between the stubs of the frame, and the whole covered over with clap boards; they were usually of one story with a hipped roof, the shops and half doors with no glass, swinging signs, and wooden shutters opening downwards, on which goods were exposed for sale. Several of these old houses were in existence in 1850, windows and doors being altered.

In 1768 and '77, there were lamp posts at all the principal corners, the town being then lighted at the public expense.

The Dutch in the north suburbs usually built with the ends of their houses to the street; those of the better sort had ornamental windows and heavy cornices with weathercocks. One or two of these old houses were to be seen in Brunswick Street about thirty-five years ago. Among the old houses which have now disappeared was one which stood in the field opposite the tower wharf, near Point Pleasant; it was built about 1770, and occupied by General Fanning about 1783.

A year or two after the settlement Mr. Gerrish built several small stone houses near the tower; the clearance east of the pine woods is still to be seen; they were occupied for a short time by the settlers from the north of Ireland who went to Cobequid.

A large wooden building stood in the centre of the enclosure now occupied by Government House, built before the American Revolution, and used as a residence for field officers and other military purposes. The public hospital stood on part of the land now occupied by Government House to the north of the present house; it was afterwards sold; probably the spot on which St. Matthew's church now stands.

The first jail stood where the late Mr. Robert Brown's house in Hollis Street stood, opposite the Halifax Hotel; the jail was kept there till 1787, or thereabouts. In 1777, the Provost Marshal was suspended from his office in consequence of the repeated escape of prisoners from this building.

In 1752, government purchased a small stone house built by Col. Horseman for a prison, probably a military one; this was near where St. Mary's Cathedral now stands.

One remnant of the first settlement, now forgotten, was an old hardwood tree which stood on the beach, just above high water mark, at the corner of the Market Slip; this tree was used as a public gallows from 1749, and was there within the recollection of one or two aged persons living in 1825; it was cut down about 1763, but the stump remained until 1784 or '5.

The progress of crime between 1749 and '54, was perhaps less rapid than might have been expected among a population of 5,000 or 6,000, composed of such materials. During the first five years there were fifty criminal trials on record, many convictions for grand larceny, which was then the subject of capital punishment. After the appointment of Chief Justice Belcher, convictions were less frequent; most of the executions, as in the time of the general court, were for stealing or receiving stolen goods.

The Dockyard was first established at Halifax in 1758. It was extended and improved in 1769. The date over the gate is 1770. The walls have since undergone several renewals.

The Town Clock was erected early in the present century jointly by the garrison and the town. The merchants of Halifax raised a subscription towards the object. It was placed at the head of George Street for the convenience of the inhabitants. It was managed by the garrison. The late James Dechman, senior, was keeper, and resided in the clock for many years; he died about 1829 or 1830.

According to the plan of the town made by Col. Desbarres in 1779 or '80, and published in his nautical charts in 1781, there was a nine-gun battery about where the Ordnance wharf now is, and the five-gun battery a little to the north, but on an angle with the other. Gerrish's wharf, since known as Marchington's wharf, was immediately north of the five-gun battery, and Joshua Mauger's wharf at the foot of Jacob Street. Proctor's wharf appears to have been situated near where Cunard's old wharf now is. The old market wharf, known as Fredericks' wharf, and afterwards as Beamish's wharf, was as at present. Fillis' wharf appears to have been that now known as Mitchell's, south of the Queen's Wharf. Terrance Fitzpatrick's wharf was situated about the spot now occupied by Esson & Boak's wharf. Crawley's was to the south of the latter, and Collier's about where Pryor's wharf now is.

There was a battery at the Commissioners' point at the south end of the Dockyard, and the storekeeper's wharf ran out to the south of the Commissioners' point somewhere, apparently, in the vacant space between the Dockyard and West's property. Joshua Mauger's Distillery was situated between the Dockyard and the present hospital grounds. Guns were mounted on the careening wharf. Three batteries with ditches and enclosures were formed by Col. Spry, Chief Engineer, on the lower side of Brunswick Street; one on the corner of Brunswick and North Streets, one on the south corner of Dockyard Lane, and the other down Gerrish Street below the Dutch burial ground. It was generally understood that these works were on the opposite or western side of Brunswick Street, but Desbarres' plan places them on the east side. The works on Citadel Hill appear to consist of a small enclosure, but no regular fortifications appear.

EARLY PRINTING IN HALIFAX.

In 1751 printing was first introduced into Nova Scotia. The first press was established at Halifax, and there was not a second in the province until 1766. Bartholomew Green, Jr., was the grandson of Samuel Green, of Cambridge, Massachusetts, and was of the firm of Green, Bushell & Allen, of Boston. He removed to Halifax with a press and type in August, 1751. He died about six weeks after his arrival, 52 years of age.

John Bushell, who had been the partner of Green in Boston, immediately succeeded him in Halifax. He printed for the government, and in March, 1752,* published the first newspaper printed in Nova Scotia. The work for government was inconsiderable, but was the chief support of Bushell. He was a good workman but had not the art of acquiring property, nor did he make the most economical use of the little which fell into his hands. Bushell died in February, 1761. The proclamation published by Governor Lawrence in 1758 for the settlement of the French lands on the Basin of Minas was printed by John Bushell. Anthony Henry succeeded Bushell as a printer at Halifax. He was a German, and had lived some time with a printer, but had left his master and became a fifer in one of the provincial regiments. With this regiment he came to Nova Scotia, but some time after obtained his discharge. There was then no printer in the province, and his pretentions to skill in this art greatly facilitated his release from the army. There appears, however, to have been a printing office at Halifax in March, 1756, conducted by one Isaac Ourry. Henry began business with the press and type which had been used by Bushell. He published the Gazette. The government, through necessity, gave him some work which was badly executed. This paper was edited for some time by the Hon. Richard Bulkeley, Secretary of the Province.

---

* See Thomas' History of Printing in America.

In 1766 a printer with a new and good apparatus came from London and opened another printing house. He published a newspaper and was employed by government. Henry, who had been inattentive to his affairs, did not despond at the prospects of a rival, but, much to his credit, exerted himself and did better than before. After a few years' trial, his rival, not finding the business so profitable, nor place agreeable, sold out his paper, and Henry was again the only printer in the province. He procured new type and a workman better skilled than himself. His printing from this time was executed in a more workmanlike manner. He remained without another rival until the British army evacuated Boston, in March, 1776, when the printers in that town who adhered to the Royal cause were obliged to leave that place, and they, with other refugees, came to Halifax. Henry continued printing until his death. He possessed a fund of good nature, and was of a very cheerful disposition. He died December, 1800, aged 66 years.

Robert Fletcher arrived at Halifax from London in 1766, with new printing materials and a valuable collection of books and stationery. He opened a book store and printing house near the parade, published a newspaper and printed for the government. Until this time there had been no book store in the province. Fletcher executed his printing with neatness, and raised the reputation of the art in Nova Scotia. He remained in Halifax until 1770, then sent his printing materials to Boston for sale and went into other business.

Alexander and James Robertson, who had been printers in New York, Norwich and Albany, went to Shelburne, in Nova Scotia, in 1783, where they printed a newspaper. John Howe began printing in Halifax in 1776, and was publisher of the Gazette in 1801. Howe commenced the Halifax Journal in 1780. In 1790 his office was at the corner of Sackville and Barrington Streets. This paper was afterwards purchased and carried on by John Munro; his office was where Mr Kenny's new stone building now is, at the corner of George and Granville Streets. The weekly Chronicle was set on foot by William Minns, a Loyalist settler, in 1786, and was continued until 1828. Mr. Minns kept a stationer's shop in Barrington Street, below the parade. This paper had the Star and Garter at its heading.

Henry's printing office was in Grafton Street, in rear of the residence of the late Attorney General Richard John Uniacke, where his descendants resided for many years. There was another printing office in the same street, further north, which is represented in the engraving of the town in 1776 with a steeple surmounted by a hand holding a pen.

After the peace of 1784, printing found its way into the Province of New Brunswick.

CHAPTER IX.

The following short sketch of some of the persons who took a lead in establishing the Colony, has been compiled chiefly from public records:

The Honorable Edward Cornwallis, the first Governor and Commander-in-Chief, was a younger son of Charles, third Baron Cornwallis by Lady Charlotte Butler, daughter of Richard, Earl of Arran and uncle to the celebrated Duke of Ormonde. He was born in 1713, was member of Parliament for the borough of Eye in 1749, and was elected member for the city of Westminster in 1753, shortly after he returned from Halifax. He married the same year, a daughter of the late Lord Townshend, but left no children. He was afterwards raised to the rank of Major General and appointed Governor of Gibraltar. General Cornwallis was twin brother of Dr. Frederick Cornwallis, Archbishop of Canterbury.

The gentlemen who composed the first Council were Paul Mascarene, Edward How, John Gorham, Benjamin Green, John Salisbury and Hugh Davidson.

Col. Mascarene was a native of Castras in the south of France, was born in the year 1684. His parents were Huguenots and were compelled to fly from their native country on the revocation of the Edict of Nantes when all Protestants were driven from France. He made his way to Geneva at the age of 12, were he received his education. He afterwards went to England, where he received a commission in the British army in 1708. He was appointed Captain in 1710 and ordered to America, where he joined the regiment raised in New England for the taking of Port Royal. He was at the capture of Annapolis Royal that year, and was for some time commander of the garrison as senior major of the regiment. On the death of Colonel Armstrong he became Lieutenant-Colonel of the regiment under General Phillips, and was third on the list of councillors in 1720, when the first Council was organized in Nova

Scotia. In 1740 he was appointed Lieut.-Governor of the fort, and administrated the government of the Province until the arrival of Cornwallis in 1749. He remained in command at Annapolis after the settlement at Halifax, and was subsequently engaged as agent of the British Government in arranging treaties with the Indians of New England and Acadia in 1751. He retired from active duties and died a Major General in the British army at Boston, on 20th January 1760. He left a son and daughter. His son was said to be living in New England in 1835, at a very advanced age. The late Judge Foster Hutchinson, of the Supreme Court of Nova Scotia and the late Deputy Commissary General William Handfield Snelling, were his grandsons. His great-grandson, Mr. W. Snelling Stirling, has his portrait, painted by Smybert of Boston about 1725.

Benjamin Green was a native of the province of Massachusetts, born in 1713, youngest son of the Rev. Joseph Green, minister of Salem, Mass., and graduate of Harvard College. He was brought up as a merchant under his elder brother Joseph in Boston. In 1737 he married a daughter of the Honorable Joseph Pierce of Portsmouth. He accompanied General Pepperal to Louisburg in 1745, as Secretary to the expedition. After the capture of that place by the Provincial army, he remained there as Government Secretary and manager of the finances until Cape Breton was restored to the French, when he removed with his family to Halifax, and was appointed to the Council by Governor Cornwallis in July 1749. After the removal of Mr. Davidson he acted as Secretary of the province. He held several other important public offices, among which were those of Treasurer and Judge of the Court of Vice-Admiralty. On the death of Governor Wilmot in 1766, Mr. Green being then senior councillor, was appointed Administrator of the Government. He died at Halifax in 1772, in the 59th year of his age. His eldest son Benjamin succeeded him as Treasurer of the province. Benjamin Green, Junior, was father of Lieutenant William Green of the Navy, and Joseph Green and Henry Green of Lawrencetown, the latter left descendants at Lawrencetown. The second son of Governor Green was many years sheriff of Halifax, and having married a Boston lady, afterwards removed to that place. His daughter was married to Mr. Stephen H. Binney, son of Jonathan Binney of Halifax, whose descendants are numerous.

John Salisbury was brother to Dr. Thomas Salisbury, the eminent civil lawyer in London. Lord Halifax was his friend and patron, and sent him out with Governor Cornwallis as one of his suite. He does not appear to have taken any active part in the settlement. He married a Miss Cotton, who brought him a fortune of £10,000, which he spent in extravagance and dissipation. He returned to England in 1753, and died at Offley, the country seat of his relative Sir Thomas Salisbury in 1762. His only daughter was the celebrated Mrs. Thrale, the friend of Dr. Johnson, afterwards married to a Mr. Piozzi.

Hugh Davidson also came out with Governor Cornwallis. He was the first Provincial Secretary; he returned to England in 1750 under charges of trading in the supplies and stores for the settlers. Governor Cornwallis in his letters to the Board of Trade, thought him innocent of the main charges made against him.

Captain Edward How was a member of His Majesty's Council at Annapolis in 1744. He was with Col. Noble at the affair at Minas and Grand Pre in 1747, where he was severely wounded and taken prisoner by the French under DeCorne. He came down from Annapolis with Governor Mascarene in June 1749, and was sworn in a member of Cornwallis' first Council. He was well acquainted with the language of the Indians and their manners, and was sent on a negotiation to the French and Indians at Beaubasin in 1751, where he was treacherously murdered by the enemy, though acting under a flag of truce, having been shot through the back from the bush. The French officers denied having anything to do with this disgraceful affair, and charged it on Mr. LeLutre, the Indian missionary, who it was said was jealous of Mr. How's influence with the Micmacs. His widow afterwards petitioned the government for pecuniary aid, in consequence of her husband's services, and for money advanced by him for public service. The late Richard W. How, captain in the 81st regiment, formerly of Halifax, was his grandson.

Colonel John Gorcham was a native of Massachusetts; he was with General Pepperal at the siege of Louisburg in 1745, as Lieutenant-Colonel of his father's regiment raised in Massachusetts. He afterwards had command of a company of Rangers at Annapolis and came down to Chebucto with his rangers to meet Governor

Cornwallis in 1749. He took precedence next to Governor Mascarene at the council board. He is styled Captain Goreham by Mascarene and by Cornwallis in his commissions and correspondence. That of Lieutenant-Colonel was probably militia rank only. It is probable he returned to Boston soon after the settlement was formed as his name does not appear on the Council books after 1752. He had a brother, Joseph Goreham, who was also a member of Council in 1766; he afterwards attained the rank of Lieutenant-Colonel in the British army. He was engaged in the border skirmishes on the isthmus from 1754 to about 1758, and was afterwards appointed Commandant at Newfoundland.

Lieutenant-Colonels Horseman, Ellison and Merser, who were afterwards appointed to the Council, were the officers in command of the regiments which came from Louisburg. They all retired soon after to England.

Charles Lawrence was a Major in Warburton's Regiment of Infantry. He came up with the army and was engaged during 1749 and '50 in the French wars at Cobequid. He acted as Brigadier General under Amherst at Louisburg; he was a member of the Council and sworn in Governor of the Province on the death of Governor Hobson; the first assembly was convened during his administration, (2nd October, 1758); he died unmarried on 11th October, 1759, it is said of an inflammation, caused by overheating himself at a ball at Government House; he was deeply respected by the whole community, and the Legislative Assembly caused a monument to be erected to his memory in St. Paul's church " from a grateful sense of the many important services which the Province had received from him during a continued course of zealous and indefatigable endeavors for the public good, and a wise, upright, and disinterested administration." This monument has now disappeared from St. Paul's Church. His escutcheon remains in the East Gallery. Lawrence, though an active and zealous governor, by his desire to favor the officers of Government with a partiality for his military friends, brought on himself an organized opposition from the leading inhabitants of the town, who petitioned the Home Government for redress of their grievances, which they in a great measure attributed to the Governor and his Lieutenant Colonel Monckton. His resistance to the desire to call a Legislative

Assembly was among the chief charges against him. His death shortly after the petition put an end to the difficulties. He was succeeded by Judge Belcher as Administrator of the Government.

Charles Morris was a native of England; he was Captain of Provincials under General Pepperal at the seige of Louisburg in 1745. He had been engaged by Governor Shirley of Boston in a survey of the interior parts of Nova Scotia with a view to British colonization, in 1745. He also commanded one of the Provincial Companies sent to Minas under Colonel Noble in 1747. He was in Halifax in 1749, and in company with Mr. Bruce the Military Engineer laid out the town and peninsula. He was appointed to the Council in 1755. Though Surveyor General of the Province he acted for some time a Judge of the Supreme Court during the time of Chief Justice Belcher, which offices were both afterwards filled by his eldest son Charles. Captain Morris died in 1781, and was succeeded in the office of Surveyor General by his son Charles, whose son, the Hon. Charles Morris, also filled the same office and was a Member of Council in 1808. He was the father of John Spry Morris, Esq., afterwards Surveyor General, who was the fourth in succession who had charge of the Surveying Department in Nova Scotia. There are numerous descendants of Captain Morris in Halifax.

Jonathan Belcher, the first Chief Justice, was a native of Massachusetts, son of the Governor of that province, of an eminent colonial family; he was appointed Chief Justice of Nova Scotia in 1754, when a young man, and administered the government on the death of Governor Lawrence; Chief Justice Belcher arranged and revised the laws as they appear on our first Statute Book, and rendered good assistance to Governor Lawrence in founding the settlements at Horton, Cornwallis, Falmouth, &c., in 1758, '9, and 1760. Judge Belcher died poor; the Legislature voted a provision to his only daughter. His son, the Honorable Andrew Belcher, was for many years a resident in Halifax and member of Council.

Captain Wm. Cotterell was the first Provost Marshal or Sheriff, (there being no county divisions at this time). He was succeeded in that office in 1750 by Captain Foy, who held that situation many years, and received a small pension on his retirement. Mr. Cotterel afterwards acted as assistant Provincial Secretary.

William Nisbett came out with Cornwallis in 1749 as one of the Governor's clerks. He practised as an attorney and solicitor. He was appointed Attorney General on the resignation of Mr. Little, which office he held for 25 years. He was one of the first representatives in the General Assembly of 1758, and was elected speaker on 4th December 1759. He continued in the Chair of the House (with the intermission of one session when sick) until 1783, when he retired on a small pension and died the following year aged 83. In 1763 he declined a seat in the Council. During the period of his being Speaker, the House sat for 14 years without being dissolved. The old house in which Mr. Nisbett resided situated in Grafton Street, Block letter E, Collins' division, mentioned in a former chapter, still remains, though much changed by the cutting down of the street many years ago. He left no male descendants. His daughter, Mrs. Swann, died in the old Grafton street house about 60 years ago.

Archibald Hinshelwood was one of Governor Cornwallis' clerks, and performed the duties of Deputy Secretary with Mr. Cotterell and others for many years. Most of the drafts of the letters sent to England by the first three Governors are in his handwriting. He was elected a member of Assembly for Lunenburg in 1759 and again in 1765. Lord William Campbell the Governor appointed him to the Council in 1773, but he died before taking his seat. His property on Argyle Street after occupied by the City Water office fell to his nephew, (he having no children), who left two sons in the navy, both of whom died young. The old property was sold about 60 years since and purchased by Mr. W. A. Black, who resided there many years.

Otis Little was Captain of one of the New England Independent Companies. He was probably a native of England. Being in England in 1749, he came out with Governor Cornwallis, who appointed him Commissary of Stores, from which office he was dismissed on suspicion of having traded in the supplies for the settlers. He acted as first Attorney General of the Colony, and was probably a lawyer by profession. He was the author of a well-written pamphlet on the resources of Nova Scotia, written in 1748, with a view to encouraging British emigration to the province. Capt. Little left a daughter, who died unmarried at Halifax early in the present century.

John Baptiste Moreau, designated gentleman and schoolmaster in the book of the settlers, had been originally a Roman Catholic priest, and Prior of the Abbe of St. Matthew at Breste. He joined the expedition under Cornwallis in 1749, and went to Lunenburg with the settlers in 1752. He received ordination as a clergyman of the Church of England in 1750, and officiated to his countrymen and the Germans in the County of Lunenburg, where he died much esteemed and regretted in the year 1770. He left a son, Cornwallis Moreau, who was the first male child born in Halifax, and was called Cornwallis after the Governor. This old man was living at La Have, in Lunenburg County, in the year 1848, being nearly 100 years of age. He received pecuniary assistance from the Nova Scotia Philanthropic Society in that year.

Doctor John Breynton came up from Louisburg with the army, where he had been acting Chaplain to the Forces. He succeeded Mr. Tutty at St. Paul's in 1751 or 1752, in conjunction with Rev. Thomas Wood. Mr. Breynton was inducted Rector in 1758 or '9, under the provisions of the Statutes of the Province, and Mr. Wood acted as Curate or Vicar. After Mr. Wood's removal to Annapolis in 1763, Mr. Joshua Wingate Weeks, from New England, became assistant minister at St. Paul's. Dr. Breynton received his degree of D. D. in 1770. He died in 17—, and was succeeded at St. Paul's, as rector, by the Rev. Doctor Robert Stanser, afterwards Lord Bishop of the Diocese. Dr. Breynton was esteemed an eloquent preacher, and was in the habit of addressing the settlers in English, French and German.

John Creighton was an officer in the army. He served in the Dragoons at the Battle of Fontenoy. Having been discharged at the peace of Aix la Chappelle, he was placed on half pay as Lieutenant of Warburton's Regiment of Infantry, and came out with the expedition in 1749. Mr. Creighton was sent to Maligash with Col. Lawrence in 1752 to assist in forming the settlement at Lunenburg, where he continued to reside until his death, which took place in 1807. He was Colonel of the Militia, Judge of the Common Pleas, and for some time a member of His Majesty's

Council, to which he was appointed in 1776. Col. Creighton was a native of the South of England. He left numerous descendants in this country. His youngest son, Col. Joseph Creighton, half pay of 56th Regiment of foot, died at Halifax about 1851. His grandson, the Hon. John Creighton, of Lunenburg, was a member of the Legislative Council. Mr. James Creighton, the ancestor of the family of that name now in Halifax, came out with Col. Creighton. It does not appear there was any relationship between them. Mr. James Creighton became one of the most thriving and influential settlers in the town, and was the ancestor of one of our most numerous and estimable families. Col. Creighton's daughters married, one to the late Judge Wilkins and another to Hon. Hibbert N. Binney, both of whom have left numerous descendants.

Perigrin Thomas Hopson, the second Governor at Halifax, was Commander-in-Chief at Louisburg when that place was delivered up to the French after the Treaty of Aix la Chappelle. He came up with the army and was sworn in a member of Council in August, 1749. He succeeded to the government on the resignation of Governor Cornwallis in August, 1753. He did not remain long at Halifax. In 1757 he was gazetted a Major General, and in the following year was appointed to the command of the forces destined for the West Indies. He died before Guadaloupe a short time before the Island was captured.

John Collier was a Captain in the army and Member of Council in 1752. He was appointed by Governor Cornwallis one of the magistrates of the town, and had command of a section of the militia; one of the divisions of the town being named after him. He died at Halifax in 1769. It is uncertain whether he left any descendants.

Richard Bulkeley accompanied Governor Cornwallis to Nova Scotia as one of his A. D. C. in 1749. He was appointed Secretary of the Province in or about 1759, which office he held until 1793 when, on his retirement, he was succeeded by his son, Michael Freke Bulkeley, who died a few years after his appointment, 1796. Capt. Bulkeley was called to His Majesty's Council in 1759, and as Senior Councillor, he administered the government on the death of Governor Parr, in 1791. He held, at various times, the offices of Judge of Admiralty, Brigadier General of Militia, and Grand Master of the Masons. He died December 7th, 1800, at the age of 83, beloved and respected by all classes throughout the province. He was justly esteemed the father of the settlement, being the only person of consideration then living who came in 1749. He had been twice married. His first wife was a daughter of Capt. Rouse, R. N.; she died in 1775. He had three sons, all of whom died before him. His residence was at the corner of Prince and Argyle Streets, opposite the south-west corner of St. Paul's Church. The old stone house built by him still remains; it was for many years the residence of the late Hon. H. H. Cogswell, and is now known as the Carlton House. Mr. Bulkeley was buried under St. Paul's Church. His escutcheon, with the bull's head crest, hangs in the west gallery. The Hon. Richard Bulkeley was the only person who ever held the rank of General of Militia in this country.

Capt. Horatio Gates was A. D. C. to Governor Cornwallis with Capt. Bulkeley. He had been in command of an independent company of provincials in New York in the year 1737. After his arrival in Halifax he was employed for a short time in the country against the Indians and French. In 1762 he was appointed A. D. C. to General Monckton, with the rank of Major, and accompanied him in the expedition against Martinique. Gates was afterwards better known as a General in the American Revolutionary Army. Sir Robert Walpole, in a letter dated 1778, says Gates was the son of a housekeeper of the Duke of Leeds. Sir Robert was his God-father.

Jonathan Binney was a native of Hull, a small village near Boston. He came to Halifax shortly after the settlement was formed, and was engaged in business. He was elected a Member of Assembly for the town in 1761, and in 1764 was elevated to the Council. In 1768 he was sent to the Island of St. John (now Prince Edward Island) as Second Judge of the Local Court, and afterwards held the offices of Collector of the Revenue at Canso and Collector of Imports and Excise at St. John Island. He was charged with errors in his accounts by Mr. Legge, the Governor of the province, under which he went to England in 1776, where he completely refuted the charges made against him. Mr. Binney married Hannah, daughter of Mr. Henry Newton, a Member of Council, and is the ancestor of the whole Binney family now in Nova Scotia.

Joseph Fairbanks was from Massachusetts. He was one of the representatives in the first House of Assembly, summoned in 1758. Mr. Fairbanks left no children. His nephew, the late Rufus Fairbanks, became heir to all his property in Halifax, which at the time of his death was very considerable. Mr. Rufus Fairbanks was for many years one of the magistrates of Halifax; he married a daughter of Charles Prescott, sister to the Hon. Charles Prescott, of Cornwallis, and was the father of the Hon. John E. Fairbanks, of the firm of Fairbanks & McNab; of Hon. Charles R. Fairbanks, many years a Member of Assembly for Halifax and Judge of Admiralty and Master of the Rolls, and of Samuel P. Fairbanks, formerly Member for Queens County, with other children.

Benjamin and Joseph Gerrish were both from New England. The former was a member of His Majesty's Council, appointed in 1768, and Agent for Indian Affairs in 1760. The latter was many years Naval Storkkeeper at Halifax. He was also a Member of Council. His appointment to the Board bears date August 16th, 1659, from which he was suspended in 1762 for non-attendance. He died at Halifax in 1774. Mr. Joseph Gerrish built a residence in the north suburbs, south of the Dockyard, between Lockman and Water Streets, and had a fruit garden, the old stone wall of which remained on the east side of Lockman Street until about 1835. One of these gentlemen carried on business for some years in company with Mr. Gray, who was connected with him by marriage. Mr. Gray was father of the late Rev. Dr. Benjamin Gerrish Gray, minister of St. George's, and afterwards Rector of Trinity, St. John, New Brunswick, who was succeeded by his son, the Rev. Dr. William Gray, lately deceased. He was also the ancestor of Mr. Charles Gray, British Consul at Virginia. The Hon. John Gray, of St. John, New Brunswick, and Benjamin Gerrish Gray, Esq., barrister at law, of Halifax, are their descendants; one the son of Mr. Charles Gray, the other of Dr. William Gray. A Mr. John Gray came out with Governor Cornwallis in 1749 as a Deputy Secretary; probably Mr. Gray who was in partnership with Gerrish was the same person.

Major Leonard Lochman, (spelt wrongfully Lockman) was a German doctor and practised his profession in early life. He came out with the settlers in 1749 and resided in the north suburbs, where he built a residence for himself and had a large garden. This old house was lately pulled down. It stood on the upper side of Lockman Street and was built with a hipped or gamble roof. He received the rank of Major in the army for services performed to the British Government. He died at Halifax, and was buried under the little old Dutch Church, in Brunswick Street, where his escutcheon and monument with armorial bearings are still to be seen. The street between Brunswick Street and the water, which was laid out between the German lots, was named Lockman Street in compliment to the Major, who was for many years a leading man in Dutchtown. It is not known whether he left any descendants in the province.

The names of Jonathan Prescott, Malachi Salter, Richard Gibbons, Lewis Piers and Otto William Schwartz appear among the principal inhabitants of the town in 1750. Mr. Salter was from New England, had been extensively engaged in the fishery, and had visited Chebucto Harbor in 1744, five years before the settlement, while on a fishing voyage along the coast. Chebucto was the frequent resort of Cape Cod and Marblehead fishermen previous to the settlement. He was a Member of Assembly and Justice of the Peace for the town in 1759. The old house at the corner of Salter and Hollis Streets, afterwards the residence of the Hon. W. Lawson, and later of Mr. Esson, was built by Mr. Salter and was his place of residence for many years. During the American revolt, Mr. Salter, with several other gentlemen of the town, became suspected of treasonable correspondence. He was twice under prosecution, but on a full investigation nothing appeared to have been said or written by him of sufficient moment to warrant the charges. Mr. Salter was the ancestor of the family of that name now remaining in Halifax. He died at Halifax, in January, 1781, aged 65.

Mr. Gibbons was acting Attorney General for several years, and a leading practitioner at the Bar of Halifax. His son, Richard Gibbons, died at Sydney, Cape Breton, at an advanced age, where his descendants are numerous. The old gamble-roofed house at the corner of Buckingham and Grafton Streets, known as Isles' corner, lately pulled down, was the residence of Mr. Gibbons.

John Duport was the English Attorney. He came out with the settlers in June, 1749, and in July following was appointed a

Justice of the Peace. In 1752 he was made Judge of the Inferior Court of Common Pleas. He performed the duties of Secretary of Council for many years. He was sent as a Judge to St. John's Island in 1770, and was afterwards Chief Justice of the Island. Mr. Duport left a daughter married to Mr. P. Skey, of Falmouth, and a son who was in the army and was father of Mr. Robert Duport, later an officer in the Purveyor's department of the British Army. Judge Duport was much esteemed, and appears to have been an active public servant during the first twenty years of the settlement.

Joshua Mauger was an English trader, who had been connected with the government contracts at Louisburg, and appears to have resided in Halifax for the purpose of commerce only. In 1751 he held the office of Agent Victualler for the navy at Halifax. In 1754 he had shops established at Pisiquid, (Windsor) Minas, (Horton) and other places, where he sold goods and spirits to the French and Indians. He had still houses in Halifax where he made rum which he supplied to the troops and the navy. Mr. Mauger had some difficulties with Governor Cornwallis regarding illicit dealing. He went back to England about 1761, and was appointed Agent of the Province in London, which he resigned in the following year, having secured a seat in the British Parliament. He owned much property in and about Halifax. The beach at the entrance of the harbor, extending westerly from Cornwallis, now McNab's Island, was originally granted to Mr. Mauger, and still bears his name.

Michael Franklin was a merchant from England who settled in Halifax about 1752 or 1753. He was elected a Member of Assembly in 1759, and appointed to His Majesty's Council in 1762. In 1766 he received the appointment of Lieut.-Governor of the Province, which he held until 1776, when he again took his seat at the Council Board. Governor Franklin was a most active and esteemed public officer. His name appears connected with almost all the transactions of importance which occurred in the town from 1763 to 1780. During the American Revolt, his exertions in support of British authority while administering the government, were in a great measure instrumental in preserving the tranquility of the province. He married a daughter of Mr. Boteneau, of Boston, whose wife was a daughter of Peter Faneuil of that city. He left several children. The late James Botenean Franklin, for many years Clerk of the House of Assembly, was his eldest son. Mrs. Fitzgerald Uniacke was his grand-daughter.

Lewis Piers was a grand-son of Sir Henry Piers, 1st Bart. of Tristernagh Abbey, Ireland.

The Hon. Thomas Saul was the wealthiest and most enterprising merchant from 1749 to 1760.

The names of Benjamin Gerrish, Charles King, Henry Ferguson, Joseph Fairbanks, William Piggot, William Fury, James Grant, Jacob Hurd, Daniel Shatford, Samuel Sellon, Carles Mason, Lewis Piers and Robert Campbell appear on the lists of the Grand Jury between 1751 and 1754.

The following names appear on the register of early settlers :— Richard Wenman, Thomas Keys, John Edes, John Gosbee, Ralph Coulston, Edward Orpen, John Christopher Laurilliard, Philip Knaut, Peter Burgman, Otto William Schwartz, John Jacob Preper, John Woodin, Andrew Wellner, Christopher Preper, Simon Thoroughgood.

APPENDICES.

A.

The following is a copy of the advertisement which appeared in the London Gazette, March, 1749:

WHITEHALL, 7th March, 1749.

A proposal having been presented unto His Majesty for the establishing a civil government in the Province of Nova Scotia, in North America, as also for the better peopling and settling the said province, and extending and improving the fishery thereof by granting lands within the same, and giving other encouragement to such of the officers and private men lately dismissed His Majesty's land and sea service, as shall be willing to settle in said province. And His Majesty having signed his royal approbation of the report of the said proposals, the Right Honorable the Lords Commissioners for Trade and Plantations do, by His Majesty's command, give notice that proper encouragement will be given to such of the officers and private men lately dismissed His Majesty's land and sea service as are willing to accept of grants of land, and to settle with or without families, in Nova Scotia. That 50 acres of land will be granted in fee simple to every private soldier or seaman, free from the payment of any quit rents or taxes for the term of ten years; at the expiration whereof no person to pay more than one shilling per annum for every 50 acres so granted.

That a grant of ten acres over and above the 50 will be made to each private soldier or seamen having a family for every person including women and children of which his family shall consist, and from the grants made to them on the like conditions as their families shall increase, or in proportion to their abilities to cultivate the same.

That eighty acres on like conditions will be granted to every officer under the rank of Ensign in the land service, and that of Lieutenant in the sea service, and to such as have families, fifteen acres over and above the said eighty acres, for every person of which their family shall consist.

That two hundred acres on like conditions will be granted to every Ensign, three hundred to every Lieutenant, four hundred to every Captain, and six hundred to every officer above the rank of Captain. And to such of the above mentioned officers as have families, a further grant of thirty acres will be made over and above their respective quotas for every person of which their family shall consist.

That the lands will be parcelled out to the settlers as soon as possible after their arrival, *and a civil government established, whereby they will enjoy all the liberties, privileges and immunities enjoyed by His Majesty's subjects in any other of the Colonies and Plantations in America, under His Majesty's Government, and proper measures will also be taken for their security and protection.*

That all such as are willing to accept of the above proposals shall, with their families, be subsisted during the passage, also for the space of twelve months after their arrival.

That they shall be furnished with arms and ammunition as far as will be judged necessary for their defence, with a proper quantity of materials and utensils for husbandry, clearing and cultivating the lands, erecting habitations, carrying on the fishery, and such other purposes as shall be deemed necessary for their support.

That all such persons as are desirous of engaging in the above settlement do transmit by letter, or personally give in their names signifying in what regiment or company, or on board what ship they last served, and if they have families they intend to carry with them, distinguishing the age and quality of such person to any of the following officers appointed to receive and enter the same in the books opened for that purpose, viz :—John Pownell, Esq., Solicitor and Clerk of the Repts. of the Lords Comrs. of Trade and Plantations, at their office at Whitehall; John Ressell, Esq., Comr. of His Majesty's Navy at Portsmouth; Philip Vanburgh, Esq., Comr. of His Majesty's Navy at Plymouth.

And the proper notice will be given of the said books being closed as soon as the intended number shall be completed, or at least on the 7th day of April.

It is proposed that the Transports shall be ready to receive such persons on board on the 10th April, and be ready to sail on the 20th, and that timely notice will be given of the place or places to which such persons are to repair in order to embark.

That for the benefit of the settlement, the same conditions which are proposed to private soldiers and seamen shall likewise be granted to Carpenters, Shipwrights, Smiths, Masons, Joiners, Brickmakers, Bricklayers, and all other artificers necessary in building or husbandry, not being private soldiers or seamen.

That the same conditions as are proposed to those who have served in the capacity of Ensign shall extend to all Surgeons, whether they have been in His Majesty's service or not, upon their producing proper certificates of their being duly qualified.

By order of the Right Hon. the Lords Comrs. of Trade and Plantations.

(Signed)   THOMAS HILL, *Secretary.*

B.

The following notices appear in the Gazettes and Magazines of the day:

LONDON, Saturday, July 1, 1749.

Three vessels came up the river with about 300 German Protestants, who were ordered to remain at Lambeth and Vauxhall till they can be conveniently shipped to Nova Scotia.

Friday 21st July, 1749.

A great number of German Protestants from the Palatinate attended the Baron Munchausen, Chief Secretary for Hanover, with a petition soliciting a passage to Nova Scotia.

Wednesday, 12th April, 1749.

A great number of disbanded soldiers, discharged sailors, poor artificers, laborers, etc., who have accepted of His Majesty's grant of lands in Nova Scotia, attended at the Plantation Office in Whitehall, and received orders for admission, with their families and effects, on board the transports.

WHITEHALL, April 18, 1749.

Lieut.-Col. Cornwallis made Colonel and Commander of the Forces destined for Nova Scotia, with a salary of £1000 per annum.

May 9, 1749.

Hon. Edward Cornwallis to be Captain General and Governor-in-Chief in and over the Province of Nova Scotia or Acadia.

C.

Extract from a letter in the Gentleman's Magazine for 1749:

BOSTON, 10th July, 1749.

We have advice that two French men-of-war of 80 guns, and 20 transports, with a Governor and troops for a garrison, have arrived at Louisburg. The French Government offered Governor Hobson to transport his garrison to Chebucto, which was accepted, and orders came to discharge the vessels taken up here for that service. Col. Cornwallis, Governor of Nova Scotia, arrived at

Chebucto on 21st June* in the Sphinx, and Capt. Rouse in a sloop of war, and fifteen transports with 2000 adventurers on board, whose first settlement will be at or near Chebucto, where the Governor intended to keep the transports till next year for the convenience of the people, especially the women and children, until houses are built. The same encouragement that has been given to the British disbanded soldiers is given to Governor Sherley's and Col. Pepperell's regiments. Rum was sold at Louisburg for 9d. per gallon, and molasses extremely cheap. The French lost a great number of men in their passage to Louisburg by the small pox, yellow fever, etc., but the transports at Chebucto lost only one child.

D.

The following account of the expenditure on the settlement for the year 1749, was submitted to Parliament by the Lords Commissioners of Trade and Plantations:

Blankets, Woolens and Shoes for the settlers, and presents for the Indians	£ 1,325	4	8
Lines, Nets and Hooks for Fishery, Stationery, Surveyors' Instruments, Bricks and Garden Seeds	2,729	12	9
Lighterage and Shipping off the settlers, package and charges of Hospital Stores, a Surgeon with medicines by the Transport from Liverpool, and the Union Snow	336	0	3
Medicines, Sugar, Live Stock, for the voyage, and Drugs, Instruments and necessaries for the Hospital	680	14	8
French Bibles	102	17	10
Cash paid for victualling for settlers	12,068	5	6
Treasurer of the Navy's account for Bedding and Victualling during voyage	7,354	19	0
Ditto, on account of the Sarah, Transport, from Liverpool	67	18	8
Treasurer of the Ordnance account for field pieces, swivel guns, small arms and powder	3,592	4	4
Printing and incidental expenses by directions of Lords Commissioners of Trade	445	19	10
Ventilators for six Transports	102	11	6
2 Fire Engines	72	16	0
Pay of Surgeons, Apothecaries, Midwife, exclusive of what they received at Halifax	860	0	0
Silver and Gold carried out by the Governor	3,922	8	0
Bills of Exchange drawn by the Governor, the account of the expenditure not yet received	11,452	13	4
Bill to Capt. Ives for a boat	40	0	0
The Treasurer for Scales and Weights	21	7	0
Bills drawn by Delancey & Watt, of New York, for Silver sent to the Province	5,523	5	9

*The memorandum on the first page of the register of settlers makes the date of Cornwallis's arrival the 8th June—the writer of this letter may have been misinformed.

Thomas Handcock, Esq., for Boards, Plank, 2 Schooners, Salt and Money shipped to purchase materials for mills	£ 1,528	15	0
Bills drawn by S. Martin, from Boston	576	5	6
	£52,804	2	7
To the Transport Service for conveying the Settlers to Nova Scotia, etc.	23,672	1	3
	£76,476	3	10
To Governor Cornwallis for personal outfit	500	0	0
	£76,976	3	10

(Signed) CHRISTOPHER KILBY.

Account submitted to Parliament by the Lords Commissioners the following year:

Blankets, Woolens and Shoes for settlers, and presents for Indians	£ 1,325	4	8
Supplies for Fishery, Surveyor's Instruments, Bricks and Garden Seeds	2,729	12	9
Lighterage and Shipping Settlers, package and charges of Hospital Stores, etc	336	0	3
Medicines, Sugar, Live Stock, Drugs, Instruments, etc., for Hospital	680	14	8
French Bibles	102	17	10
Cash paid for Victualling Settlers	12,068	5	6
Treasurer of the Navy's account for Bedding and Victualling during voyage	7,354	19	0
Ditto on account of Sarah, Transport, from Liverpool	67	18	8
Treasurer of the Ordnance account for field pieces, swivel guns, small arms and powder	3,592	4	4
Printing and incidental expenses by directions of the Lords of Trade	445	19	10
Ventilators for 6 Transports	102	11	0
Two Fire Engines	72	16	0
Bill to Capt. Ives for a Boat	40	0	0
The Treasurer for Weights and Scales	21	7	0
Thomas Handcock, Esq	1,528	15	6
Pay of Surgeons, Apothecaries and Midwife, exclusive of what they received at Halifax	860	0	0
To Transport Service for conveying settlers to Nova Scotia	23,672	1	3
Fees thereon	147	19	9
Fees on money received from the Exchequer, exclusive of the sums charged on the foregoing articles	473	4	6
To Freight, Bed, Bedding and Cabins for 514 passengers on board the Alderney, Nancy, Fair Lady and Two Friends, Transports, and incidental expenses attending embarkation, etc., etc	3,144	4	4
To expenses repairing and fitting Sloop, New Casco	833	19	6
Gratuities 322 Foreign Protestants from Holland	338	2	0
Cash paid on account of Victualling settlers	4,500	0	0
Cash to Treasurer of Ordnance for Bills drawn by Governor	1,000	0	0
To Governor Cornwallis for the purchase of stores, payment of officers, package of stores, artificers and laborers, and contingent expenses, exclusive of £2,500 paid to his regiment for the four pence stopped for provisions to 11th Sept., 1750	25,268	0	2
Lieut. Martin's disbursements at Boston, for materials, vessels and stores	6,503	18	2

	£	s	d
To Apthorp & Handcock, disbursements at Boston, for materials, vessels and stores	6,924	14	6
Thos. Gunter's Bills remitted him at Boston, on account of Expedition to Chignecto	2,600	0	0
Benj. Green, Treasurer, by his account from Sept. 20, 1750, to Nov. 30, 1750	3,621	14	0
Richard Bulkley, Paymaster of Works, from 1st August, 1750, to Nov. 30	4,073	16	3
To hire of Transports retained in the service and not paid by the Navy	4,002	2	4
To Foreign Settlers employed in public works at 12d. per day, till the money advanced is thereby reimbursed	1,003	0	0
To Col. Phillips' (now Cornwallis') Regt., to return deductions for provisions to Christmas, 1750	3,919	5	8
To provisions supplied Cols. Warburton's and Lascelles' Regts., Artillery Company, Independent Companies, seamen in vessels, laborers and artificers	17,832	3	8
Victual and transporting Lascelles' Regt. from Ireland	8,581	3	9
To Office of Ordnance for Timber, Materials and Tools sent from Annapolis, hire of vessels, magazine of powder and payment of officers and artificers employed by the Board	10,417	15	3
	£173,838	2	3

CR.

	£	s	d
By account of Money granted by Parliament for Nova Scotia Colony Regiment, March 23, 1748, granted upon account towards the charge of transporting to His Majesty's Colony of Nova Scotia, and supporting and maintaining there such reduced officers, etc., etc	40,000	0	0
1749. Granted upon account for defraying the charges incurred by transporting to H. M. Colony of Nova Scotia, and supporting and maintaining settlers not provided for by Parliament	36,476	3	10
1749. Granted on account for supporting, maintaining and employing the settlers, March 19, 1750	39,778	17	2
Exceedings	57,682	19	3
	£173,938	2	3

CHRISTOPHER KILBY.

The charge for contingencies, and the last charge of £10,417 15. 3., probably embrace the expenditure on Government buildings—the two churches of England, St. Paul's and St. Matthew's; also the fortifications and other government works then in progress.

WHITEHALL, February 20, 1750.

Estimate for		Estimate for	
1751	£74,070	1756	£61,657
1752	96,639	1757	40,068
1753	58,559	1758	15,753
1754	47,741	1759	13,081
1755	55,799		

E.

The following extracts are from the letters of a French officer after the siege of Louisburg:

"The eyes of all Europe are fixed on this formidable armament; they have assembled an army of 22,000 men, 1600 brought from Europe, the remainder provincial militia, with a large train of artillery and munitions of war, 22 line of battle-ships and 200 transports. Yet Admiral Holburn, who appeared off Louisburg with 22 sail of men-of-war, took it into his head that our numbers were equal to his own, and has made his way back to Halifax. They will ask him there, why did you run away? Oh! says he, a superior force venit, vedit, fugit. It is vexatious that the first squadron which France has equipped since 1703 should be shackled with orders only to keep a look out. If ever there was a certainty of firing gunpowder to the renown of the white flag, it was on the 19th August, when Holburn appeared off Louisburg."

In some of his subsequent letters he appears to give a very accurate account of the seige, and some facts relative to the war not to be found in any history of that period. In speaking of the landing of Wolfe at the head of the Highlanders and the American Light Troops—

"It is the interest of the conquered not to diminish the glory of the victor, and besides it is our duty to do justice even to our mortal enemy, for which reason I confess that the English on this occasion behaved with such valor as before the event must have appeased temerity. Yet it must be allowed that at the same time the difficulty of the enterprise does them infinite honor, it saves ours; who would have forseen that they would have ventured to have climbed rocks till then rendered inaccessible, under a heavy fire from our batteries, notwithstanding their boats were every moment knocked to pieces in the surf, which drowned great numbers.

In speaking of the capitulation he says:

"Though reduced to the last extremity we demanded far more advantageous terms than we had reason to expect. After a consultation between Admiral Boscawen and General Amherst, an unconditional surrender was demanded. Dracourt, the Governor, extremely exasperated at those terms, resolved to hold out, but was compelled to give in on receiving a most peremptory petition on the part of the inhabitants, presented by M. Prevost. The capitulation was signed on 15th July, 1758, after a bloody siege of two months. On the day following, our troops were drawn up, and the colors and arms surrendered to General Whitmore, who took command of the town. The evening before the English took possession of the town, we suffered our soldiers to plunder the magazines, and the priests spent the whole night in marrying all the girls of the city to the first who would have them. No one here can perceive, at least by any personal inconvenience, that we are in a conquered town. The garrison has embarked with as much tranquility as if it had been going on a voyage of pleasure. Every soldier has taken away whatever belongs to him without suffering the least injustice. M. De Dracourt has received all the honors which a person of his rank deserved; Admiral Boscawen has shown all the respect to Madam De Dracourt as were due to her merits. This lady has performed such exploits during the siege as must entitle her to rank among the most illustrious of her sex, for she fired three cannon every day in order to animate the gunners. After the surrender she interested herself in behalf of all the unfortunates; in this number M. Maillet de Grandville was a striking instance of the instability of fortune. He left France at the age of 17, arrived at Quebec in indifferent circumstances; by his industry and application to business, he accumulated a vast fortune which enabled him to purchase the Lordship of St. Louis, which cost him 80,000 livres; but now, by the taking of Louisburg, he is left quite destitute with a numerous family."

F.

HALIFAX, July, 1752.

A list of the families of English, Swiss, etc., which have been settled in Nova Scotia since the year 1749, and who now are settlers in the places hereafter mentioned.

NORTH SUBURBS OF HALIFAX.

HEADS OF FAMILIES.	Males above 16.	Females above 16.	Males under 16.	Females under 16.	Total.
John Seutt	2	1			3
Edmund Dwight	1	2	1	2	6
Benjamin Brown	5				5
William Gindler	1	3	1	1	6
Samuel Shipton	3	3	3		9
Charles Procter	2	2	5		9
Jonathan Hoar	2				2
Gerchon Tuffs	1	2		2	5
Preserved Cunnable	2	2		2	6
William Bourn	9	1			10
Matthew Barnard	2	3			5
William Rundal	1				1
Anthony Caverly	1				1
Charles Hay	2	2			4
Nathaniel Henderson	1	1			2

NORTH SUBURBS.—(CONTINUED.)

HEADS OF FAMILIES.	Males above 16	Females above 16	Males under 16	Females under 16	Total
Henry Chadwick	2	1		1	4
Samuel Lyne	1	1	2	2	6
Thomas Fitzpatrick	1	1	3		5
Judah Riger	1	1			2
Ezekiel Gilman	6	1			7
John Kinselagh	3	2			5
Benjamin Ives	5				5
Mrs. Decorot		2	1	2	5
Josiah Crosby	1	1	1	2	5
William Harris	3	1		2	6
Benjamin Phippeny	1	1		2	4
George Gerrish	3	1	1	5	10
Robert Norman	1	1			2
John Cox	1	1			2
Edward Bowden	1	1	1	1	4
John Tongue	2	1	1		4
Samuel Tanner	1	1		2	4
Samuel Chandler	1	1	1		3
George Sanders	2	1	2	1	6
John Christian Mulblhe	2	3	2	1	8
Ernst Preper	2	1	1		4
Christopher Harness	1	1	1	3	6
Charles Robins	1	1	1	1	4
Ezekiel Wildman	3	1		1	5
Walter Motley	2	1		1	4
Charles Christ	2	2	1	2	7
Peter Schahlan	1	1			2
Peter Mozar	2	3	2	3	10
John Hoffens	1	1		3	5
Peter Wayte	1	1	1		3
Thomas Hay	3				3
Jacob Cheney	2	1	1	2	6
John Jones	2	1			3
Mary Birin	1	1	2	1	5
Charles King	1	1	1	2	5
John Porter	1	1	1	4	7
Joseph Pratt	1		1	1	3
Daniel Brewer	2	1			3
William Husstable	6	1	1		8
Benjamin Storer	3	1		3	7
Jasper Battel	1	1		2	4
Ulrich Dithoe	1	1			2
Hans. Geo. Kohl	2	2			4
Joseph Chadwick	2	1			3
Christopher Warner	1	1	1		3
John Christopher Rodoph	1				1
John Burger Erad	6			1	7
John A. Le Mand	3	1		4	8
Ludovick Schnerr	1	2	2	1	6
	130	75	42	63	300

Swiss and Germans in the North Suburbs.

Heads of Families.	Males above 16.	Females above 16.	Males under 16.	Females under 16.	Total.
Chs. Lndk. Hagelsieb	2		1	2	5
John Peter Tahn	2	1		1	4
Michael Brier	1	1	1	1	4
Lorenz Buagler	4	3	2	3	12
Leonhard Urich	1	1		1	3
Jacob Craft	1	1	1		3
Wendal Ramjer	1	1	1	1	4
George Storch	1	1	1		3
Peter Klattenburger	2	1	1	1	5
Michael Clouser	3				3
Michael Morash	2	2		1	5
Jacob Schmidt	1	2			3
Joseph Ley	2	1			3
Barthel Hans	3	3	1		7
Jacob Moser	2	1	1	4	8
Conrad Hall	1	1		1	3
Jacob Hall	2	1	2		5
Joseph Bley	3	1		1	5
Michael Ley	1	1	1		3
Elizabeth Werner		1		2	3
Magdalen Orell		2			2
Benedict Mayhofer	1	2			3
Andreas Kalb	1	1	1		3
Adam Rundl	1	1			2
Urich Seeger	3			4	7
Daniel Schumaker	1				1
John Jacob Schmidt	1	2			3
Adam Luty	1	1			2
Conrad Mucher	1	1			2
Godfried Knotz	3	2		1	6
Peter Lawner	2	2	1		5
Godfried Torpel	2	1	2		5
Jacob Tanner	1	1	2	2	6
Johannus Buhofer	1	1			2
George Nagel	1	1	1		3
Rudolph Pense	1	1	2	2	6
Adam Wambolt	2	2			4
Peter Wambolt	1	1			2
Ruchart Schup	1	1	1	1	4
Michael Hagg	2				2
Michael Gimber	1	1	1		3
Adam Buhler	1	1			2
Andreas Young	1	1			2
—— Beringer	1	1			2
Casper Hickman	1	1	1		3
Henrick Oxner	2	1	1	3	7
Jean Mange	1	1	2		4
Casper Lehry	1	1			2
Peter Estmann	1	1		1	3
Johannus Lonus	1	1	4		6
Loui Eouton	1	1	1		3

NORTH SUBURBS.—(CONTINUED.)

HEADS OF FAMILIES.	Males above 16	Females above 16	Males under 16	Females under 16	Total
Casper Trillian	1	1			2
Augustin Wolf	1	1	2	1	5
Anton Halton	1	1		3	5
Matthias Nagel	2				2
Franciska Schnider	1			1	2
Ledwig Koenig	2	1		3	6
Nicholas Wolf	1	1		1	3
Johannes Schroeder		2			2
Johannes Loesten		3			3
Utrick Klatt	1	1			2
Maria Schlitter		2	1		3
Johannus Miller	1	1		3	5
Johannus Hoalf	1			1	2
George Vogler	6	2		4	12
Jacob Paulus	2	2	1	1	6
Conrade Werner	2	2	1	2	7
Matheus Finer	1	1		1	3
Andreas Sronnagel	1	1		2	4
Jacob Heish	2	1	1		4
George Polleber	1	1			2
Christian Finis	1	1		3	5
Gotleib Schermuller	5	2		1	8
Adam Schmidt	3	1	1	2	7
Christian Perfek	1	1	2		4
Christian Ernst	2	1			3
Frederick Auremburg	2	2	2	2	8
Nicholas Eggly	6	1			7
Henrick Kuhn	4	2			6
Ulrick Schanskill	2	3	2	1	8
Jacob Shaffhouser	1	1			2
Johannes Simon	1	2	1	1	5
Assmus Diel	5	2			7
Jacob Sperry	2	2			4
Adam Jung	4	2		1	7
Johann Jung	4	1	1	1	7
	61	41	13	26	141

South Suburbs.

Heads of Families.	Males above 16.	Females above 16.	Males under 16.	Females under 16.	Total.
Mary Rance		1	2		3
Thomas Latham	3	1			4
Jonathan Prescott *	11	1	1		13
Joseph Kent	1	1	1		3
Edmund Crawley †	4	1	1	1	7
John Winiton	3	1		1	5
William Trefoy	4		1		5
Darby Cavannugh	1	3	1	2	7
Edward Lush	5	1	1		7
Alice Twyny		2			2
James Ridder	4				4
John Crooks	2	1	2		5
James Hickens	1	1		1	3
James Pierpont	1	2		1	4
John Shippey	2	3	2		7
Peter, a negro	1	1		1	3
John Call	2	2		1	5
Ruth Wheeler	5	2			7
Joseph Harris	8				8
Richard Peirie	1	1			2
Francis Coburne	5	1	1	1	8
Charles Terlaven	5	1	2		8
Darby Sullivan	1				1
John Jackson	3	1		2	6
Gregory Ives	1	1			2
Samuel Sellon	2				2
Isaac Underdunk	1	1	2	2	6
George Featherstone	1	1	1	2	5
Maurice Welsh	1	1		1	3
Andrew Shepperd	2	1		1	4
William Mallus	4	1	4	1	10
Phillip Hammond	1	1		2	4
Solomon Reed	1	1	2		4
Joseph Evans	2				2
John Walker	1	1	2	2	6
Thomas Nunan	3	1			4
George Knox	1	1			2
Joseph Gullison	1	1		2	4
Jason Chapman	3	1		2	6
Rebecca Baldwin	1	1	2	1	5
Richard Manning	3	2			5
James Cane	1				1
Dennis Hieffernon	2	1	1	1	5
William Wickham	1	1			2
John Rider	2	1	2		5
Josiah Marshall	2	2	2		6
Joseph Pierce	2	1			3
John Steel	4	3			7

* Father of the late Hon. Charles Prescott.
† Afterwards Member of Council.

SOUTH SUBURBS.—(CONTINUED.)

HEADS OF FAMILIES.	Males above 16	Females above 16	Males under 16	Females under 16	Total
Malachy Salter	3	2	1	2	8
Charles Kanier	3				3
Jeremiah Rogers	3	1		3	7
* Peter, Marquis D'Conti and Gravina	2				2
Samuel Cleveland	2	1	2	4	9
Richard Graham	2	2			4
William Nesbitt	4	3			7
Isaac Knott	12	16	2	1	31
Daniel Tappoon	3		1		4
Hannah Hutchinson		1		1	2
Isaac Basset		2		1	3
Thomas Clarke	1	1	1	1	4
Robert Davis	1	1	1	1	4
William Lawson	1	1	2	1	5
John Eustace	1	1			2
John Miller	1	1	1	2	5
James Grimes	2	1	1		4
John Griffin	1	1	3	1	6
Joseph Mehany	2	2		1	5
Josiah Cleveland	1		3	1	5
Felix McMehan	2		2		4
Josiah Nottage	3	1		2	6
Mathew Mullens	2	1	2	1	6
Henry Ferguson	5	2	3		10
Jean Campbell		1		3	4
Ezekiah Averil	1	2	2	3	8
Thomas Hardin	1	1	2	1	5
Thomas Magree	1	1	4	1	7
Robert Brooks	1	1			2
James Jordan	1	2	1		4
John Poor	2	2		1	5
Thomas Lamb	1	1	2	2	6
Thomas Collicut	2	1			3
John Barry	1	1			2
Maurice Driscoll	1	1		1	3
John McCuller	2	1			3
Benjamin Child	2	1	2	2	7
William Wallace	1	1	1		3
John Murphy	1	1			2
Henry Rigby	1	1	1	2	5
William Peters	2				2
David Carmer	2	1			3
Patrick Mahoney	1	1			2
Samuel Fulton	2	1			3
Dennis Sullivan	1		2		3
Stephen Wisdoms	1	1	3	3	8
Richard ———	1	1	1		3
Bartholomew Calahan	1	1		1	3

* A Sicilian Nobleman, who came with a number of settlers from the West Indies. He was afterwards a Lieutenant of one of the companies of Rangers.

South Suburbs.—(Continued.)

Heads of Families	Males above 16	Females above 16	Males under 16	Females under 16	Total
Cornelius Crowley	3		1	2	6
Nathaniel Millett	1	1	1		3
Peter Wallace	1				1
John Slayter	1				1
Martin Ludovig	1				1
John Wisdom	1	1		1	3
George Cheshire	3	1			4
George Featherstone	1	1		1	3
Richard Sparks	2	1			3
Jacob Hurd	3				3
William Williams	3	1	1		5
Jedediah Harris	2	1	1	1	5
Abraham Slayter	3	1	1		5
Richard Winter	1	2			3
John Arbuckle	1	1	3	3	8
Perfect Miller	3	1			4
Mary Miller		1		1	2
Samuel Greenfield	1	1			2
Moses Clarke	1	2			3
—— Lewis	1				1
William Matthews	1	1		1	3
William Christopher	1	1		1	3
Thomas Walker	1	1	2		4
Daniel Hills	4		1		5
Richard Williams	1	1			2
Daniel Farrel	5	1	1	1	8
James Fullerton	1	1	2		4
Nathaniel Mason	1				1
Aaron Porter	4				4
Jacobus Derkindrekin	1	1			2
William Seward	5		1		6
Joshua Orne	6				6
Elias Girott	3	1	1		5
Richard Wenman	3				3
Daniel Shatford	1	1	2		4
Charles Henderson	5	1			6
Jonathan Harris	2	1			3
Patrick Cambell	3	2			5
Aaron Cleveland	1	1	1	2	5
James Monk	1	1	2	4	8
Samuel Crafts	7	1			8
William Russel	65	1			66
Ann Wenmen, in Orphan House		4	4	11	19
Joseph Palmer, in Hospital	21	1			22
Michael Naddow	1				1
Joseph Gerrish	27		1		28
Dennis Mehaney	1	1			2
John Conway	1	1	3	1	6
Mrs. Taylor		1			1
Michael Lawler	1	1			2

SOUTH SUBURBS.—(CONTINUED.)

HEADS OF FAMILIES	Males above 16	Females above 16	Males under 16	Females under 16	Total
Peter Murpil	1	1		1	3
John Gallant	17	2	1	1	21
Nicholas Nagler	1	1	3		5
1 Swiss	1	1	2		4
Josiah Bracket	3	1	1		5

WITHIN THE TOWN OF HALIFAX.

HEADS OF FAMILIES	Males above 16	Females above 16	Males under 16	Females under 16	Total
Thomas Power	11	2	1	1	15
Joshua Mauger	14	3	2	1	20
William Steele, Esq.	2	2			4
Benjamin Gerrish	2	2			4
Robert Cowey	7	2	1	1	11
Abigail Ward		1	1		2
William Austin	1	1		1	3
Thomas Matterson	1	1		1	3
Frederick Beeker	1	1		1	3
William Schwartz	1	1	1	1	4
Isaac Deschamps	1		1		2
Madam D'Pacquet	3	5		1	9
John Brown	2	2		1	5
Thomas Fulford	1	1			2
Lewis Pierce	1	1	1	1	4
Thomas Grenoak	1	2	2	2	7
Leonard Lockman*	5	4			9
William Ford	1	2			3
John Johnstone	1	1	1	1	4
Thomas Lake	1	1	1	1	4
Leonard Cotton	5	1	1	3	10
William and Edward Nichols	3				3
James Brenook	1	2	1	1	5
Thomas Oakes	2	1		1	4
Mr. Wheyland		1		2	3
John Wellemon (Wellenor?)	1	1	3		5
Thomas Price	1		2		3
Vernon Merefield	1	1	3		5

* Leonard Lockman was a German. In early life he practised medicine. He afterwards held the rank of Major in the army, which he received for services rendered to the British Government. He came out with the settlers in 1749, and eventually settled in the North Suburbs. He died at Halifax, and was buried beneath the old German Church on Brunswick Street, where his monument still remains. Lockman Street was named after him.

WITHIN THE TOWN OF HALIFAX.—(CONTINUED.)

HEADS OF FAMILIES.	Males above 16.	Females above 16.	Males under 16.	Females under 16.	Total.
John Brown	3	3	1		7
Allen Usher	1		1		2
Jeremiah Fitzsimons	3	1	2		6
Daniel McCylster	2	1	3	1	7
John Panier	2	1			3
Peter Anchoto	2	2			4
John Aubony	7	2	1		10
David Loyd	1	1			2
Thomas Saul	10	1			11
Alexander Keddy	1	2			3
Jane Knight		1	1		2
William Brew	1	2			3
John Marlow	1	1			2
Jacob Cone	2	1	1	1	5
George Twelve's wife		1		2	3
John William Hoffman	2		1		3
Mr. Surgot	2			1	3
James Fitzgerald	1	1			2
James Stewson	1	1			2
—— Redman	1				1
James Colbeck	1	2	2		5
Alexander Abercrombie	1				1
John Baxter	1	2		1	4
Giles Harris	3	1	1	1	6
William Pierce	1	2	2		5
Edward Luky	1	1	1		3
James Patfield	1	1			2
Widow Clerk		1			1
William Davis	1	1	1		3
—— Melony		1			1
John Steinford	1	1		1	3
George Suckling	1	1		1	3
Alexander Allen	1	1			2
Widow Henry		1		1	2
Thomas Frost	1	1			2
Ephraim Cook	12	4			16
by Mr. Brown					
James Colvill	3	2		1	6
Thomas Moore	1	1	1	2	5
Joseph Mascon	1	1	1		3
Edward Potter	1	1	1	1	4
China Brownjohn	1	1		1	3
Francis Lock	1	1	1	1	4
Daniel Stewart	2	3	1	2	8
Robert Grant	3	1	2		6
John Stockley	1	3	1		5
Edward Marguin	3	2			5
George Greenwood	1	1	1		3
James Smith	1	1	2	1	5
John Collier, Esq	2	2			4

WITHIN THE TOWN OF HALIFAX.—(CONTINUED.)

Heads of Families.	Males above 16	Females above 16	Males under 16	Females under 16	Total
William Piggott	7	1	3	4	15
William Best	6	2	2	1	11
William Henderson	3	2			5
Anne Woodside	2	1	2		5
John Connor	3	1			4
Richard Barry	2	3	1		6
William Heyslop	1	2	2	2	7
John Peter De Brace	3	1			4
John Rast	1	1			2
John Mundy	1	1	4		6
Richard Stritton	1	2	1		4
Joseph Churchill	1	1			2
Laurence Collins	1	1		1	3
John Humphreys	1	1		1	3
Joseph Coeishton	6	1			7
Ebenezer Petty	1	2	1	2	6
Robert Howden	1	1			2
Thomas Newman	7	2		2	11
William Griffin	3				3
James Ruston	4				4
Thomas Hagan	2				2
Thomas Manneu	1	1		1	3
Edward Butler	1	1			2
John Grant	3	2			5
Edward Orpin	4	1			5
John Vintenon	2				2
Thomas Branham	2				2
Henry Wilkinson	1	1		2	4
William Wright	1	1	1	2	5
Henry Wyan	4	1		1	6
Paul Pritchard	1	2		1	4
Alexander Forbes	2				2
William White	3	1		2	6
John Hall	1	1	2	1	5
Thomas Wilder	5				5
Thomas Greensword	1	1			2
George Nelson	1	1			2
Robert Parfect	1	1			2
William McCarty	2	1			3
John Ewes	1	1			2
James Fallon	5	1	1	1	8
William Johnson	2	1			3
Thomas Campbell	1	1	1		3
James Porter	3	1		2	6
William Vanfelson	1	1			2
James Ford	1	1	2	3	7
Robert Freeman	1	1	3	2	7
John Wooden	2	1	2	2	7
William Roscock	1	1	1	1	4
Peter Parkman	1	1			2

WITHIN THE TOWN OF HALIFAX.—(CONTINUED.)

Heads of Families.	Males above 16.	Females above 16.	Males under 16.	Females under 16.	Total.
Matthew Hopkins	1	2	2	1	6
James Douglass	1				1
John Meeds	1	1		1	3
Mary Robertson	5	1	3		9
Mary Williams		3			3
Nathan Nathans	5				5
George Taylor	3		1		4
Patrick Furlong	2	1			3
John Slayter	1	1	3		5
John Ker	2				2
John Clewley	8	2			10
Garret Mead	2	2			4
Charles Mason	3	1		1	5
Matthew McNemara	3	2			5
George Frank	1	2		1	4
John Webb	1				1
Robert Ewer	14	1			15
Peter Martin	1	4			5
Michael Mullineaux	1	2	1	2	6
Thomas Reeve	1	1			2
John Bohanan	1	1	2	1	5
——— Ray		1		2	3
Eusta. Butter	1	1		1	3
Thomas Golden	2	2			4
William Williams	1	1			2
Edward Lee	1	1	5		7
James Bannerman	2	1			3
Richard Bulksley	3	2			5
John Franks	1	1	1	1	4
Christopher Cooke	1	1	1	3	6
Robert Dickie	2	2	2		6
Joseph Wakefield	1	1	2		4
Thomas Bryant	1	1			2
Edward L'Cras	3	3	1		7
Lawrence Ren	1	2	2		5
John Fenly	1				1
William Walker	1	2			3
Mr. Bruce	2				2
Thomas Rnudal	1	1			2
——— Wigel	1	1	1	1	4
Mark Cullymore	1	1	1		3
Nathaniel Gosford	2	2			4
John Naymers	1	2	3	2	8
Davis Townsend	1	1	2		4
John Cleary	2	2			4
John Kent	4	1			5
William Crafts	1	3	2	1	7
Rosana Scott		3	2		5
Patrick Britt	2	2		1	5

WITHIN THE TOWN OF HALIFAX.—(CONTINUED.)

HEADS OF FAMILIES.	Males above 16	Females above 16	Males under 16	Females under 16	Total
William Bearsto *	1	1	3	1	6
Joseph Ford	3	2	1	1	7
William Eaton	1	1	...	1	3
James Tate	1	1	...	1	3
Samuel Sprague	1	...	...	...	1
Stephen McKine	1	1	3	1	6

WITHIN THE PICKETS† OF HALIFAX.

HEADS OF FAMILIES.	Males above 16	Females above 16	Males under 16	Females under 16	Total
James Vickars	1	1	...	...	2
Joel Waterman	1	1	1	1	4
Catherine Austin	...	1	...	...	1
Andrew Maxwell	4	1	...	1	6
John Gaffar	2	2	...	...	4
Luke Shippey	1	1	1	...	3
Henry Sweetland	2	...	...	...	2
Jonathan Markham	3	1	...	...	4
Francis Porter	4	3	...	...	7
Matthew Corker	1	1	1	...	3
Thomas Landerkin	1	1	...	...	2
Griffin Jenkins	1	1	...	...	2
Mary Hollowell	...	2	...	...	2
Edward Castle	6	1	...	...	7
Mrs. Whitehand	2	2	1	...	5
John Crowley	1	1	...	1	3
Philip Knaut	1	2	1	...	4
Storker Nelson	3	2	1	...	6
John Lowrey	1	1	...	1	3
Joseph Scott	2	1	1	...	4
Israel Abrahams	2	5	1	2	10
Thomas Ames	2	...	...	...	2
Thomas Dame	1	1	1	1	4
Benjamin Lee	1	2	1	...	4
Mary Cooper	...	1	1	...	2
Michael Sexton	3	2	...	...	5
George Popplewell	1	1	...	...	2
John Beswick	1	1	1	...	3
John South	1	1	...	...	2
Richard Hollis	1	2	1	...	4

* Captain in the army.
† Between Buckingham Street and the present Blowers Street.

WITHIN THE PICKETS OF HALIFAX.—(CONTINUED.)

HEADS OF FAMILIES.	Males above 16.	Females above 16.	Males under 16.	Females under 16.	Total.
Mr. Reynolds	1				1
James Whellon	1	1		3	5
William Giles	1	1			2
Frederick Barley	1				1
Ezekiel Budd	1	1			2
Josiah Hardy	1	1	3	1	6
John Edmundson	1	1			2
James Thompson	1	2	1		4
Mary Webb		1			1
Timothy Cane	1	1		1	3
James Banfield	1	1	1		3
James Babrig	3	2			5
Isaac Solomon	1	1		1	3
James Thorp	1	1		1	3
Samuel Blockden	1	2	2	4	9
Elizabeth Gunnel	1			2	3
Eleanor Cannon	1			1	2
Thomas Walker	3	1		1	5
Charles Morris	5	2		1	8
Josiah Millekin	2	1			3
John Codman	2				2
Lewis Hays	2	2	1		5
William Moore	4	1			5
William Cannon	1	1			2
Samuel McClure	1	2	1	1	5
Henry Fielding	1	1		1	3
Patrick Kennedy	2	2		1	5
John Walker	3	1	1		5
Benjamin Fogg	2	2		1	5
William Foye	2	4			6
Otis Little	4	2	1	1	8
Hugh Vans	3		1		4
Lewis Frignot	4	1			5
Joseph Antrims	2	2		1	5
Benjamin Green, Esq	3	2	3	1	9
H. J. O'Brien	2	2	1	2	7
Bartholomew Kneeland	2	1			3
Joseph Fairbanks	9	1			10
James Fillis	1		1		2
John Rous	2	4	1	2	9
Joseph Rous	4	2	1		7
John Greensword	17	4			21
William Fury	3	1	1	1	6
Debtors in Gaol	19				19
Criminals	8				8
William Falkner	1	1			1

On Several Islands and Harbors, Employed in Fishery.

Heads of Families.	Males above 16	Females above 16	Males under 16	Females under 16
On Cornwallis Island:				
Capt. Joseph Rouse	4			
" Manger	7			
" Cook	5			
——— Bradshaw	16	1		
	32	1		
At Ketch Harbor:				
John Grace	10	2	1	
Capt. Gill	6			
——— Brown	3	2	1	
	19	4	2	
At Sambro Island:				
Capt. Matterson	21	1		
Thomas Youngston	1	1	1	1
	22	2	1	1
At St. Margaret's Bay:				
Benjamin Frog	10	1	2	
James Ford	13			
Adam Clown	1	1		1
——— Allen	5			
	29	2	2	1

Laborers Employed in His Majesty's Works on George's Island.

Heads of Families.	Males above 16	Females above 16	Males under 16	Females under 16	Total
Richard Reeve	1	1	1		3
Thomas Leak	1	1	1		3
Patrick Hamilton	1	1			2
Cornelius Larigas	1	1			2
Laborers	11				11

AT THE BLOCK HOUSE AND THE ISTHMUS.

HEADS OF FAMILIES.	Males above 16.	Females above 16.	Males under 16.	Females under 16.	Total.
Adam Schafner	1	2			3
Jacob Soloer	1	1	1		3
Johannes Frederick	1		1		2
Peter Moeser	1	1			2
Richard Voleker	1				1
Adolph Henokel	1	1	2	2	6
Philip Krepof	1	1	1	1	4
Casper Meisner	1	3	2		6
Johannus Hoars	1				1
Henrick Hiltz	2	1		1	4
Henrick Mertz	1	1			2
Johanna M. Girtler		2		1	3
Margaretta Hoars		1	2	2	5
Philip Spounagel	1	1	1	1	4
Michael Westhoefer	1	2			3
Wilhelm Wensell	1	2	2		5
Johannes Forrokner	1	1			2
Ferdinand Shultz	1	1	1		3
Christian Schmidt	1	1	1		3
Johannus Schuok	1	1	1		3
Christopher Schafner	1	1			2
Lorentz Conrat	4	1	2	1	8
Jacob Braude	1	1			2
Philip Winter	1	1			2
Johannus Knaut	1	1			2
Wenel Wust	1	1	1	1	4
George Evalt	1				1
Adam Lehnhart	1	1	2	1	5
Conrad Graff	1	1			2
Jacob Berger	1	1			2
Philip Sigler	1				1
Frederick Heison	2	1		2	5
Henrick Lehn	1	1			2
Johannas Barget	1	1		2	4
Andrew Walter	1	1	1	1	4
Henrick Minok	2	1	1	2	6
Wilhelm Knveller	1	2		3	6
Adam Fileoh	1	1			2
Andrew Sauer	1				1
Eva Gibbart	1	4		2	7
Peter Krauner	1	1	2	1	5
Jacob Seely	1	1	1	2	5
Adam Boettinger	1	1			2
Caspar Ditrich	1	1			2
Christian Gothart	1				1
Johannes Schmidt	1	1			2
John Sebastian Nicolas	2				2
Ditrich Klauter	1				1
Ludovig Feller	1				1
Leonard Anton Freher	1	1		1	3

AT THE BLOCK HOUSE AND THE ISTHMUS.—(CONTINUED.)

HEADS OF FAMILIES.	Males above 16	Females above 16	Males under 16	Females under 16	Total
Laurens Lahn	2	1	2	......	5
Andreas Velocker	1	2	......	2	5
Ladovig Schnoer	2	1	1	2	6
Philip Hirchman	1	1	1	......	3
Anne Lees	1	......	......	1	2
Caspar Qonok	1	1	2	1	5
Philip Ritchauser	1	2	1	2	6
Conrad Teele	1	1	1	2	5
Michael Merokel	1	......	......	......	1
George Grant	1	......	......	......	1
Partel Hoarse	2	5	1	......	8
Alon Ostertay	1	......	......	......	1

	Families	Males above 16	Females above 16	Males under 16	Females under 16	Total
Within the Pickets of Halifax	468	846	622	279	285	2032
Within the North Suburbs	169	317	205	105	138	765
Within the South Suburbs	151	429	169	115	105	818
Within the Town of Dartmouth	53	81	47	29	38	195
On several Islands and Harbors employed in Fishery, etc.	......	168	13	18	3	202
On the Isthmus and the Peninsula of Halifax.	65	73	66	38	39	216
	906	1914	1122	584	608	4248

    906 families.
    1914 males over 16.
    1122 females over 16.
    584 boys under 16.
    608 girls under 16.

1914
1122
----

792 excess of males over females (over 16).

The foregoing is copied from a book in the Crown Land Office, having been in the Surveyor General's office, apparently, since 17th May, 1779, as the blank leaves contain memoranda of different warrants of survey from that date to June, 1781. Copied 4th December, 1862.

G.

From the Gentlemen's Magazine, Vol. 20, 271.

HALIFAX, NOVA SCOTIA, December 7, 1749.

DEAR SIR,—I have at various times given you the last account I was able of the state of affairs in this Colony. The summer was beautiful beyond description and even the conception of those who are always confined within the liquid walls of Britain. As to the winter, which you know I always dreaded, I do assure you I have felt severer weather in England. The people acquainted with this climate say that it began this year sooner than was ever known in the memory of man, and assure me likewise that it will not be more severe than it has been already; if so, there is no danger to be apprehended from it. This you will readily grant when I tell you, notwithstanding the tenderness of my constitution, to which you are no stranger, that I have not added a single thing, not so much as a great coat, to my dress since I have been in this Province. When I look back upon the 21st June, the day of our arrival, I am astonished to see the progress made; there are already about 400 habitable houses within the fortifications and not less than 200 without. So surprising is the growth of this colony, so great the happiness of being ruled by one who has no other interest at heart but that of making thousands happy.

From my soul I wish that all other governors would copy such an amiable example of imitation; he does not, like most others gripe and squeeze to accumulate a fortune; on the contrary, he derives no profit to himself from anything, but, with the most unexampled generosity, gives all places and commissions gratis to the most deserving, nor suffers his officers to take any fees at present. You know what an English rabble is (and the greatest part of this colony was such.) You know they are generally tumultuous, refractory, full of discontent and murmuring, capricious in demanding favors, not long satisfied with present concessions, and not seldom abusing them by restless importunity for more. Such generally is the rabble of mankind, and such were many of the settlers of this province, but by his prudent management and proper generosity, by his condescension, candor and affability, the Governor has charmed the tiger's fury and turned a sad tumultuous rabble into a tractable and quiet people. They now work with ten times the alacrity they did at first, are patient under disappointments, and when they meet with a repulse, they conclude their petitions to have been unreasonable, from a firm persuasion that His Excellency has their true interest at heart; they cannot ask with reason, but what he grants with pleasure.

Yours, etc., etc.,

* * * * *

H.

COPY OF MINUTES OF COUNCIL OF 12TH JUNE, 1752, REGARDING THE ERECTION OF A LIGHT HOUSE AT SAMBRO.

At a Council holden at the Govrs. House at Halifax, Fryday, June 12th, 1752.*

PRESENT—His Excellency the Govr.
Benj. Green,   Wm. Steele
John Collier,   Geo. Fotheringham, } Esqrs.

Resolved, That, Whereas a Light house at the Entrance of the Harbor of Halifax, would be greatly beneficial to the Trade, Navigation, and Fishery of this Colony, and might be the means of preserving the Lives and properties of many of his Majesty's Subjects, and whereas altho' many persons might willingly contribute towards so good a Work without any Expectation of a Reimbursement, yet probably many may more readily be concerned therein, when attended with any hopes of promoting their own Interest at the same time.

A Lottery, according to the following Scheme, be set on foot for raising a sum of £450 towards building a Lighthouse at or near Cape Sambrough, (whereby, besides the advantages before mentioned,) a considerable number of Settlers will be usefully employed for some time, and a great & lasting Benefit to the province be gained, by a voluntary Tax upon those persons (amongst others) who at present contributed nothing towards the Expence of the Government whose protection & favour they enjoy.

Scheme of a Lottery for Raising £450 towards building a Lighthouse at or near Cape Samborough :—

The number of Tickets to be 1000 at £3 each, £3000.
The number of Benefit Tickets to be 200, vizt. :

1 Prize of £500	....	£500
1 Ditto of 300	....	300
2 Ditto of 100 each	....	200
5 Ditto of 50 each	....	250
10 Ditto of 30 each	....	300
40 Ditto of 10 each	....	400
140 Ditto of 7 each	....	980
1 The first drawn	....	70
200 prizes.		£3000

---

* At a previous meeting of the Council held on the 3rd of February, a public ferry was established between Halifax and Dartmouth, and John Connor of the latter place appointed ferryman, with the exclusive privilege for 3 years to keep boats constantly passing and repassing, between Sunrise and Sunset, every day in the week, except on Sunday, when the boats should pass only twice—the ferriage to be 3d., and 6d. after hours, for each Passenger, and a reasonable price to be paid for goods, other than baggage, etc., carried in the hand, which passed free.

Fifteen per cent. to be deducted from the fortunate Tickets, and the remainder to be paid, without any other Deduction, to ye possessors of the sd. Tickets, as soon as the drawing shall be over— To be drawn publickly in the Town House, at Halifax under the Direction of managers to be appointed by his Excelly. the Govr. as soon as all the Tickets shall be disposed of, and in case the said Tickets shall not be all disposed of, before ye 31st Augt. next, the money recd. for any sold to be repaid to the possessors thereof on Demand.

ED: CORNWALLIS.

I.

Governor Cornwallis* to Duke of Bedford.
(COPY.)

CHEBUCTO, 22nd June, 1749.

MY LORD DUKE,—

I arrived here yesterday,—this morning a Sloop arrived from Mr. Hopson, which I am obliged to send to Boston in case any ship should be going thence to England. I would not neglect an opportunity of writing to your Grace. I met the "Fair Lady" storeship at sea the eleventh, after we had been from England four weeks, who told me the Transports arrived at Spithead the day before he sailed, and were to sail in three days after him, we were then off the island of Sable, and except the first eight days had met with contrary winds all the passage, besides we had steered our course for Cape Race but was forced off the banks by a gale of wind from the North West so that I had reason to think the Transports might be soon at Chebucto—we had nobody on board that knew anything of the coasts nor of the Bay of Funday, so were to cruize off the coasts till we met with a pilot, we made the Coast of Acadie the 14th, but met with no pilot till the 20th, when we met with a sloop from Boston to Louisburgh with two pilots on board, for the use of the Governor,—the wind not serving for the Bay of Funday, and the officers assuring me in case of foggy weather (not unusual upon those coasts) we might be a fortnight getting to Annapolis. The wind was fair for Chebucto, so I thought it advisable to go in there rather than risk the being some weeks, perhaps, after the settlers arrived.

---

* The Honorable Edward Cornwallis was fifth son of Charles, third Baron Cornwallis, by Lady Charlotte Butler, daughter of Richard, Earl of Arran, and uncle to the celebrated Duke of Ormonde. He was born 22nd February, 1712-13. He was Member of Parliament for the borough of Eye in 1749, and in 1753, shortly after his return from Halifax, he was elected for the city of Westminster. He married, the same year, a daughter of the late Lord Townshend, but left no family. In 1759 he was made a Major General, and was afterwards Governor of Gibraltar. General Cornwallis was twin brother of Dr. Frederick Cornwallis, afterwards Archbishop of Canterbury, and uncle of the Lord Cornwallis who defeated General Gates at Camden, South Carolina, in 1780, and afterwards surrendered at Yorktown, to the Revolutionary General Lincoln.—*Collins' and Debrett's Peerages.*

I could save the garrison of Louisburgh the bad and long navigation to Annapolis, so I sent to Governor Hopson that I was going for Chebucto and desired him to transport the garrison thither, imagining he had transports ready; by his sloop that came in this day I find him in great perplexity, the French arrived, and he no transports.—The Council of War it seems were of opinion that the orders from the Secretary at War did not empower him to hire transports, but to wait my arrival and that I was to send the transports that brought the settlers here. As I cannot know when the transports will arrive, in what condition, nor how many I can spare, I think it absolutely necessary for the service to send the sloop to Boston with orders to Apthorp and Hancock, who Mr. Hopson has recommended as the persons who have been always employed on the part of the Government, to hire vessels with all expedition for the transportation of these troops from Louisburgh to Chebucto. I send a letter by the same sloop to Colonel Mascarene in case he should meet at sea any vessel going to Annapolis. I likewise send a Frenchman that knows the country over land, by Minas to Annapolis. I have ordered Colonel Mascarene to come here with a quorum of the Council as soon as possible that I may open my commission, take the oaths and appoint another Council, according to His Majesty's instructions.

I can give Your Grace little information as yet as to this country—the coasts are as rich as ever they have been represented. We caught fish every day since we came within fifty leagues of the coast, the harbor itself is full of fish of all kinds; all the officers agree the harbor is the finest they have ever seen—the country is one continual wood, no clear spot to be seen or heard of. I have been ashore in several places—the underwood is only young trees so that with difficulty one might walk through any of them; D'Anville's fleet have only cut wood for present use, but cleared no ground, they encamped their men upon the beach. I have seen but few brooks nor have as yet found the navigable river that has been talked of—there are a few French families on each side of the bay about 3 leagues off; some have been on board. As to the disposition of the French or Indians I can give Your Grace no account till I see Colonel Mascarene, when I shall write more fully and continue from time to time to acquaint Your Grace of our proceedings. I wish the French may not be uneasy at waiting so long on board for the evacuation of Louisburgh as it may be some time before Mr. Hopson will get transports—it will, I fear, retard the settlement.

I am &c.,

ED. CORNWALLIS.

P. S.—I expect the transports daily.
His Grace the Duke of Bedford.

(From the Duplicate.)

We came to anchor in Merliguiche Bay, where I was told there was a French settlement. I sent ashore to see the houses and manner of living of the inhabitants—there are but a few families with tolerable wooden houses covered with bark, a good many cattle and clear ground more than serves themselves—they seem to be very peaceable, say they always looked upon themselves as English subjects, have their grants from Colonel Mascarene, the Governor of Annapolis, and showed an unfeigned joy to hear of the new settlement. They assure us the Indians are quite peaceable and not at all to be feared—there are none hereabouts.

I have, &c.,
ED. CORNWALLIS.

(From the Duplicate.)

This Frenchman will be there in three or four days—'tis 25 leagues from hence to Minas, and the French have made a path for driving their cattle over here.

Governor Cornwallis to Duke of Bedford.*

CHEBUCTO, JULY 23rd, 1749.

MY LORD,—

My last to Your Grace was of June 22nd, a duplicate of which is enclosed,—the 27th, the transports appeared off the harbor and in a few days most of them got in. As their passage had been extremely good and none of them had in the least suffered, I found they would be ready to sail the moment the settlers should be put ashore. I despatched a sloop to Boston to countermand the order I had given, and sent to Mr. Hopson to let him know I would send in a few days transports to bring away his garrison. Mr. Hopson had wrote me that he had agreed with Desherbier, the French Commissary, to make use of the French transports upon condition that in case the English ships should arrive before they were all on board he should be at liberty to disembark them. I sent him one the 1st of July and four more, the largest of the fleet, the 5th. I own I was much disappointed in finding Mr. Hopson unprovided with transports as I never had the least intimation that he was to wait for the ships that should bring the settlers. I have an account from Boston of July 3rd that my second order got there soon enough to prevent all but one from sailing, but as they were all hired this will cause some expense; they write me it will not be much.

---

* John Russell, 4th Duke of Bedford, was appointed Secretary of State in 1747-8 and resigned the office in 1751. He was afterwards Minister Plenipotentiary to France. He died in 1771.—*Collins' Peerage.*

July 8, I received from Mr. Hopson copies of letters from Governor Shirley and Colonel Mascarene giving an account of the French having begun a settlement and a fort at the mouth of the St. John's River. As my instructions direct me to prevent all such encroachments, and particularly mention that River as of the greatest consequence, I next day sent Capt. Rous of the Albany with a small sloop to attend him with orders to the commanding officers at Annapolis to furnish him with troops if demanded. Copies of my letter to Capt. Rous and one to the commander of St. John's, I send Your Grace enclosed. I hope what I have done in this affair will meet with Your Grace's approbation. July 12th I heard from Governor Shirley, that he had sent the Boston to Annapolis to receive my instructions about the affair of St. John's. I sent Capt. Pearse the same directions I had given to Capt. Rous, and a copy of the declaration asserting His Majesty's rights. As to Port Mouton which is mentioned in these letters, I believe it was a mistake occasioned by the French having put in there in their way to St. John's.

I shall now lay before Your Grace our proceedings at Chebucto.

Colonel Mascarene arrived here on the 12th with five of the Council; next day I opened to them His Majesty's commission, and took the oaths; the day following I nominated the members of a new Council:

Colonel Mascarene.*   Mr. Benj. Green.
Capt. How.   Mr. Salisbury.
Capt. Gorham.   Mr. Davidson.

I have added since, Mr. Steel.

As, perhaps, no copies were taken of the plans sent me of the harbor, I send along with this a copy of Durel's plan. Your Grace will see that the place I have fixed for the town is on the west side of the harbor—'tis upon the side of a hill which commands the whole peninsula and shelters the town from the north-west winds. From the shore to the top of the hill is about half a mile, the ascent very gentle, the soil is good, there is convenient landing for boats all along the beach and good anchorage within gunshot of the shore for the largest ships. In Durel's plan the two points that make the entrance to Bedford Bay are marked as the places proper to fortify, which is likewise taken notice of by Mr. Knowles. Their view must then have been to have the settlement within that bay. This would have been subject to great inconveniences. In the first place, it would be too far up for the fishermen, it being about five leagues from the entrance of the harbor to these points, and the

---

* Col. Mascarene was the Lieut. Governor of Annapolis; Capts. How and Gorham were two of his councillors. Mr. Green was secretary to Governor Hopson at Louisburg. Messrs. Salisbury and Davidson came out with Governor Cornwallis. Mr. Steel, afterwards added to the Council, was one of the settlers from England.

beach all along as proper for curing their fish as can possibly be imagined, so that no fisherman would ever have thought of going within these forts—indeed no ships would choose to go so far, as no finer harbor can be than that of Chebucto, which reaches from these points to Sandwich River,* so that notwithstanding of any forts upon these points an enemy's fleet might lie secure and indeed block up all ships within the bay. The proper places to fortify for the defence of the harbor seem to be Sandwich Point and the bank opposite to it. George's Island lies likewise very convenient for a battery to defend both the harbor and the town. It contains about ten or twelve acres. It was there I landed the settlers from on board the ships sent to Louisbourg—I have now a guard there and stores, and propose to build a magazine upon it for powder.

As there was not one yard of clear ground, Your Grace will imagine our difficulty and what work we have to do. However, they have already cleared above 12 acres and I hope to begin my own house in two days; I have a small frame and planks ready.

The Indians are hitherto very peaceable, many of them have been here with some Chiefs; I made them small presents, told them I had instructions from His Majesty to offer them friendship and all protection and likewise presents which I should deliver as soonas they should assemble their tribes and return with powers to enter into treaty and exchange their French commissions for others in His Majesty's name.

Three of the French Deputies have been here to know what is to be their condition for the future; I gave them copies of His Majesty's Declaration and copies of the Oath of Allegiance which I told them they must take without any condition or reservation, but in the same manner as His Majesty's English subjects;—they pretend their only difficulty is from fear of the Indians in case of a French war. I have ordered all the Deputies to come here and expect them in a few days. I think 'tis necessary to show them that 'tis in our power to master them or to protect them, and therefore I design to send as soon as possible two companies to Minas with orders to build a barrack and stay there the winter. I shall also send an armed sloop into the Bay of Minas to prevent all correspondence with the French by sea; another company I shall send to the head of the bay where the road to Minas begins. I propose, likewise, a blockhouse half way for the conveniency of travellers, and then to employ all the men I can get together, soldiers and inhabitants, to clear the road from hence to Minas; 'tis about 30 miles in a direct line—whether this can be executed before winter I cannot say. Had the garrison of Louisbourg been arrived,

---

* North-west Arm.

they would have been of infinite advantage; at present I have only one company of Hopson's, one of Warburton's and 60 of Gorham's Rangers.*

A list of the civil officers I shall be able to send Your Grace by the next ships that sail, with an account of what further progress we shall have made.

I am, &c.,

ED. CORNWALLIS.

To His Grace the Duke of Bedford.

J.

NAMES OF THE MEMBERS OF THE SUN FIRE COMPANY OF HALIFAX IN THE YEAR 1819.

John W. Pyke.	Robert Lyons, Jr.
John Tremain.	John Howe, Jr.
Michael Tobin.	James T. Alport.
Stephen W. DeBlois.	Henry Austin.
Charles Hill.	John Carroll.
John Owen.	Joseph Allison.
Richard Tremain.	Lewis E. Piers.
Henry Taylor.	W. Bremner.
J. E. Butler.	Samuel Story.
David Shaw Clarke.	George N. Russell.
James Grant.	James Russell.
James Kerby.	E. J. Hopson.
William Bowie.	Samuel Cunard.
Alexander Creighton.	Enos Collins.
John Letson.	James Cogswell.
Alexander Fiddis.	John Dupuy.
William Lawson.	Lewis DeMolitor.
Adam DeChezeau, Jr.	Temple F. Piers.
Andrew Smith.	Edward Alport.
John Liddell.	John Salter.
Joseph Dolby.	John Moody.
William Milward, Jr.	George Mitchell.
Azor Stephens.	S. Morris.
Joseph Marchington.	John Ferguson.
Lawrence Hartshorne, Jr.	W. N. Silver.

---

* These Rangers came from Annapolis; they had been enlisted in New England and were chiefly composed of Indians of half blood.

James Bain.
William K. Reynolds.
Charles Boggs.
Miles W. White.
A. McDonald.
H. Ford.
D. McColl.

ABSENT MEMBERS.

P. Senncrats, London.
Mark Etter, Trinidad.
James Barlow, London.
John Telford, Scotland.
G. W. Anderson, Glasgow.
James Walker, Chester.

MEMBERS LATELY DECEASED.

John Henry.
Thomas Leo DeWolf.
James Bell.
Robert Lyon.
Samuel T. Prescott.
Winkworth Allen.
John Buchan.
Thomas Austin, Jr.
Peter Bain.

K.

From the Gentlemen's Magazine, Vol. 20, 1750. (June.)

The Town of Halifax is entirely built according to the plan given in our last February number, and many additional buildings are carrying on. The barracks for the soldiers are completed and the fort at the mouth of the harbor will soon be in a good posture of defence.

The story in the papers of the Indians burning a town of 200 houses is without foundation.

Major Lawrence, of Warburton's Regiment at Nova Scotia, appointed Lieut.-Col. of Governor Cornwallis' Regiment and Lieut. Governor of Annapolis Royal. (July number of the Magazine, 1750.)

August, 1750. Halifax, Nova Scotia.—The fishery here is extremely good, one company only having 1400 or 1500 quintals of good dry fish ready to ship for a foreign market, and others also have been very successful. Mr. Brown, gardener to Governor Cornwallis, with his son and four others, going out two or three miles from the town, were beset by the Indians, who killed him and his son; the latter they buried, but the other body was found on the ground scalped, and brought hither and buried; the four others, it is feared, are killed or carried off. The Indians have also attacked and scalped seven men that were at work on the other side of the harbor. Parties are gone out to repel them.

L.

RETURN OF THE 1ST COMPANY OF HALIFAX VOLUNTEER ARTILLERY, UNDER THE COMMAND OF CAPTAIN RICHARD TREMAIN, 6TH JULY, 1812.

Peter Robb, Sergt. Major.

John Brown, \
Wm. Forsyth, } Sergeants. \
Thos. Fenerty, \
John Rogers,

Charles Dunbrack, \
Thomas Nelson, } Corpls. \
John D. Scott, \
William Rudolf,

David Muirhead, \
William Story, Jr., } Bomb'rs. \
Martin Piazza,

John Tremain.
Frederick Major.
William Gorham.
James McAllen.
John Miller.
William Bond.
John Peeples.
William O'Brien.
Alexander Smith.
George Morin.
Francis Story.
George Nock.
Samuel Lydiard.
Benjamin Marshall.
Benjamin Kingston.
Peter Hay.
Frederick Kringle.
John Henry.
William Smith.
Martin Gay Black.
Leslie Moffatt.
John Phillips.
Frederick Ruuvell.
Francis Muncey.
Robert Grinton.
George O'Brien.
Morgan Doyle.
Daniel Fraser.

Alexander May.
Thomas Gentles.
John Pendergrass.
William Stairs.
John N. Ford.
Nicholas Wright.
Samuel Black.
Azor Stevens.
Henry Monson.
Dennis Connor.
Paul Cermanatti.
Henry Wright.
Abner Stowell.
William Schwartz.
Peter McNab.
Thomas Muirhead.
Alexander Fiddis.
Herven Cameron.
Thomas Simmons.
William H. Barry.
John Hussey.
Thomas Richey.
John McPherson.
Fred'k John Knight.
John Cobb.
Thomas Smith, Jr.
Daniel Ferguson.
Charles W. Hill.
William Murray.
Thomas Beamish.
Nicholas Vass.
Alexander Clarke.
Joseph Lordley.
Henry Boyer.
John Bonnell.
Henry Warner.
David Hutton.
Ralph Turnbull.
Donald Fraser.
James Wilson.

272   *Nova Scotia Historical Society.*

John Forrest.
John F. Salter.
John Fillis.
Richard Scott.
William Strachan, Jr.
John Simpson.
Robert Fraser.
James Cogswell.
John Buchan.
Wyndham Madden.
James Leishman.
Hugh Gall.
Alexander Smith.
Joshua Lee.

Robert Field.

Halifax, July 6th, 1812.

Sgd.   RICHARD TREMAIN,
Capt. H. V. A.

www.ingramcontent.com/pod-product-compliance
Lightning Source LLC
Chambersburg PA
CBHW031251250426
43672CB00029BA/2037